Asian Churches

The Future of the Asian Churches

The Asian Synod and
Ecclesia in Asia

James H. Kroeger • Peter C. Phan

CLARETIAN PUBLICATIONS
Quezon City, Philippines

THE FUTURE OF THE ASIAN CHURCHES:
The Asian Synod and *Ecclesia in Asia*

Copyright © 2002 by: **James H. Kroeger**
                          Peter C. Phan

Published 2002 by:
      Claretian Publications, Inc.
      U.P.P.O. Box 4 Diliman, 1101 Quezon City, Philippines
      Tel.: 921-3984 • FAX: 921-7429
      E-mail: claret@cnl.net Website: www.cnl.net/claret

Claretian Publications is a pastoral endeavor of the Claretian Missionaries in the Philippines. It aims to promote a renewed spirituality rooted in the process of total liberation and solidarity in response to the needs, challenges, and pastoral demands of the Church today.

Cover Design: F. Alvarez
Photographs: J. Kroeger, *World Mission*

Library of Congress Cataloging-in-Publication Data

Kroeger, James H., 1945-
Phan, Peter C., 1943-
      THE FUTURE OF THE ASIAN CHURCHES:
            The Asian Synod and *Ecclesia in Asia*
            viii + 206 cm. 15.24 x 22.86
            ISBN 971-501-936-6

      1. Catholic Church—Asia. 2. Catholic Church—Bishops—Asia.
      3. John Paul II, Pope, 1920-
      I. Kroeger, James H. 1945- II. Phan, Peter C. 1943-
      III. Catholic Church. Asian Synod (1998: Rome, Italy):
      Ecclesia in Asia.

            BX1615 F88 2002
            282'.5—dc 21

CONTENTS

PREFACE

The Special Assembly of the Synod of Bishops for Asia, popularly called the "Asian Synod," has often been described by participants and commentators as an "event." Indeed, an "event" is more than a common experience or happening. It cannot be simply captured by a detailed chronology, an exhaustive list of participants, or a lengthy narrative. How does one adequately describe an event such as the Asian Synod, with all its ramifications for Church life—particularly in the Asian context?

Three elements enter into an "event." First, an event contains something **new**; it generates surprise. There is a break from the ordinary and routinary. New vistas, possibilities, and options are opened. Secondly, an event happens in a specific **context**; history, people, stories, emotions and concerns, great diversity and complexity all coalesce to shape an event. Thirdly, an event implies celebration and **continuity**; there is a perduring quality to an event as it affects the ongoing life of the community.

This modest book attempts to capture *some* of the newness, context, and continuity of the Asian Synod as a pivotal event in the life of the Asian Churches, charting their future in the third millennium. Most certainly, only a partial glimpse of the event will be achieved.

Part One focuses on the Synod itself, its preparation and celebration. The nine pieces in this section include two general overviews (Kroeger, Dupuis) and two responses by Asia's bishops, one before and one during the Synod (*Tablet* synthesis, O'Connell). Four reactions to the Synod by participants and observers (Menamparampil, Evers, Hong-Soon, Somchai) help capture the context, spirit and newness of the event. The comprehensive "Message to the People of God" expresses the central themes of the Synod, giving evidence that the local Churches of Asia "are very much alive and some of them manifest an extraordinary dynamism.... The Spirit of the Lord is obviously at work in Asia" (7).

Part Two, composed of ten contributions, is focused on the proclamation and "reception" of the final Synod document, the apostolic exhortation *Ecclesia in Asia* (EA). The beautiful editorial from *Vidyajyoti* sets a positive mood in which to view the papal visit to India. The pope's homily and Bishop Tagle's reflections bring to life this Asian phase of the Synod. Two synthetic overviews follow: Kroeger introduces the central themes of EA, while Phan outlines the challenges facing the Asian Churches in discovering their own identities. Topics central to the Synod and EA are discussed by recognized experts: Proclamation (Neuner), Inculturation (Roest Crollius), and Interreligious Dialogue (D'Ambra). Brief assessments of EA, both negative and positive, round out the presentation (Amaladoss, Van Noi, Shwe, Phimphisan).

Part Three and **Part Four** are designed to facilitate the appreciation and "reception" of EA. The full text and notes are presented; a detailed index, the first of its kind, enables ready access to the rich mine of themes and challenges discussed in EA.

This collection of materials ranges from the scholarly and academic to the popular and pastoral. The authors represent over a dozen nationalities, including many Asians as well as experts who have made their home in Asia for decades. The book consciously limited the bibliographies; however, attention is called to a comprehensive new book by Peter Phan, *The Asian Synod: Texts and Commentaries* (Orbis Books, 2002). Minor modifications in original texts have been made to have uniformity in presentation (e.g. Scripture, Church documents, English usage). The editors express gratitude to all publishers for permission to use their materials.

The "event" of the Asian Synod has not concluded; one trusts that, in the power of the befriending Spirit, it is just beginning. The full assimilation or "reception" by the Churches in Asia remains the task at hand. We are living in a new age of the Spirit, a time of an ongoing Pentecost in Asia, a fresh experience of a "new way of being Church-in-mission" in Asia; we are invited to fully participate in shaping *the future of the Asian Churches.*

Part One

Synod of Bishops
for Asia

Experiences - Reflections

SYNOD OF BISHOPS FOR ASIA
Panoramic Overview

James H. Kroeger

The Special Assembly of the Synod of Bishops for Asia, popularly known as the "Asian Synod," was held in Rome April 19 to May 14, 1998. As the Church of Asia swept into Saint Peter's Basilica and the Synod Hall, she brought with her all her wealth and variety of faith, experience, traditions, and customs. Pope John Paul II presided at the Synod's opening concelebrated Eucharist; Indonesian and Indian dances contributed to the beauty and prayerfulness of the liturgy, which employed ten different Asian languages for readings, prayers, and songs.

The Holy Father reminded the participants of their task: "During the Synod we would like to witness to *what the Spirit of Christ says to the Churches on the great Asian continent.* Ours is the task of writing new chapters of Christian witness in every part of the world and in Asia [and this] calls for *respectful attention to 'Asian realities' and healthy discernment in their regard.*"

Asian Context. The 252 participants (188 Synod Fathers, 6 Fraternal Delegates, 18 Experts, 40 Auditors) explored the Synod's theme: "Jesus Christ the Savior and His Mission of Love and Service in Asia: '...that they may have life, and have it abundantly' (Jn. 10:10)." The deliberations emerged from "Asian realities" personified in the participants themselves. As Cardinal Kim (Korea) noted, Asia is not only made up of "various nations, but, one might say, many worlds." Truly, there are many Asias, extending from Lebanon to the Philippines, from Siberia to Indonesia.

Asia, a conglomerate of "continents" and giant archipelagoes, possesses a rich mosaic of cultures and subcultures; it also has a wealth of spiritual heritages. 85% of all the world's non-Christians live in Asia. Catholics

(105.2 million in 1997) represent only 2.9% of the nearly 3.5 billion Asians (over 60% of humanity). Significantly, well over 50% of all Asian Catholics are found in one country alone—the Philippines; thus, Catholics in many Asian nations are a small—even tiny—minority. Islam numbers some 700 million followers in Asia alone. The world's two largest Islamic nations are found in Asia: Indonesia and Bangladesh; each has well over 100 million Muslims.

The Asian Synod set its deliberations within these realities. Such religious, political, social-cultural facts challenge and startle; yet, they also concretize the Church's mission of evangelization. These statistics have great implications; they focus the pope's words: "We ask ourselves: *what must we do to proclaim and bear witness to Christ before the men and women living in Asia*"?

Synodal Procedure. The Asian Synod followed the usual Synodal pattern: (1) consultation with the episcopal conferences through a series of questions in the *Lineamenta*; (2) publication of the *Instrumentum Laboris*, the main guide to Synod discussion; (3) interventions on the Synod floor; (4) group discussions; (5) reports before and after the discussions; (6) presentation of propositions; (7) approval of propositions; (8) Final Message of the Synod Fathers. This outline of the Synod's overall structure and inner dynamics helps one appreciate the actual Synod process.

The final official document is the apostolic exhortation that the Pope issues after the close of this assembly of shepherds [bishops] from Asia. *Ecclesia in Asia* was issued in India on November 6, 1999.

Preparatory Phases. The *Lineamenta* for the Asian Synod was published on September 3, 1996 and circulated among Asia's episcopal conferences. Reactions were forthcoming; many were quite negative. These thoughtful, extensive responses were widely publicized in Asia, particularly in *Asia Focus* and the *East Asian Pastoral Review*.

Some reasons for these unfavorable reactions may be noted: (1) The theological vision of the Church's mission in the Asian context, consistently elaborated by the Federation of Asian Bishops' Conferences (FABC) for over two decades, was ignored; (2) The *Lineamenta* proposed a narrow, ecclesiocentric perspective of mission theology; (3) The document lacked a solid pneumatology which would permit a more positive valuation of Asian religious traditions and the importance of interreligious dialogue;

(4) There was a failure to incorporate ways that Asian reflection understands the imperative for the local churches to put on an "Asian face."

On February 20, 1998 the *Instrumentum Laboris* (working document) was released; improvements were apparent. The structure of the document changed; elements of the FABC vision were included. A narrow ecclesiocentric perspective gave way to a Regnocentric perspective; action for justice and interreligious dialogue found a more generous place; Asian realities and the concomitant approach of integral evangelization were more adequately portrayed. Viewing the Church in Asia as a communion of local churches received its rightful place. In a word, the Synod now had a serviceable instrument for undertaking its work.

Synod Sessions. The actual sessions began on April 20 in the Synod Hall; Cardinal Paul Shan Kuo-hsi, S.J. from Taiwan, the Synod's general relator, gave an extensive introduction (*Relatio ante Disceptationem*). His overview was very well received; he provided a comprehensive framework for discussion, elaborating all the great themes of an Asian vision of evangelization.

Enumerating these themes actually captures the central agenda of the month-long synod: (1) broad notion of the Church's evangelizing mission; (2) emphasis on FABC's triple imperatives for justice, inculturation, and interreligious dialogue; (3) positive approaches to Asian religious traditions and the role of God's Spirit; (4) central role of the local churches and the ecclesiology of communion; (5) the Church at the service of the Kingdom; (6) a humble, *kenotic* Church with an Asian face; (7) importance of Asian approaches to evangelization (e.g. experience over dogma; witness of life over doctrines). Cardinal Shan's presentation was considered one clear high-point of the Synod.

Days of interventions followed. Participants were permitted to speak once in the plenary sessions—eight minutes maximum for bishops, five for others. Most episcopal conferences carefully planned their allotted interventions; topics were wide-ranging. Each speech brought new content; interest was high; there was attentive listening. Noteworthy was the freedom, insistence, and even critical stance with which the Asian bishops spoke and pursued their points. Many bishops were straightforward and frank; the interventions of the observers, especially the laity, were spontaneous and courageous, manifesting the laity's loyalty, intelligence, and dedication.

An analysis of the content of the interventions reveals that 76% dealt with aspects of four main topics: (1) interreligious dialogue; (2) the Church becoming Asian through her dialogue with living cultures; (3) the Church learning to dialogue with the poor; and, (4) the Asian local churches as churches of the laity. These topics quite remarkably parallel the thinking that has characterized the quarter-century evolution of the FABC.

The Synod's activities—interventions, group discussions, reports, summaries—moved the process forward. One bishop noted how the Synod was very human, being composed of people and their ideas; he also emphasized that as an ecclesial assembly one could palpably experience the presence of Christ and the Holy Spirit.

Integrating the Insights. Two important moments in the Synod process were the small group discussions and the formulation of a series of propositions to be forwarded to the Holy Father for his guidance in composing the post-synodal apostolic exhortation. There were eleven discussion groups (8 English; 2 French; 1 Italian). In broad strokes, one observes that the insightful exchanges and comments addressed concerns focused on Christ and the Holy Spirit, the Church in the Asian context, and the contemporary mission of evangelization, expressed in terms of love and service.

Employing the rich material of the eleven working/discussion groups (along with the plenary interventions), a list of 59 proposals was finally approved, none receiving fewer than 140 votes out of the maximum number of 168. Although a secret document, the proposal list soon found its way into publication in various languages. One proposal (No. 3) even requested that the final apostolic exhortation "have an Asian way of presenting its contents." Ultimately, all the propositions (except seven) directly appeared in *Ecclesia in Asia*, forming nearly half (49.6%) of the footnoted documentation.

The Synod deliberations in Rome emerged from the concrete situations and challenges of Asia, intending to serve the Asian peoples and their varied needs in diverse contexts. Dramatic events occurring in Asia were felt inside the Synod hall: riots in Indonesia, shootings in the West Bank, Muslim-Christian tensions in Bangladesh, detonation of several nuclear tests in India, the suicide-sacrifice of Pakistani Bishop John Joseph protesting Islamic blasphemy laws. The presence of bishops from the new, independent Central Asian Republics and their witness of Christian survival under persecution brought sincere edification; the absence of the Mainland Chinese bishops brought sorrow to the participants. The Synod proved to be a "reality-centered" gathering of Asian pastors, assembled "...that they [Asia's peoples] may have life and have it abundantly."

Several noteworthy thematic syntheses of the Asian Synod content are available [consult bibliography]: Theological Perspectives (Arokiasamy, Dupuis, Tagle), an "Asian" Church (Carrera), Mission Themes (Kroeger), Consecrated Life (Prior, Wang), Justice and Solidarity (Rogers), Women (Gajiwala). Beyond the limits of this short piece, these authors examine some of the richness that was the Asian Synod.

People and Events. Pope John Paul II led and guided the Synod through his presence and occasional remarks at all the plenary sessions. He noted how the Church in China remains his special concern and the focus of his first prayer each morning. Two bishops from Mainland China (Matthias Duan Yinming of Wanhsien [Wanxian] and his coadjutor Joseph Xu Zhixuan) received a special invitation to the Synod, but were unable to travel to Rome.

One morning the pope casually noted: "Jesus was born in Asia." This delighted the participants; Jesus like them was Asian. The pope added: "Oh, in that part of Asia that looked out to Europe." The pope was maintaining the particular and universal dimension of Jesus and his mission. Participants appreciated the pope's invitation to come in small groups and share lunch or dinner with him.

Several Japanese bishops played an important role in the Synod; many spoke on the first day of the interventions. Their boldness and courage in proposing questions for the Synod both set the tone and encouraged all to be frank in their statements. Bishop Nomura (Nagoya) challenged the Church to be a more authentic witness, noting: "In Japan, like the rest of Asia, the eyes have a more central role than the ears in the process of insight and conversion." Cardinal Shirayanagi (Tokyo) emphasized the dialogue approach to evangelization fostered by the FABC.

Bishop Hamao (Yokohama) highlighted the Church's mission of peace-making. His intervention was almost like a "public confession." He emotionally recalled World War II and the atrocities of the Japanese military, noting that the Church in Japan did not raise its voice against such inhumanities. He exhorted the Church to be committed to peace promotion. Bishop Hamao's intervention, spoken by an Asian to fellow-Asians, evoked healing, forgiveness, and reconciliation.

Some additional "pivotal personalities" in the Synod's proceedings were Cardinal Paul Shan Kuo-hsi, Archbishop Oscar Cruz, and Cardinal Julius Darmaatmadja. As noted earlier, Cardinal Shan served as the general relator for the Synod; his opening overview-report (April 20) was a masterful document. Shan's mid-Synod *Relatio post Disceptationem* was deemed "dry and incomplete" and prompted renewed efforts by the Synod Fathers to have their "Asian" voices heard. His overall performance was much appreciated.

Archbishop Oscar Cruz (Philippines), FABC Secretary General, was the principal redactor for the final Synod "Message to the People of God." It creatively captured the mood and central themes of the Synod: the Asian Church's triple dialogue with Asian religions, cultures, and people (especially the poor); the centrality of interreligious dialogue as the mode of evangelization in Asia's multiethnic, multireligious, and multicultural situation; the importance of local church, spirituality, laity, and inculturation in the Church's mission; the role of Christ and the Holy Spirit for holistic evangelization.

Cardinal Julius Riyadi Darmaatmadja (Indonesia) gave a beautiful closing Synod address on May 13. "We argued when we had differences of opinion," the cardinal noted, "but what has been really good is that we have been able to try to listen to the opinions and ideas of others ... and to seek what is positive in them." He described the synod as a search "for a fuller way for the Church to be rooted in Asia"; he believes that "the effort to be a Church with a truly Asian 'face' ... is nothing other than cooperating so that Christ's own efforts will succeed more fully." In Asia, "the credibility of the evangelizer lies in his or her being a man or woman of God more than a scholar, in being a person who lives simply but with depth." The cardinal recalled that "as in the Council of Jerusalem, Saint Peter gave the final view. So also we await the last word from the Holy Father in the forthcoming post-synod apostolic exhortation."

A Success Story? Although formally concluded by Pope John Paul II on May 14 with a concelebrated Mass in Saint Peter's Basilica, the Asian Synod is best understood in the fuller context of the Church's celebration of the Great Jubilee Year 2000. All the continental synods formed a special preparatory phase for that millennium event. The fruits of the

Synod enabled the emergence of *Ecclesia in Asia*, a programmatic and visionary papal document for the universal Church as well as for the local churches of Asia.

However, in and of itself the Synod proved to be a Spirit-filled event for the Church, particularly in Asia. Bishops met their colleagues from all parts of Asia; the universality and catholicity of the Church took on human faces; there was a strong consolidation of common Asian perspectives in evangelization; Asia was listening to its own Spirit-inspired voices providing an enriching exchange of ideas; the quarter-century labors of the FABC were affirmed; the Church as a "community of communities" gathered around the chief shepherd was celebrated.

A major ecclesial event always engenders renewal, change, solidarity, visioning, dreaming, faith, discontinuity, surprise, expanded consciousness, an experience of transformative grace, commitment to a renewed evangelization, a palpable encounter with Christ and his befriending Spirit; such was the Asian Synod. The local churches of Asia will treasure this event for many years, even after they have crossed the threshold of the new millennium.

SELECTED BIBIOGRAPHY

Arokiasamy, S. "Synod for Asia: An Ecclesial Event of Communion and Shared Witness of Faith," *Vidyajyoti* 62/9 (1998): 666-675.

Carrera, F. "Becoming an Asian Church," *World Mission* (Manila); 10/5 (1998): 21-25.

Claver, F. "Personal Thoughts on the Asian Synod," *East Asian Pastoral Review* 35/2 (1998): 241-248.

Cummins, J. "Synods in Contrast," *America* 179/5 (1998): 9-12.

Dupuis, J. "Premier échos du Synode pour l'Asie," *Etudes* No. 3893 (1998): 215-227; "First Echoes of the Synod for Asia," *Landas* 12/2 (1998): 13-28.

Gajiwala, A. "The Asian Synod of Bishops and Women: Sipping the Same Cup?" *In God's Image* 17/4 (1998): 57-62.

Kroeger, J. "Asia, A Continent of Emerging Missionary Hope," *Landas* 12/2 (1998): 35-56; *Verbum SVD* 40/3 (1999): 329-337.

Phan, P. *The Asian Synod: Texts and Commentaries.* Maryknoll, New York: Orbis Books, 2002.

Prior, J. "Apostles and Martyrs: Consecrated Life at the Bishops' Synod for Asia," *Review for Religious* 58/1 (1999): 6-27.

Rogers, A. "Challenges for the Church in Asia in the 21ˢᵗ Century: Reflections in the light of the Synod of Bishops for Asia," in: Federation of Asian Bishops' Conferences: Office for Human Development, *Special Assembly of the Synod of Bishops for Asia.* Manila: FABC: OHD, 1998: 22-37.

Seigel, M. (Ed.). *A Church on the Threshold: SEDOS Symposium to Accompany the Asian Synod.* Rome: SEDOS Research Center, 1998.

Tagle, L. "The Synod for Asia as Event," *East Asian Pastoral Review* 35/3-4 (1998): 366-378; "The Theological Perspectives of the Asian Synod," *Diwa* 24/1 (1999): 2-13.

Wang, J. "Sharing My First Hand Experience of the Asian Synod," *Religious Life Asia* 1/1 (1998): 24-39.

ASIA'S BISHOPS RESPOND TO ROME*

Tablet Documentation

The Asian Synod process involved the preparation of an outline and discussion questions (*lineamenta*), which was circulated to the Asian bishops' conferences in late 1996 for their discussion. Many reactions and comments were severely critical of this preparatory document; a synopsis of some reactions follows.

The Asian bishops criticized the outline document for being too Western in approach. Indeed, the Japanese bishops felt that the questions it contained were so far from Asian realities that they could not even answer them. Instead the Japanese bishops drew up their own list of questions.

They also detected overtones of Roman imperialism. "From the way the questions are proposed, one feels that the holding of the synod is like an occasion for the central office to evaluate the performance of the branch offices," they said. "That kind of synod would not be worthwhile for the Church in Asia."

This awareness of their own dignity and responsibility as local Churches was echoed by the suggestion from one Indonesian diocese that the synod should explore the possibility of an East Asian Patriarchate endowed with similar autonomy to the partriarchates of the Eastern Churches in communion with Rome. "This would relativize the primacy of the 'Western' Church," they said, and would help the Asian Churches to earth themselves in the local cultures.

The Japanese bishops called on Rome to take a new look at the connection between the Churches in Asia and the Holy See. They asked

*Original Text: *The Tablet* (May 2, 1998): 571.

the Holy See to "give more recognition to the rightful autonomy of the local Churches." As an example, they found it "strange" that approval should have to be obtained from Rome for Japanese translations of liturgical texts already approved by the Japanese bishops' conference.

The Japanese also drew attention to the disadvantages of forcing people to work in a language not their own. "Among all the countries of Asia there is not one which has as a native language those ordinarily used by the Holy See—Italian, English, French, German, Spanish," they said. Given that it took just over three months to have the outline document translated into Japanese and distributed to the dioceses, they asked for a period of preparation of "at least six months" between the publication of the subsequent working document and the convening of the Synod. [The working document was published in February and the synod met on April 19.] "The bishops of Japan consider it most important to translate the working document, study it carefully, and prepare themselves in prayer," they said. "And for the same reason we request that, together with determining English and French as the languages to be used at the synod, provision be made for simultaneous translation from English and French to Japanese, and other languages as requested by the other conferences."

They also had a suggestion for the working of the Asian synod itself. This was that the small discussion groups into which the bishops divide after the first two weeks should be based not on language but according to background culture—Islamic, Hindi, Hinayana Buddhist, Mahayana Buddhist, or Confucian.

A number of bishops conferences underlined the need to develop a specifically Asian theology or theologies. "Western and especially scholastic, theology is not adapted to the religions of Asia because it is too rational," explained the Vietnamese bishops. "For the Asians, one cannot analyze the truth or explain the mystery. And there is a preference for silence over words and not getting entangled in quarrels over words," they said. They noted that the word is only the finger pointing to the moon, and what matters is the moon and not the finger.

Similarly, the Korean bishops said that what was needed most of all was "a theological development based on Asian religious sentiments," while the four bishops of Laos listed among the areas calling for particular attention the formation of an Asian way of thinking and special studies of the sacred books of India.

Noting that "there is more than one theology evident in the New Testament," the Indian bishops declared that it was not possible to formulate a common method and expression for preaching the Gospel to the people of Asia. Rather, the local Churches themselves should develop their own methods according to their pastoral needs. This should be done under the guidance of a teaching authority which was "predominantly pastoral in character" (a quotation from Pope John XXIII's opening address to the Second Vatican Council).

The Philippine bishops said that "Christian life must become 'at home' in Asia." They called on the Synod to assess "the development of an Asian theology which may or may not follow the thought processes and expressions of Western, and particularly Roman, theology," while abiding "in dynamic fidelity" to the teaching authority.

The Indian bishops were positively scathing about the instruction on non-Christian forms of meditation issued by the Vatican Congregation for the Doctrine of the Faith in 1989. "Though no doubt well-intentioned, this instruction could have been much more effective if only there had been the necessary preliminary consultation among the Churches concerned," they said, citing it as an example of the way in which "much unnecessary embarrassment and pain" could be avoided by "timely dialogue" between the local Church and the universal Church.

The Sri Lankan bishops pointed to the way in which the controversy sparked by Pope John Paul II's remarks about Buddhism in his 1994 book *Crossing the Threshold of Hope* had "triggered a host of unpleasant feelings and seriously hampered the work of dialogue." They noted that the enthusiasm for dialogue which had been apparent immediately after Vatican II "seems to have faded away."

Another major theme of the Asian bishops' responses was the importance of dialogue with non-Christian religions, which are dominant in most of the countries concerned. Indeed, the Indonesian bishops stated that for them, as for the Federation of Asian Bishops' Conferences [FABC], "interreligious dialogue is the primary mode of evangelization." To them the outline document seemed to have as its dominant concern a fear that too much emphasis on dialogue would not place enough stress on proclaiming the faith. "Interreligious dialogue is distinct from proclamation, but may not be opposed to it," they said, "since in dialogue Christians give witness to their faith, and in proclamation Christians respectfully encounter in the hearers of the Word the truth and goodness that comes from the God of salvation and leads to him."

A common theme was the way in which the Church had learned from non-Christian religions how to be more tolerant and the need to build on this. The bishops of Malaysia, Singapore and Brunei listed what the Church could learn from dialogue with other religions:

- From Muslims the Church can learn about prayer, fasting, and almsgiving.

- From Hindus the Church can learn about meditation and contemplation.

- From Buddhists the Church can learn about detachment from material goods and respect for life.

- From Confucianism the Church can learn about filial piety and respect for elders.

- From Taoism the Church can learn about simplicity and humility.

- From animists the Church can learn about reverence and respect for nature and gratitude for harvests.

- The Church can learn from the rich symbolism and rites existing in their diversity of worship.

- The Church can, like the Asian religions, learn to be more open, receptive, sensitive, tolerant, and forgiving in the midst of a plurality of religions.

EVANGELIZATION: THE ASIAN WAY*

Gerard O'Connell

The Synod for Asia has revealed an Asian approach to preach Christ and be the Church. Key insights into the Church's mission emerged from the small group discussions that formed the second phase or "heart of the synodal process," coming after the delegates had finished their speeches (interventions) in the synod hall. There were eleven such working groups: eight English-speaking, two French-speaking (participants were mainly Middle Eastern and Vietnamese), and one Italian-speaking.

Participants could raise any matter they wished in the groups, but most were guided by the questions contained in the rapporteur's second report. These questions, however, did not flow naturally from the interventions and were theologically framed in a Roman way. Several bishops queried them and one group—English A—even recorded its "dissatisfaction" with them.

Proclaiming Christ. The first question was *how should Christ be proclaimed in Asia?* Despite centuries of evangelization, Catholics are still a tiny minority there: 100 million in a population of 3.5 billion. It is difficult to get their message heard in Asia. A new, more effective way must be found.

The best witness to Jesus, according to the group reports, is "the witness of life." But, as English D insisted, one must "have the God experience," as Jesus did, before one can effectively proclaim him. "Saints are the best proclaimers of Jesus"; there is a great need for prayer and holiness.

---

*Original Text: *The Tablet* (May 16, 1998): 647-649.

They agreed that a more scriptural, "less theological, more human" presentation of Jesus was needed (English D). It should "emphasize the human traits of Jesus" (English C) as a compassionate teacher of truth, guru (English A, D and French B), and a holy man, healer and prophet (English A, D, G). The Italian group questioned the guru concept, however. Everyone felt it necessary to show Asians that Jesus is the one who understands the suffering of the weak and downtrodden and identifies with the poor (English A). Some favored presenting him as "liberator" (French B, English A), but through non-violence, love and reconciliation (English B), and as the one who harmonizes (English H).

Jesus should also be presented as "the fulfillment of the yearnings of Asia expressed in the mythologies and folklore of Asian peoples" (English D). It should be shown how God's plan for salvation was "already operative 'in a certain way'" in the pre-Christian religious traditions of the East (English F).

Others, like English F, proposed starting with what the Christian message has in common with the cultures of other peoples: mercy and submission to God's will (Islam), compassion (Buddhism), non-violence (Hinduism), harmony with creation (cosmic religions). They shared English B's view that there should be "no arrogance in the proclamation of Jesus, who emptied himself."

Many Saviors? Significant differences of approach appeared in response to another question: *How can Jesus be presented as more than simply one of the saviors?* All agreed that Christ is the one and only savior, but many advised a gradual unfolding of that message in Asia. Some felt "it would not be prudent" to present Jesus as the only savior "immediately" (English C). First he should be presented as a perfect human being. English D agreed that "the uniqueness of Jesus, though theologically correct, may not be the best place to start." The first step was to show that Jesus is "not distant" from Asian realities.

For some, the expression "Christ the only savior" was "too aggressive" in the context of interreligious dialogue (French B). They advocated a more humble formulation. English A warned of announcing the uniqueness of Christ in a way that "smacks of arrogance and superiority on our part" and is even "insulting." For English G, though Jesus is the one and unique mediator of salvation, that "does not mean that there are no other mediators" although "in a participative sense only."

Theological Debate. One question seemed to come from nowhere, and certainly not from any of the Asian bishops: *How can the Church deal with some unorthodox trends among some theologians* with regard to the divinity of Jesus and his unique mediation of salvation? Some groups did not even address the subject. Others agreed with English A: "just one or two theologians" in Asia have come up with unorthodox views "but it is not the general trend." What Asian theologians need is encouragement.

English B felt that the accusation of "unorthodox trends" referred to theologians attempting "to build a bridge between Christianity and other religions." On the contrary, they expressed appreciation for their work and advocated that they should be given "some freedom or elbow room." They proposed "a permanent structure of dialogue and consultation" between these theologians and church authorities "to prevent misunderstandings" or "hasty publication of theological opinions" which could create tensions among Catholics. The Italian group was concerned by some theologians—"especially Indians"—who had over-emphasized the salvific value of other religions; this was a minority view.

The Church's Image. The groups were asked how they saw *"the image of the Church in the light of other religions."* They provided a remarkably frank picture. Though it is a minority in all countries except the Philippines [and Timor], the Church in Asia is widely perceived as rich, powerful and well organized (English A, French A). It is seen as Western (French A) and foreign, not having fully severed the umbilical cord of colonialism (English C). It is renowned for delivering excellent health care, social work and educational services (English A, French B), but is also perceived as a political power-broker and moral arbiter (English B, French A).

Significantly, however, many Asians do not appreciate the religious dimension of the Church, because they do not see it as a sign of God's presence (English B and C) or as a teacher of spirituality (French B). It is not seen as a praying Church, responding to their spiritual needs.

This stark analysis led many groups—using language reminiscent of Vatican II—to call for a humble, not triumphant, servant Church (French A, English F), a Church with the poor, a contemplative and self-emptying Church (English F), a Church of the poor and for the poor (English H). It should have the image that God intended for it (English B).

Intra-Church Communion. Next came the most delicate question of all. The concept of the Church as communion was prominent at Vatican

II and came to the fore in the 1985 Extraordinary Synod. It has been central in every synod since then. The groups were asked: *How can greater communion be promoted between the local Church and the universal Church, among the particular Churches in Asia, and within the particular Church? How can tensions be avoided among the particular Churches and between particular Churches and the Roman dicasteries?*

English A put it this way: "Communion recognizes differences." They recalled how Pius XI, in his *Quadragesimo Anno* (1931), formulated the principle of subsidiarity and how the 1985 Extraordinary Synod referred to it. "This principle in governance has to be practiced," English A said. It means that when possible "decision-making has to be shared in all levels"—which means that "more trust has to be manifested."

English C said the local Church must be looked upon as a reflection of the universal Church. There must be "unity in diversity." Local Churches can do things in different ways and yet maintain communion. "Unity not uniformity is the goal." Local Churches must have their legitimate freedom to grow; their growth contributes to and ensures the growth of the universal Church.

Many groups spoke of the need for greater trust, especially between Rome and the local Church, but also between local Churches and within the local Church. In the same vein, many groups urged that the laity be trusted more and given responsibility in the Churches in Asia. English D said the synods "would be more productive if more lay people were invited." English E said that for the development of a truly participative Church, "there is need to change the unwelcoming attitude of many among the clergy on the question of greater lay participation in the Church."

English D proposed the creation of a Catholic Conference of Asia, which would include bishops, clergy, religious and laity from all the Asian Churches, as a way of promoting communion in the Church. Finally, English D spoke of the Church as a "communion of communities," and the majority of the group said that basic ecclesial communities (there are thousands of these in the Philippines) should be promoted.

Most groups called for greater autonomy for the local Churches in liturgical matters and inculturation. A particular source of frustration is the requirement that Rome should approve translations of liturgical texts. The bishops are not trusted with such decisions and the attitude of the Roman dicasteries is "not at all positive" about the need to express the liturgy in the context of local cultures, English H said. Others said national episcopal conferences should be given "full authority" over liturgical translations (English B and E). Some groups advocated greater internationalization of the Roman Curia through recruitment of personnel from Asia (English C, D, G and H) and Africa (English D).

The Church's Mission. A third set of questions related to *the Church's mission of love and service*. The discussion here was about the priorities. In Asia, the Church has "a serious duty" to take action to protect human rights (English E and H). It must combat discrimination based on caste (English A) or other status (English E), and speak in favor of the fisherfolk of south India (English B), migrants (English D), AIDS victims—"the new lepers" (English E). Others called for action against drugs, prostitution (French A), abortion (many groups), and child labor (English B). One group urged a freeze on the international arms trade (English F).

Many groups discussed the advance of a single world order— "globalization." Participants focused more on the negative effects, especially on poor countries (English A). It is a new kind of colonialism, high economic power subjugating weaker economic power (English C). It introduces false models of development, eliminates jobs, promotes dehumanizing labor, and marginalizes people (English D). Globalization is pushing many Asian Churches to greater involvement in the social apostolate (English E). The Church should highlight the negative consequences (English H) and make a statement on globalization (Italian group).

English B and G appealed to the Churches in the First World to join the Asian Churches in a crusade for justice and solidarity. Several groups called for cancellation of Third World debt. The French suggested work for reconciliation among Christians, but the issue got little attention. English F urged the Synod to express its concern for Jerusalem. English G noted a serious omission in all the synodal documents: not a word about the Israeli-Palestinian question. There was discussion on youth, women, education and families.

These are the messages from the discussion groups, the heart of the synodal process; this is what should be reflected in the propositions forwarded to the Pope and in the final apostolic exhortation, *Ecclesia in Asia.*

SYNOD FOR ASIA: FIRST ECHOES*

Jacques Dupuis

Asia extends from West to East, from the lands of the Gulf to Japan. The southern part of the continent includes Southern Asia, Southeastern Asia and East Asia. In the North are found the republics of Central Asia; in the Northeast, Siberia and Mongolia. This immense territory covers a multitude of races, religions and cultures. Asia represents more than three-fifths, almost two thirds, of the population of the world, with one of largest proportions of young people. All economic models and all political regimes are represented there. Alongside countries with flourishing economies and others in the process of rapid development, Asia includes many of the poorest countries in the world, in which masses of men and women live in dehumanizing poverty. It has become banal to describe the Asian reality as composed of three elements: masses of humanity in need of liberation; a wealth of numerous ancient cultures; a multitude of religious traditions.

Asia, taken as a whole, is the cradle of all the great religions of the world: Hinduism, Buddhism, Judaism, Christianity, Islam. Asia is also the home of numerous other religious traditions: Taoism, Confucianism, Zoroastrianism, Jainism, Sikkhism, and Shintoism. With the Philippines as the sole exception, Christianity represents only a tiny minority. For example, China and India at present together number over two billion people, out of whom the entire Christian population is estimated to number only a little over 25 million! These figures suffice to demonstrate the magnitude of the challenges that the Asian continent poses to the mission of the Church as it moves toward the third millenium of Christianity.

---

*Original Text: *Landas* 12/2 (1998): 13-28.

Mark of Service. The millenium, in Asia more than in other parts of the world, should thus be celebrated under the mark of humility and service. It should be an occasion for Christian Churches to become more conscious of, and to make more evident in action, their vocation to be at the service of human beings and peoples, in view of the Kingdom inaugurated by God in Jesus Christ, which embraces all humanity and goes far beyond the frontiers of Christianity and the Churches. Is not the model to follow that which Jesus himself taught us, he who came not in order to be served but to serve? The Church, which continues his mission, must follow him on the narrow way and reproduce in herself the *kenosis* of the incarnation. In Asia specially, she is called to be the yeast that disappears into the dough to make it rise, the salt of the earth that must likewise disappear. The Church must empty herself of herself, in order to be entirely centered on the Lord.

Many of the responses of the Episcopal Conferences to the *Lineamenta* for the Synod noted this need for service in forgetfulness of self. One reads in the *Instrumentum Laboris* (13): "In the work of evangelization, the Church in Asia needs to be aware of the image she has among believers of other faiths and non-believers. While the Church is admired for her organizational, administrative, educational, and health services as well as developmental works, these same people often do not see the Church as totally Asian.... In many cases, the Christian faith itself is perceived as something that has been imported into Asia from the outside. This is the reason why some people do not accept Christianity, fearing a loss of their national identity and culture.

Similarly, the responses note that "the Western Christian missionary approach to other Asian religions ... oftentimes lacked a full appreciation of these elements.... The Church's rediscovered appreciation of other religions and cultures should find greater expression in her missionary approach" (Ibid., 14). These affirmations are very measured and made with great discretion. They hardly reveal the magnitude of the problems; they say enough however to allow one to glimpse the immense challenges which the mission of the Church encounters today in the Asian context, challenges the continental synod had to face....

***Lineamenta* critiqued.** Produced, as is the custom, by the Roman Curia under the responsibility of the General Secretariat of the Synod of Bishops, the *Lineamenta* was published on September 3, 1996. Circulated among all the Episcopal Conferences, it was the object of numerous reactions, mostly negative. It is not necessary to examine in detail this provisional text. It is useful, however, to take note of the most important negative reactions submitted to the Vatican by the Conferences on the subject of this first document, and to note the remarkable convergence existing among these different responses.

The first negative comment was that the theological and pastoral reflection developed for over twenty five years by the Federation of Asian Bishops' Conferences (FABC), given eloquent witness by an impressive number of documents, was, if not entirely passed over in silence, at least hardly represented—and this itself under an unfavorable light. The theological vision of the mission of the Church in the Asian context, elaborated by the Federation with a remarkable consistency over the course of the years, was thus totally ignored.... Taken as a whole, according to the responses of the Episcopal conferences, the attitude of the *Lineamenta* to the Asian Churches is paternalistic, and its theological perspective, centralist and Eurocentric.

A second negative comment made concerning the *Lineamenta* was the narrow, ecclesiocentric perspective of its theology of mission.... This explains why the document adopts of a notion of the mission of the Church which insists in a unilateral fashion on the proclamation or announcement of Jesus Christ, while the role of interreligious dialogue and that of involvement for justice are, if not passed over in silence, at least greatly diminished. A Regnocentric perspective on mission, conceived in the manner of the documents of the FABC, would have permitted the development of a holistic vision of evangelizing mission.

The responses to the *Lineamenta* underline too the absence of pneumatology. The universal presence of the Spirit of God, especially in Asian religious traditions, should have been spoken of, for this would have permitted the development of an open and positive theology of the value of religious traditions and their significance in the order of salvation. The forgetfulness of the pneumatological dimension in the *Lineamenta* resulted in the loss of the meaning of interreligious dialogue; for if it is true that the Church must witness to her faith in dialogue, it is also her duty to recognize what the Spirit has accomplished and continues to accomplish in others.

A further critique of the *Lineamenta* is that it does not take account of the way in which Asian reflection insists on the felt need of the Churches to put on "an Asian face." The theology of the local Church is underdeveloped in the document. Now, for such a development to become a reality, it is necessary to emphasize, not only in theory but also in praxis, the ecclesial reality of the local Church in its relationship to the universal Church, through the concrete application of the principles of collegiality and subsidiarity, against a tendency to an exaggerated centralization. It is necessary that the local Church enjoy a "legitimate autonomy" in order for it to able to develop its own identity in different aspects of ecclesial life.

In this regard, the vision of the first General Assembly of the FABC in Taipei in 1974 should be recalled, a vision which has remained constant through the years. There, mission in Asia was spoken of as the construction of a truly local Church, that is to say, a Church engaged in a triple dialogue with cultures, with religions, and with the poor. From this vision are drawn the threefold priority tasks of inculturation, interreligious dialogue, involvement toward human liberation. These three tasks, moreover, are inseparable, and should be pursued together.

A Recentered *Instrumentum Laboris*. Considerable difference exists between this new document and the preceding one. A detailed comparison of the two documents would demonstrate this clearly. The very structure of the document changed, to give place to new sections responding to the requests of the Conferences, which were taken seriously into consideration. Something of the ecclesiological and missiological vision of FABC now becomes more transparent: the negative and defamatory references are suppressed; the overly narrow ecclesiocentric perspective gives way to a Regnocentric perspective, in which the Church is understood as placed at the service of the Reign of God (# 34). As a result, a more generous place is granted to interreligious dialogue and action for justice. "The need to elaborate an Asian understanding of evangelization in which interaction, dialogue, witness, service, and proclamation are all seen as integral elements of the Church's evangelizing mission" (# 47) is now noted.

Explicit reference is made to the triple dialogue with the poor, with cultures and with religions, envisaged by the documents of the FABC since its creation (# 37). An entire section is devoted to the presence of the Spirit of God in cultures and religions, from which the salvific role the latter plays among the peoples is inferred (# 31).... The presence of the

Spirit among others is the foundation of a dialogue that can be the source of mutual enrichment for both partners in the dialogue.

Another important new element of the Working Document, compared to the *Lineamenta*, concerns the Church as a communion of local churches and the necessity of applying "the principles of unity of faith, charity, collegiality and subsidiarity" (# 38) to the relationship between the local Churches and the central authority. This means that "more autonomy should be given to the local Churches in areas of dialogue, inculturation, and adaptation," in view of which the Church must determine the necessary structures. The need for inculturation is brought out, even in the fields of theology and theological formation (# 50). Without wishing to say everything, one can affirm that, taken as a whole, with this new document, the Synod had in its hands a useful instrument to undertake its work....

A First Report. The opening salvo was made through the Preliminary Report by Cardinal Paul Shan Kuo-hsi, bishop of Kaohsiung, reporter general of the synod, on April 21. From the start the Cardinal-reporter constantly referred to the Working Document, an evident sign that the latter represented a valuable point of departure in view of the work of the Assembly.

The report brought out all the great themes of an Asian vision of mission. They can be mentioned rapidly: the broad notion of the mission of evangelization, with its triple imperatives of action for justice, inculturation and interreligious dialogue; a positive theological evaluation of Asian religious traditions, based on the active presence of the Spirit of God in cultures and religions; the urgent need of inculturation in all aspects of ecclesial life, including theology (particularly, Christology), liturgy, sacred art, spirituality, social organization; an ecclesiology of communion in which the principle of collegiality is operative (the principle of subsidiarity was passed over in silence), in view of a greater autonomy of the local Churches, which must present themselves with an Asian face; the Church at the service of the Kingdom of God; a Church which reproduces in herself the model of the "Suffering Servant" and follows her Master in his *kenosis*; a Church which is not only for the poor, but with the poor; the primacy in the Asian context of the experience of God in Jesus Christ over doctrines; an experience which is transmitted though witness which incarnates the values of the Gospel. In brief, Churches which are not or no longer "copies conformed" to the model of Western societies.

Days of individual interventions of the fathers in the General Assembly followed. These interventions re-enforced in many places the perspectives first recovered by the Working Document and corroborated afterwards by the first Report. It is neither necessary nor possible to go over, even rapidly, these interventions of the synodal fathers. These were, in their turn, incorporated, although imperfectly, in the second Report of Cardinal Paul Shan....

New Document ... New Requests. Some of the salient features of the *Relatio post Disceptationem* (Second Report) can be noted. An inculturated liturgy is a part of evangelization. In view of this, the use of sacred texts of other religions in the liturgy and prayer of the Church is suggested (# 16). The local Church, subject of evangelization, should be an inculturated Church. This means that local Churches should enjoy a "legitimate autonomy" within the unity of the faith, and thus, that the "principles of collegiality, subsidiarity and legitimate autonomy" (# 18) be respected. Local Churches should also be "communities of participation" at all levels, a "communion of communities" (# 22). Priority should be given to the evangelization of indigenous populations and minority groups (# 26). Education should be perceived as a true activity of evangelization (# 28).

Local churches should assume "an Asian face" in all their dimensions: theological, liturgical, organizational and spiritual; this is what "a new way of being Church in Asia" means. Only an authentic process of inculturation can change "her western image and give an Asian countenance to the Church" (# 32). The vocation of the Church is to become "an even more perfect image of the Kingdom of God and to invite others to do the same" (# 33); she must "take on the image of a servant." "Since she desires to be of service to the peoples of Asia, she is to pursue in Asia the values of the Kingdom" (# 34). "The Church has a duty to engage in a manifold dialogue with the followers of other religions in order to build more just, humane and harmonious societies" (# 38).

Integral human development implies not only the promotion of the values of the Kingdom of God in the world, but also the struggle against the structures of sin in society (# 38-39). Inculturation is the call made to Christians to root the values of the Gospel in every culture. It can perhaps be seen as "a dialogue between people and the Holy Spirit" (# 48). It should inform every aspect of the life of the Church. In the field of liturgy, "there is a need for greater flexibility and creativity." In the area of theology, inculturation will lead to bringing out certain aspects of the person of Jesus; for example, presenting him as Guru or as Liberator (# 49). Interreligious dialogue, in its different forms, takes on a special importance in Asia; in dialogue, Christians must learn not only to speak, but also "to listen and learn" (# 51). The scandal of the division of Christians remains "one of the great obstacles to evangelization" (# 52). The question of whether the discipline of the Church could be reconsidered was raised, so that Eucharistic hospitality might be extended "to all Christians who believe in Christ's real presence in the Eucharist" (# 53).

These remarks obviously do not exhaust the content of the *Relatio post Disceptationem*. They are highlighted as signs of openness in a text which was not afraid to put forward suggestions or requests of far-reaching impact, made in the Assembly of the Synod. These suggestions take up, in fact, reflections and hopes kept alive for many years in the Asian Churches during the period of the renewal of the Church which followed the Second Vatican Council. Are these hopes, unfulfilled at that time, closer to fulfillment today? One can get some idea of an answer by examining what sort of echo the official propositions of the Synod furnish.

Final Propositions, Perspectives for the Future. The final list of propositions handed over to Pope John Paul II by the Synod contains fifty-nine propositions. They cannot all be reviewed here. One must be content with showing that, on certain important points, they adequately reflect the Second Report, although certain more controversial points are passed over in silence.

The concern for inculturation of Asian Churches remains primordial. These Churches must be immersed in the diverse Asian realities, contrasting and perhaps even conflictual (# 3). The different aspects of evangelization are enumerated as follows: witness, dialogue, proclamation, catechesis, conversion, baptism, insertion into the ecclesial community, implantation of the Church, inculturation and the integral human promotion (# 6)....
The proclamation of Jesus Christ remains primordial, but it must be inculturated. Jesus will thus be presented as the Teacher of Wisdom, the Healer, the Liberator, the Spiritual Guide, the Enlightened One, the Compassionate Friend of the Poor, the Good Samaritan, the Good Shepherd, the Obedient Servant (# 6).

The Synod encourages theologians to pursue their work, which consists of developing an inculturated theology, in sincere union with the

Magisterium (# 7). The Spirit of God, who has been at work since creation (# 11), must be discovered in Asian realities, cultures and religions; he is the principal agent of evangelization in the multi-cultural and multi-religious context of Asia (# 12).

The Church-communion, "communion of communities," must be marked at all levels by participation; the spirit of communion and of collegiality is recommended (# 13-15). "Basic ecclesial communities" represent "a new way of being Church in Asia" (# 30). The Church must institute "new ministries for women," in view of their effective participation in the Church's mission (# 35). Religious life should be inserted in the reality of Asia, while remaining faithful to respective charisms (# 27); mission societies are to be promoted (# 28). Action for justice is an integral aspect of evangelization (# 22). Human promotion is a constitutive dimension of evangelization. The "preferential love for the poor" presupposes on the part of the Church that she make their cause her own, by becoming a Church of the poor and for the poor (# 44). Indigenous and tribal populations are specially disposed to receive the message of Christ; the Church must respond to their expectation (# 38). Interreligious dialogue seeks to promote mutual collaboration and enrichment in respect for one's distinctive religious identity (# 41). Concerning ecumenism, it is suggested that Episcopal Conferences explore with other Churches the possibility of new structures, in view of promoting the union of Christians (# 42).

Coming to the inculturation of the Gospel in the diverse cultures of Asia, the different fields of application are enumerated as follows: theology, liturgy, the formation of priests and religious, catechism, spirituality, and popular religiosity (# 43). One might note the absence of the structural aspect of the Church and her legislation from this list. It is said, moreover, that "local Churches need the authority and freedom to inculturate the liturgy by adapting it to local cultures, while recognizing the need for dialogue and communion with the Holy See, principle of unity in the Church" (# 43). In particular, the Synod asks the concerned Roman congregations to accord to Episcopal Conferences "the authority or competence to approve translations of liturgical texts in the vernacular" (# 43). That is all and that is so little! This request is limited to a relatively derisory application of the competence that should be recognized of Episcopal Conferences, if it is true that they enjoy an authority, equally doctrinal, in their respective territories. The "legitimate autonomy" of the local Church is not spoken of, nor is the principle of subsidiarity, which, as was noted, appeared and then disappeared along the way in the preceding synodal documents.

Contrasting Assessment. The last observation above brings us to some reflections on the Synod itself. Should one have expected more? The situations are in fact so diverse in all their elements, including ecclesial traditions from the "Middle East" (referred to as Western Asia) to Southeast Asia, or again from the countries of the Gulf to Japan, that a common synod for all of Asia was doubtless condemned to content itself with generalities.

In his remarks at the end of the Synod, Cardinal Julius Darmaatmadja, archbishop of Jakarta, president delegate of the Synod, noted: "We have been able to try to listen to the opinions and ideas of others, which have been influenced by different situations, and to seek what is positive in them. We may still find ourselves in disagreement with certain propositions.... But, as in the Council of Jerusalem, Saint Peter gave the final word. So also we await the last word from the Holy Father in the forthcoming post-synodal apostolic exhortation" (# 8).

In fact, the theological vision developed through the years by the Federation of Asian Bishops' Conferences (FABC), the absence of which in the *Lineamenta* was regretted by Episcopal Conferences, appeared little in the final propositions. The hope was expressed that the apostolic exhortation, which should serve as the crown of the synodal process, could itself, in its presentation, reflect an Asian character [proposition 3]; but this hope is poorly served by the propositions, of which all the references come from, besides the texts of the Second Vatican Council, documents of the Central Magisterium. There is not a single reference to the documents of the Asia Federation, often so rich and more adapted to the context.

Words and Silences. Without doubt, the subjects that have become in fact essential in all continents were treated. The different dimensions of the evangelizing mission of the Church were spoken of; in this case, the triple dialogue of the local church with cultures, religions and the poor. But the place given to interreligious dialogue seems meager in comparison to that given to proclamation of the Gospel, especially if one considers the minority status of the Church in so many Asian countries, where the witness of life or interreligious dialogue often represent the only possible ways of evangelization. In other situations, dialogue with the majority religion is almost non-existent, if not perhaps impossible. The imperative of inculturation in local Churches is emphasized; however, the necessary conditions for its realization, touching on the relationship between local Churches and the central authority of the Church, are hardly touched upon, and the concrete suggestions articulated during the course of the Synod's work either disappear entirely in the final propositions, or are no longer found except in a form so toned down that they have become insignificant.

One cannot obviously claim to make a final assessment at this time, before even the publication of the forthcoming apostolic exhortation. But one cannot fail to raise questions concerning the vitality of the synodal institution in its present form. It is, doubtlessly true to say, that all the questions posed here have been raised before, perhaps at a more profound level, without receiving, all the same, the pertinent answers. There will be occasion later, no doubt, to speak of the "words and the silences" of the Asian Synod....

ASIA THROUGH ASIAN EYES*

Thomas Menamparampil

The Asian Synod has come and gone. Historically speaking, the Asian Synod was the most important ecclesial event for Asia from the time of the great Councils (Nicaea, Ephesus, Chalcedon). It reminded us of the Asian roots of Christianity, of Christ and His disciples, of the early theological formulations, of liturgical and monastic traditions and forms of spirituality which we today unconsciously associate with the West. In fact, the West took at least a millennium to inculturate these beliefs and practices and make them its own.

It is good to be reminded and to be convinced that Christianity is an Asian religion. The entire Biblical drama (except some of Paul's travels) was enacted on Asian soil. The Wisdom literature in the Scriptures reflects the sayings of our ancients and the teaching of our sages. Family bonds, master-disciple relationships, and spiritual experiences described in the Bible have an Eastern quality about them. We do not have to take extra troubles to make Christianity Asian. When Christianity is true to itself, it is all too Asian.

Contrary to fears expressed in many quarters and rumors spread, all documents relating to the Asian Synod (*Lineamenta, Instrumentum Laboris, Relatio ante* and *post Desceptationem*, and Propositions) were drawn up by Asians themselves. The drafting team felt no pressure from anybody to accept any particular point of view. And in the General Assembly, everyone had the same length of time to speak and the same opportunity to be

---

*Original Text: *The New Leader* 111/16 (1998): 21-22.

heard. No one was specially privileged. Group discussions were guided by elected members who ensured that everyone had a chance to contribute.

Western observers of the Asian Synod were surprised at the issues that came up on the floor of the Assembly almost from the very beginning. They seemed to differ greatly from those that were prominent in the other continental Synods. While evangelization was the general theme, Asian Bishops kept repeatedly referring to the sturdiness and strength of the ancient religions of Asia, the need for dialogue, the need for approaching people of other religious persuasions with respect and humility. They spoke of the importance of God-experience for an evangelizer, of contemplative depth, personal witness, spirit of sacrifice, ascetical image, humble attitude, simplicity of lifestyle, closeness to the poor, commitment to the marginalized and oppressed, transparency of character and other qualities. The urgency of being at the service of the down-trodden like the tribals and dalits received attention. There is no room for any sort of arrogance or triumphalism in sharing one's faith; it would be self-defeating.

The interventions at the Synod made it very clear that we should search for Asian ways of presenting Christ. Generally, theological abstractions do not attract Asian people. A narrative style with the use of song and story, proverbs and parables, would be more relevant. Christ should be presented to Asians as a spiritual master, healer, a messenger of peace, author of harmony, helper of the poor, a person of service, a compassionate friend, the Good Shepherd, the giver of life, the suffering servant, the one who forgives and reconciles. It was recognized that there was a pedagogy in introducing Christ to those who were new to Christianity and graduality is needed in fostering their understanding and accepting Him and His message. Ways of approach also would differ, depending on the community to which the Gospel is addressed, e.g. tribal people, dalits, Hindus, Muslims, Buddhists or other groups.

Asian Churches desired greater freedom for inculturation and for the translation of liturgical texts. The pastoral care of Asians in the Western world and those of the Oriental Churches out of their own homeland is to be ensured. Ecumenical efforts should be intensified. In all these matters, one is to be guided by the Petrine office.

The important role the laity plays in the mission of the Church received much attention. Catholic educational endeavors should specially aim at the formation of lay leaders and encouragement of Catholic intellectuals. Catechists and renewal movements have proved to be powerful agents of evangelization. Youth are the best evangelizers of their own companions. Women bring the feminine genius to the service of God's message. Family values are cherished in Asia; they ought to be defended against forces that threaten cohesion within the family.

While globalization can offer new economic opportunities, it often threatens weaker economies, local cultures, and traditional values. There is need for the development of global ethics and fairer norms to regulate international market forces. Individual nations too must put their own houses in order, ensuring transparency, good governance, fair distribution of the benefits of development, and preventing anything that looks like corruption and nepotism. Environment needs to be protected; migrants, refugees and the poor should be specially assisted.

Formation of priests and religious was another topic that received the special attention of the Synod Fathers. A missionary spirit should be inculcated in seminaries and houses of formation, and a spirit of service fostered. Sacramental life should lead to a deepening of God-experience in the future missionary. This is a brief sketch of the themes that came on the floor of the Synod; it is certainly not exhaustive. However, what one may ask is: Will the Asian Synod give a new direction to the Church in Asia?

It will be for history to tell what the Synod for Asia has achieved. But, a beginning has been made. The countries of Central Asia have sought to be admitted into the FABC, and those of West Asia have decided to maintain on-going contact with the rest of Asia. Asian Bishops, for the first time, came to know each other closely and admire the greatness of their traditions. In spite of the many differences, they have noticed a cultural closeness and similarity of perception. There are things in common that they can build on. It is right that we take greater interest in Church events in Asia. We may be better informed about events in Europe or America than in our own immediate neighborhood, e.g. Myanmar, Laos or Cambodia. Even what we know about different parts of Asia may be material presented to us through non-Asian sources of information. It is good for us to look at Asia with Asian eyes.

It is important to emphasize that being a loyal Asian does not mean being virtually anti-Western, or forever brooding over the grouses of our colonial past, or an exaggerated flattering of our collective ego. Living on a continent with 5,000 years of history, we need not easily be blinded by the events of just the last 500 years. The best in Asian traditions tells us to develop a universal outlook and work for the common good of humanity. Euro-centrism is not to be replaced by Indo-centrism or Sino-centrism, but genuine universal brotherhood. Asians are capable of forgiveness and of building on ancient ruins. Serenity and self-confidence are more important today than aggressive self-assertion, which would merely serve to reduce our stature.

The future of Asia depends on the ability of Asian nations to resolve their differences in a non-military manner. Our national leaders had vowed commitment to humanity when our nation was coming to birth. That was perfectly in keeping with the best of Asian traditions. We seem to have forgotten such noble ideals. In Church circles too, when we foster aggressiveness in vocabulary and action, whether it be in the name of language, or culture, or ethnic identity, or caste, or rite, or perceived injustice, we are betraying the core values that have made our civilizations great. In return to genuine Asian values lies Asia's salvation.

ACHIEVEMENTS OF THE SYNOD*

Georg Evers

If one considers only the official synod message from the Synod for Asia, then it appears that not much has been achieved by this gathering of so many Asian bishops from April 19 to May 14 at the Vatican. The official final document, the post-synodal exhortation, will likely be promulgated by Pope John Paul II next year, somewhere in Asia.

The real outcome of the synod, however, is to be seen in the interaction of the Asian bishops in and outside the aula, in reports and discussion in formal and informal sessions, in conferences organized by Rome-based SEDOS (*Servizio di Documentazioni e Studi;* Center for Documentation and Studies), in the activities of the International Catholic Movement of Intellectual and Cultural Affairs (ICMICA - Pax Romana), and other reactions and publications on the content and aim of the Special Assembly of the Synod of Bishops for Asia.

The Synod showed the value of the Federation of Asian Bishops' Conferences (FABC) and vindicated the spiritual and theological work done during its more than twenty-five years of existence. FABC secretary general Archbishop Oscar Cruz of Lingayen-Dagupan, the Philippines, stated that the Synod with its peculiar way of working confirmed the course of the FABC, even if it remained behind the achievements of the FABC with regard to theological insights and statements.

The cardinals of the Roman Curia, who are used to dealing separately with individual bishops, were somewhat surprised that "these Asian bishops know each other," as reportedly expressed by Cardinal Jozef Tomko, prefect

*Original Text: *Asia Focus* 14/27 (1998): 3.

of the Congregation for the Evangelization of Peoples. Other observers who participated at other continental bishops' synods confirmed that the Synod for Asia was exceptional in the outspokenness of the contributions made by some Asian bishops who took up the crucial issue of the relationship between local Churches and the Roman Curia.

Several Asian bishops stressed in their interventions the need for more latitude in the process of inculturation, such as in the "minor" issue of translation of liturgical texts into Asian languages. They proposed more respect for the competence of the Asian Churches, their leaders and theologians, in dealing with the issues of the position of Christ, the salvific meaning of other religions and interreligious dialogue.

An assessment of the synod outcome should also consider the whole process beginning with the announcement during the Silver Jubilee celebration of the FABC in Manila in January 1995, and the publication of the synod *Lineamenta* (outline). Critical responses by the Japanese, Indonesian, Indian and Vietnamese bishops' conferences pointed out that the tone set by the *Lineamenta* was heavily tainted by a Western theological approach and did not contain and express the achievements made by Asian theologians in general and the work of the FABC and its many conferences and publications in particular.

At this stage, Asian bishops followed the lead of the Japanese bishops' conference rather than that of Vatican authorities, who followed a strict policy of keeping most synodal procedures *sub secreto* (under secrecy). The publication of the *Instrumentum Laboris* (working paper), though barely a month before the Synod, showed that the criticisms of Asian bishops had been taken into account. The working paper was a big improvement over the *Lineamenta*.

The synod procedure of allotting only eight minutes each for the initial interventions, which followed each other without coordination according to the topics treated, was not conducive to a fruitful interaction between the bishops and members of the Roman Curia. Nevertheless, the central issues of the Asian bishops—inculturation, interreligious dialogue, the present Asian situation, decentralization in the relation between local Asian Churches and the Roman Curia—were expressed clearly.

The controversial issue of Jesus Christ as the "only and universal savior of humankind" was treated by several Asian bishops. There was agreement that in the multireligious context of most Asian countries, statements about the uniqueness of Jesus Christ and the absoluteness of Christianity are putting an end to any form of dialogue before the dialogue can even start. The bishops stressed that the presentation of the human features and message of Jesus should proceed in stages following the so-called "principle of graduality," which leads in time to the proclamation of faith in the person of Jesus Christ as the "only and unique savior."

That the Synod included other Asian countries besides FABC member countries proved to be an asset. The presence of bishops from Lebanon, Iraq, Syria, Jordan and Israel with their different Church structures made some Asian bishops dream of setting up some form of patriarchal Church structure in other parts of Asia as well. For the small Churches of Kazakhstan, Kyrgizstan, Siberia, Tajikistan, Turkmenistan and Uzbekistan, the Synod for Asia was an important event, especially the contact with the FABC, of which these isolated Churches became members in June. The Churches that have faced persecution in Cambodia, Laos and Vietnam renewed their contact at the Synod with other Asian Churches.

It is too early to make a final assessment of the Synod for Asia, but it can already be said that the Synod was better than many observers had predicted on the basis of the defects in its preparation and procedures and other negative factors. At the Synod, the Asian bishops were able to articulate their concerns and to show the degree of cooperation already existing within the Asian Churches, particularly within the FABC.

SYNOD FOR ASIA, A TIME OF GRACE*

Thomas Han Hong-Soon

Crossing the threshold of hope, the threshold of evangelization in the third millennium, was the primary concern of the Synod for Asia.

Keenly aware of the challenges confronting the Church in Asia, the synod participants rightly emphasized the urgent need for dialogue with the cultures, religions, and peoples of Asia as an effective means to carry out the Church's mission. They also emphasized that such a dialogue needs to be based on the Church's social doctrine, which they affirmed as a valid instrument of evangelization.

While emphasizing the need for dialogue, the Synod itself proved to be an excellent forum for dialogue. Deeply impressive was the constant openness for dialogue among the Synod Fathers. They were sincere and open to each other and, notably, to the lay auditors, who they encouraged to make interventions both at the general congregations and at the small group meetings.

The lay participants were not meant to be mere "listeners," as the word "auditor" literally means. All the participants were eager to share with each other their own thoughts and experiences for the good of the Church. This is an asset of which our Church can be proud.

All the members of the Church—bishops, clergy, religious and lay people—gathered around Pope John Paul II to "walk together" [literal translation of "synod"] in order to continue *Redemptoris Missio* [the 1990 papal mission encyclical] more effectively. This is really what a synod is. This is really the driving force of the Church. During the Synod each and

*Original Text: *Asia Focus* 15/42 (1999): 3.

every participant felt immersed in the salvific atmosphere of communion that dominated the Synod Hall.

Central and decisive was the pope's presence at every day's work. He almost literally took our hands to lead us to the heart of the problems. It was always inspiring to listen to his remarks, brief but full of wit and spiritual insight. It was indeed a great joy for all the participants to see him at all the general congregations and to feel all the more heartily that he is the unshakable center of Church communion, and the solid rock and hope of the Church.

Very notable also were the two vacant seats reserved in the Synod Hall for two mainland Chinese bishops who were appointed members of the Synod for the first time in the Church's history. Sadly enough, they could not join the Synod for political reasons. Those empty seats eloquently symbolized the voice of the silent Churches and the living communion of the universal Church with them.

Although there was no presence of the Churches of mainland China and North Korea at the Synod, a delightful fact was the participation of the Churches in Siberia and the Central Asian republics of the former Soviet Union. Their stories of rebuilding their harshly persecuted Churches, still facing adversities of every sort, made us realize once again that Asia is a continent of martyrs. No other continent on the globe has offered as many martyrs as Asia. The Asian Church shows vividly that the blood of martyrs is the seed of Christians.

Since 1988, the average annual growth rate of the number of Catholics in Asia has been more than double that of the worldwide rate. As the pope reminded us during his homily at the concluding Mass, Jesus Christ was born in Asia and he sowed in this continent the seed of salvation for all the peoples of the world. This eternal "seed" cannot but bear abundant fruit if taken care of in a proper way.

The Synod for Asia was indeed a time of grace to renew apostolic missionary zeal to proclaim Christ in Asia without being afraid. Now it is up to all of us in Asia to make good by deeds and words the great springtime for evangelization in Asia in the new millennium, and thereby to consecrate Asia as a continent of hope for humanity.

8

YOUTH INVOLVEMENT
IN THE ASIAN CHURCH*

Nicholas Somchai Interview

What will you remember most about the Asian Synod?

I will remember the generosity of the people from the Federation of Asian Bishops' Conferences [FABC] who helped me. Before going to the Synod, I had no idea what the Synod was all about. After my arrival in Rome I was informed that I was a youth representative as an auditor at the Synod. When I needed more information, FABC people such as Cora Mateo, executive secretary of the FABC Office of the Laity, and others helped me. These people worked really hard to help others actively participate in the Synod, not only in terms of preparation of documents, but also in sharing of ideas and conviction.

What is your assessment of the Synod?

The Synod was a good opportunity for the bishops from Asia to share the situations in their particular countries, and it helped them to learn from their colleagues about the life of people in other countries. It was also a forum where the prelates in the Vatican and the Asian bishops could discuss their understanding of the local Churches in Asia. We came together and talked about problems in Asia, though we didn't have any action plans when we went home.

---

*Original Text: *Asia Focus* 14/22 (1998): 8.

Were there any surprises?

Yes! I was in the first group of auditors to have dinner with Pope John Paul II. I did not know that I would have such an opportunity, so I did not prepare anything. I wore just a simple jacket and slacks. I wish I had worn a Thai-style suit or offered the Holy Father some souvenir from Thailand. During the private audience, I couldn't speak too well. When the pope spoke to me, I was so overwhelmed that all I could say was "Yes" or something like that. Nevertheless, it was a very special time for me.

What youth issues were brought up by other Synod participants, and how are they related to your concerns?

Sister Victoria Lau Suk-chun, an auditor from Macau, said the youth there want to participate in the parish and in the Church's decision-making process, because they feel that they are not a part of the Church. They feel like they are merely an object of a Church outreach.

During the Synod sessions I listened to Synod Fathers talking about youth issues. From some 180 bishops, only two or three Synod Fathers talked about youth problems or concerns. This presents a credibility problem when the Synod document describes youth, comprising some 60 percent of the Asian population, as the majority in Asia. Most importantly, it is not so much that we are the largest group, but rather it is the situation that youth often face. They are targets of many social problems including materialism, child abuse, and prostitution.

These issues are related to my concerns because they ask the same question: How can we help youth become a part of the Church? For example, in a local church meeting on any projects related to youth, all decisions seem to come from priests. If youth are allowed to take part in decision-making, it will greatly benefit any program in which they are involved.

Was there any response to your call for a role in decision-making in the Church from the Synod participants or the Roman Curia?

There was some response, but it had no weight. For example, the final message of the Synod says that the Church must "take proper care of the millions of young people in Asia," but it does not spell this out in practical terms. How does the Church take care of youth? What will the Church do to help youth participate and have an important role in the Church?

What messages did you want the Synod for Asia to give to Asian youth?

Let youth be involved in the life of the Church at all levels. On every occasion that involves youth, they should be invited to participate in the decision-making process so that they can better impart their own situations and reality. The local Church must help youth develop their thinking and express their social concern for the local reality through exposure, immersion, reflection and actions programs. Most importantly, the local Church must help youth develop their faith life. I don't think most youth really understand what the Catholic faith is.

In concrete measures, how did the Synod benefit Asian youth?

I and the other young auditor from Jordan were invited to share our concerns with the bishops. It was a good occasion to raise awareness on youth issues among them. I talked to many bishops during the Synod who told me when they go home they will be mindful of those issues and concerns.

Did the Synod change or reaffirm your perceptions of the Catholic Church?

The meeting has somewhat changed my mind about the Catholic Church. The Synod helped me reflect about things more deeply. For example, I don't normally read the Gospel on a regular basis. I just accept whatever the Gospel says without reflecting deeply on what Jesus has to say. The experience in Rome has helped me to reflect more deeply on my faith and to understand how the Gospel is significant for my life. How are we going to live our faith life with intensity in society?

Another thing that has affected my thinking is the dedicated lifestyle of the people I met and who helped me during the Synod. Those people work very hard and offer their lives to the Church. It makes me want to do something like that as well.

9

MESSAGE TO THE PEOPLE OF GOD

Synod of Bishops for Asia

Dearly Beloved Sisters and Brothers in Christ:

1. Called by the Holy Father Pope John Paul II, on the eve of the Third Millennium, we the Fathers of the Special Assembly for Asia of the Synod of Bishops, together with the Fraternal Delegates and other Invitees, met in Rome from 19th April to 14th May, 1998. United with you all, our hearts are filled with profound gratitude to God the Father. He loved the world so much that he sent his only Son Jesus our Savior, so that all may have life and have it abundantly (cf. Jn. 10:10).

A Time of Grace

2. Our coming together, for the first time, from all parts of Asia, made this Synod a unique experience and a foundational event upon which our particular Churches could build. From the very start, we gathered round the Holy Father to offer the Eucharistic Sacrifice near the tomb of Saint Peter. We prayed and sang in the different languages of Asia. We invoked the martyrs and saints of our people, and we worshiped the Lord with gestures taken from our own cultures. We listened to the Apostle John sharing with us the revelation he received: "Listen to what the Spirit says to the churches..." (Rev. 3:6) of Asia. "Write what you see in a book and send it to the seven Churches..." (Rev. 1:11).

This Synod brought together participants from all over Asia as well as representatives from other continents. We thank God for the profound sense of communion we have felt in Christ, for the sincere sharing of pastoral concerns and for the deep solidarity we have experienced. The presence of delegates from countries such as Myanmar, Vietnam, Laos, and Cambodia, as well as from Central Asia, Mongolia, and Siberia was a special reason for us to thank God. Previously, persons from these places had difficulties participating in such assemblies. We were sad that the two Bishops, who were expected to bring us the voice of the Church in Mainland China, could not be with us, but we prayed for them and benefited by their prayers.

All the testimonies of the great work done by the thousands of missionaries in Asia from the time of the Apostles down to our times evoked in us a deep sense of gratitude. We are thankful for all the help received from the various mission agencies, especially the Pontifical Mission Societies and other Church organizations, which generously assisted the Church in Asia.

We are grateful to God for the inspiration and heroic example we have of many missionaries and Asian martyrs. We also thank the Lord for our sisters and brothers who today carry on the Church's mission in challenging circumstances in different countries. Their trials were recalled on various occasions during the Synod.

Greeting the Peoples of Asia

3. We respectfully greet all our sisters and brothers in Asia who have put their confidence in other religious traditions. We gladly acknowledge the spiritual values of the great religions of Asia such as Hinduism, Buddhism, Judaism, Islam. We esteem the ethical values in the customs and practices found in the teachings of the great philosophers of Asia, which promote natural virtues and pious devotion to ancestors. We also respect the beliefs and religious practices of indigenous/tribal people, whose reverence for all creation manifests their closeness to the Creator.

Together with all Asian peoples, we wish to grow in sharing our richness and in having mutual respect for our differences. We resolve to work together to improve the quality of life of our people. We consider our faith as our greatest treasure and would like to share it with all, fully respecting their religious beliefs and their freedom.

Listening to the Spirit

4. We prayed together and listened every day to the one among us who had been chosen to comment on the Word of God for us. The interventions in the plenary assembly, the group discussions, and the peaceful and orderly dynamics of the entire Synod, made us experience day after day that the

Spirit of the Lord was by our side. He made us aware of our shortcomings and failings because of which we may be poor witnesses of Christ's saving love. We ourselves need to be evangelized while we strive to evangelize others. We wish to so live, that by seeing us, others may catch a glimpse of the marvelous riches that God has bestowed on us in his Son Jesus.

It is the Holy Spirit who helps us to understand what vision of the Church in Asia we should have as we stand on the threshold of the Third Millennium. The presence among us of representatives of particular Churches who were persecuted in the past and of those now facing increasing intolerance, has added to our understanding of the situation of Christians living in difficult circumstances.

The Fraternal Delegates from other Christian Churches rekindled in us the longing for unity of all Christians which Our Lord desired and prayed for. This reminded us of the urgent need to foster ecumenism. The contributions of special guests and representatives from the laity, religious, and apostolic associations have sharpened in us our awareness of our pastoral ministry beyond our traditional and institutional concerns.

Mission of the Church

5. The Church was entrusted by the Risen Lord with the task of proclaiming the Good News of God's Kingdom in the power of the Holy Spirit. It takes as its model the early Christians who "devoted themselves to the apostles' teaching and fellowship, to the breaking of bread, and the prayers" (Acts 2:42).

Our understanding of mission is that all may have life and have it abundantly (cf. Jn. 10:10). Having its source in the Blessed Trinity, this life is communicated to us by Jesus, the Son of God, sent to save all humankind from sin, evil, and death, and bring us to the dignity and unity to which we are called by God.

The Word of God should have central place in our lives and should nourish us spiritually. The Bible is not an ordinary book, but rather the living voice of the living God who calls us every day to carry out his plan for our lives and our world. We are happy to note that thanks to good Bible translations available in local languages, people have access to "the Words of Eternal Life" (Jn. 6:68).

All Christians have the duty to proclaim Christ. The urge to do this springs from the joy of having found a treasure and the desire of sharing it. In Jesus Christ, the unknown and inaccessible God fully reveals and communicates himself. The living Father sent Jesus, who draws his life from him (cf. Jn. 6:57). This is the life Jesus has come to share with us. It is the source of all life and lasts forever.

Many creative ways, in consonance with Asian cultures, were suggested to present Jesus to our sisters and brothers. We acknowledge the wonderful service being rendered by those who bring the Good News to Asians who have not heard about Jesus Christ. We believe that the presentation of Jesus as the personification of God's love and forgiveness has great relevance for Asia.

We are all aware that the liturgy has a key role in evangelization. It is an event where people may touch God and experience him as the One who takes the initiative to meet them. This evokes our response in adoration, contemplation, and silence. For this, however, the liturgy must be participatory. The gestures should convey that something solemn and holy is happening. Even though we felt the urgent need to take more and more into account the local cultures in our liturgical celebrations, we note with joy that practically everywhere in Asia the liturgy is held in the language of the people.

Above all, it calls for a deep missionary spirituality, rooted in Christ, with special emphasis on compassion and harmony, detachment and self-emptying, solidarity with the poor and the suffering, and respect for the integrity of creation. The witness of monastic and contemplative communities is particularly called for to reveal the authentic countenance of Jesus; likewise, the life and work of consecrated men and women. For this purpose, we need formation programs to train priests and religious who are men and women of God devoted to prayer and living deep spiritual lives and who are able to guide and accompany others on their road to God.

Christians in Asia need to have zealous pastors and spiritual guides, and not simply efficient administrators. The personal example of formators has a crucial role to play in the formation process.

We highlighted the importance of inculturation so that "the Church becomes a more intelligible sign of what she is and a more effective instrument of mission" (*Redemptoris Missio* 52). In the Asian context of a multi-ethnic, multi-religious and multi-cultural situation, interreligious dialogue has clearly become a necessity. In our times, the Church is making major efforts to encounter the millennia-old religions in a serious manner. Interreligious dialogue is a respectful and sincere meeting in which the encountering parties want to know each other, to learn from one another, to enrich each other and to love one another, as Christians and Muslims are trying to do in Lebanon, where their mutual relationship augurs well for the future. For the Christian believer, this will include the desire of sharing the saving message of Christ.

The Church in Asia is called upon to enter a triple dialogue: a dialogue with the cultures of Asia, a dialogue with the religions of Asia, and a dialogue with the peoples of Asia, especially the poor. To carry on such a dialogue, formation for dialogue is all-important, especially in our formation centers.

We acknowledge the wonderful service in the field of education rendered by priests, brothers, sisters, and the lay people in Asia. We commit ourselves to promote Gospel values and foster Asian cultures and traditions, such as hospitality, simplicity, respect for sacred persons, places, and things. The curriculum must foster critical thinking, equipping our students with the skill of analyzing the various forces at work in society and to discern situations when people are exploited. We must pay greater attention to non-formal education. From time to time, we must evaluate our education system, its contents, its methodology, the benefit to its recipients, the relationships engendered, the values inculcated, and the impact on society.

A pastoral plan for social communications should be made in all dioceses so as to include a public relations office. Due attention should be paid to media education, the constructive use of the media, such as press and publications, television, radio, and the Internet. The media is rightly called the modern Areopagus, and it is here, as in other fields, that the Church can play a prophetic role and, wherever necessary, become the voice of the voiceless.

Entrusted by God the Creator to be stewards of his creation, we must have a respect for mother earth and the life systems which nourish us. We should do all in our power to prevent the degradation of the environment, which is the consequence of unbridled greed among other causes. If not, the result will be the pollution of land, rivers, and air and the cutting down of forests. We must work for ecologically sustainable development, particularly in the agricultural sector.

The laity has an important role to play in the mission of the Church. Many signs indicate that the Spirit is empowering them for an even greater role in the coming millennium which could be called the Age of the Laity. Some signs are: their commitment to evangelization, their involvement in ecclesial life, and their active and enthusiastic participation in small Christian communities. Renewal programs, catechesis, and Catholic educational institutions have a decisive role to play in forming our laity to be missionaries. To equip them for the transformation of the socio-cultural and politico-economic structures of society, we must impart to them a thorough knowledge of the social and ethical teachings of the Church.

The family is the most endangered institution in Asia. Population control tends to discriminate against the girl child in some countries and targets the poor of the Third World. Traditional family values are being overturned and replaced by egotism, hedonism, materialism, and greed. Direct assaults on life are made by contraception, sterilization, and abortion. We must save the family, which, because it welcomes and protects human beings, is the basic cell of society and the Church. If the family is destroyed, society is destroyed. The family is the domestic Church located at the core of the Christian community. The home is the first school. Parents are the first teachers. The first textbook for the child is the relationships within the family, between parents themselves and with their children and with other families.

One of the significant signs of the times is the awakening of women's consciousness of their dignity and equality with men. The Church in Asia, to be a credible sign of the respect and freedom of women, must give witness to Christ as the promoter of the true dignity of women. This can be done by encouraging active participation of women as equally responsible for Christ's mission of love and service.

Youth are the hope of Asia and of the Church. The need of the hour is that the Church gives youth the formation they need to face the challenges of our fast changing society and our quite uncertain future. By taking proper care of the millions of young people in Asia, we fill their hearts with hope and enable them to be evangelizers. We recognize with gratitude and wish to harness the evangelizing power of youth already at work in the shaping of a better future for the Church and society.

Special attention must be paid to migrant workers. Millions of them leave their families to earn their livelihood in other countries. Pastoral care for them in their own ecclesial tradition is most necessary. If they are Christians, a proper formation will enable them to be evangelizers in their host countries.

Another group of people that should cause us concern are the refugees. There are millions of them in Asia who have left their countries and are in great need of all kinds of assistance.

Appeals for Justice and Peace

6. We could not help but feel deeply concerned when hearing of the hardships people have to undergo in several countries of Asia on account of recurring violence, internal strife, tensions and wars between countries.

There is also the problem of Jerusalem, the heart of Christendom, a holy city for the three monotheistic religions: Judaism, Christianity, and Islam. We appeal to all concerned to do everything within their power to preserve the unique and sacred character of this Holy City.

When considering the suffering of the people of Iraq, especially women and children, we strongly urge that steps be taken to lift the embargo against that country.

Elsewhere in Asia, people are suffering under political regimes that pay no heed to their legitimate claims for more freedom and greater respect for their basic rights. Others are struggling to regain sovereignty or greater autonomy.

We need to create a greater awareness of the dangers of the development and expansion of the armaments industry. These trends serve to suppress the people's demand for justice and democracy.

While there are beneficial effects of globalization, we are concerned about its harmful effects. We call on the particular Churches of the First World to be in solidarity with the poor in Asia and to be their advocates with their own governments and with world economic institutions such as the World Bank, the International Monetary Fund, and the World Trade Organization so as to bring about what Pope John Paul II called in this year's World Day of Peace Message: "Globalization without marginalization. Globalization in solidarity."

We strongly recommend that during the Jubilee Year 2000, the Third World debt be re-negotiated and its crushing burden alleviated.

Reasons for Hope

7. Our greatest reason for hope is Jesus Christ who said: "Take heart, it is I; have no fear" (Mt. 14:27) and "I have overcome the world" (Jn. 16:33). Another reason for hope is the religiosity of our people who have great resilience even in the most difficult situations.

In the midst of these peoples—who are obviously called to play a more and more important role in the evolution of humankind—the Church is already present. Barring the special case of the Philippines, Christians are everywhere a minority and in some cases, a tiny minority. Nevertheless, particular Churches in Asia are very much alive and some of them manifest an extraordinary dynamism.

Practically everywhere, we see a high number of vocations to the priesthood and religious life, but we are equally happy to see that in many countries of Asia a high number of lay people are fully conscious of their Christian responsibilities. They take part in the activity of the Church in many ways. Moreover, among them, some are very much conscious of their obligation to be authentic witnesses of Christ and to contribute to the progress of God's kingdom.

Wherever the Church has taken root, she renders highly appreciated services to the people. Though it may happen that some institutions are not truly at the service of the poorest, we are happy to note that more and more efforts are being made to ensure that the Church's institutions are truly helping the most needy. At the same time, we are happy to see that some do not hesitate to get out of institutions to share the life of the most oppressed and to struggle with them to defend their rights.

So let us be confident. The Spirit of the Lord is obviously at work in Asia, and the Church is quite active in this continent. With Christ, we have already defeated death; with him, we have already risen.

Without being self-complacent about our past achievements we should preserve our fervor of spirit as Pope Paul VI said, "Let us preserve the delightful and comforting joy of evangelizing even when it is in tears that we must sow. May it mean for us ... an interior enthusiasm that nobody and nothing can quench ... and may the world of our time which is searching sometimes with anguish, sometimes with hope, be enabled to receive the Good News, not from evangelizers who are dejected, discouraged, impatient or anxious, but from ministers of the Gospel whose lives glow with fervor, who first received the joy of Christ, and who are willing to risk their lives so that the kingdom may be proclaimed and the Church established in the midst of the world" (*Evangelii Nuntiandi*, 80).

In this message, we refer only to a few issues raised during the Synod. Many other matters were discussed which will be taken up in the various propositions to be presented to the Holy Father and eventually to be incorporated in the Post-Synodal Apostolic Exhortation which we await.

Concluding Prayer

8. As we began the Synod so we conclude it with the same Eucharistic Sacrifice, wherein through the words of consecration the bread and wine become the Body and Blood of Christ, and where the assembly is transformed into "one Body and one Spirit" in Christ. This encounter with Jesus must now continue in a greater measure all over Asia. This is the work of the Holy Spirit who is always the One at our side to help us. We turn to Mary in whose body Christ was formed by the Holy Spirit. We pray that she may intercede for us so that, like Jesus her divine Son, the Church may become ever more a Servant Church to continue its mission of love and service to the people of Asia, so that "they may have life and have it abundantly" (Jn. 10:10).

Vatican City: May 13, 1998

Part Two

Ecclesia in Asia

Proclamation - Commentaries

ECCLESIA IN ASIA: AN ECCLESIAL EVENT*

Vidyajyoti Editorial

What happened in Delhi in early November was not merely the conclusion of the Special Assembly of the Synod of Bishops for Asia, but a rich moment in the life of the Church in the continent. For a few hours the capital city of India, illumined with the lights of Diwali, became the Catholic capital of Asia. The events at the Cathedral, at the Jawaharlal Nehru Stadium and at the elegant Vigyan Bhavan, official venue of many national and international conventions, must be seen as one whole and as the symbolic expression of the life of the Church in Asia. The event holds many lessons for us, some of which we will mention here, others will be perceived by other participants and observers. They all call for reflection.

The first obvious lesson of the days before, during, and after the visit of the pope, is that we live in a world where our presence is noticed. Never, probably, had there been so much reporting in the press, positive or negative, about the Christian activity and presence in the country, both in the past and in the present, as during these weeks. The centuries of ghetto Christian life are over. What we do, what we say, and even what we think in our beliefs, is done, said, and professed publicly. This means that our expressions need to be understandable to the larger public that interprets words by the meaning they have in the media. We cannot respond to misinterpretations of our intentions by appealing to hidden theological meanings if our words suggest different meanings to people. What we say in our theological discourse must be understandable, even if not acceptable

---

*Original Text: *Vidyajyoti Journal of Theological Reflection* 63/12 (1999): 877-880.

to everybody. Words like conversion, evangelization, proclamation, mission, are often heard with different nuances than those they have in our internal forum. We need to reformulate our expressions. Not that we want to camouflage our faith, are ashamed of Jesus Christ. But the way we articulate our beliefs must convey the Christian message of Good News, an announcement of the universal and self-sacrificing love of God.

Another lesson we learned from the Delhi event is that we live in history. Our history is with us, for joy and proclamation, or for sorrow and repentance. This is natural and in many ways to be welcome. Not only our personal, but also our missionary past is with us, and we cannot afford to ignore it or be too selective in what we want to remember and what to forget. The history of the Christian community affects the way in which its present words and deeds are judged. This history itself needs redemption, and in the Catholic tradition forgiveness involves confession.

The event of Delhi had a pastoral core: as the conclusion of the Synod, it showed the Church of Asia acquiring a new consciousness of its call to serve at the beginning of the third millennium. This consciousness pervaded the deliberations of the Synod and found a papal expression in the Post-Synodal Apostolic Exhortation *Ecclesia in Asia*. We hope eventually to pay a more detailed attention to this important document which has been called, not without a certain exaggeration, the Magna Carta for the Church in Asia in the third millennium. The Exhortation is not a Conciliar Constitution like *Gaudium et Spes*, nor a Conciliar Decree like *Ad Gentes*, not even a doctrinal Papal Encyclical. It is what its title says, an Apostolic Exhortation, which offers guidelines from the Supreme Pastor of the Church for the practical involvement of the community in this vast continent. The pope presented the Exhortation as the fruit of a collegial deliberation of the Synod. This it clearly is, but he has made the themes of the bishops, Asian or Roman, his own, and added to them his insights and reflections. There is symbolic meaning in his will to sign it in Asia, perhaps the first ever document signed in our continent by the Bishop of Rome. The Exhortation was received with love and gratitude.

It is necessarily phrased in general terms: a document meant for the whole of Asia, from Siberia to East Timor, from Japan to Palestine, cannot but use general terminology and draw from the millennial faith of the Church. Each country, each cultural group, needs to make a re-reading of the document and apply it to its specific social and historical context. As the pope said in *Fides et Ratio*, his letter on the relationship between faith and reason, "In India particularly, it is the duty of Christians now to draw from this rich heritage the elements compatible with their faith, in order to enrich Christian thought." The pope naturally makes no apology for being rooted in the Church's faith, as some comments in the media have pointed out. Like every good, this faith is self-diffusive and the pope encourages us to share the memory of Jesus with all. We all need this encouragement in times when the Christian witness is often misrepresented in its intentions, its methods and its effects—whether in good or bad faith.

The teaching of the pope in the Exhortation acquired new tones in his personal address to the bishops gathered in the Cathedral of Delhi.... He clearly felt at home in what he called the "blessed soil of Asia" (Hindus often call India *punyabhumi*), "cradle of great religious traditions and ancient civilizations," and he is moved by its "ceaseless passion for the Absolute." If he spoke of the Lord's command to preach the Gospel he sees this as a consequence of our faith in Jesus Christ calling *us* to conversion. This witness, he knows, means often a Calvary, the way of the cross, the way of the martyrs, as it has been for many Asians in history. It is a witness to love, a love whose fruit is justice. "It is surely the work of the Holy Spirit that Asian Christians are turning more and more to the defense of human dignity and the pursuit of justice." In obedience to the Lord's command of love we "expend immense energies in practical charity and in human promotion and liberation." "Let no one fear the Church!," he reassured his larger audience outside the Cathedral.

The pope encouraged the Church to engage in a "dialogue of salvation," and told us what is the specific Christian contribution to this dialogue: "*The word which we must speak is the word of the cross of Jesus Christ.*" The pope thus called the Asian Church to a spirituality of *kenosis*, at the same time inviting all Asians "to contemplate *the figure of the crucified Jesus*" [italics in Vatican text].

No human word in history is a final word. The word is always pronounced and heard in dialogue, and the dialogue continues as long as the human pilgrimage continues. The Church is always in "syn-odos"— walking together. As the Word of the Gospel is heard and given new expression in every era and cultural situation, so also the papal teaching is read in each specific context that gives it more concrete shape. Theologians speak of a re-reading of the Church's doctrinal documents in every generation. *A fortiori* this applies to pastoral documents. We experienced firsthand this activity of re-reading in the Delhi event: Cardinal Darmaatmadja, President Delegate of the Synod and Archbishop of Jakarta, gave the first response to the Apostolic Exhortation of the pope. He spoke the language of the concrete Asian experience, and one could feel at once how his words found deep resonance with the listeners in the Cathedral. He said that Christ is already present in the reality of Asia, and spoke of service, liberation, love, dialogue, within which the Christian announcement of Jesus Christ is made. The teaching was the same: the stresses, the context, the language were different....

If the session in the Cathedral was the final "working session" of the Synod, the Nehru Stadium became the next day the Cathedral where the Asian community celebrated with its Supreme Pastor the Light of Christ and the proclamation of the Synod, and gave thanks to God for this privileged moment of Asian ecclesiology which was the Synod. There the pope encouraged specially the laity of Asia (many lay representatives came and received personal copies of *Ecclesia in Asia*) to fight for justice and for a right order of society. The mission, as it touched the laity, was clearly a mission of transforming society. The homily [included in this volume] and other addresses at the stadium also deserve a close study.

Perhaps we could venture to say that the climax of the Delhi event was beyond the Cathedral and beyond the sacred liturgy. It was when the Church, in the person of the pope and many other followers, laity, religious, priests, and bishops, met with representatives of other religions at New Delhi's "Vigyan Bhavan" or "Hall of Wisdom." This was living dialogue wherein each participant gave witness to the strength and inspiration she or he received from their respective faiths. Such personal testimonies were received gratefully. Here we communicated with the heart, as was clear in the loud applause and cheers of the participants when the Sankaracharya Madhavananda Saraswati and the pope joined hands and raised them together for the whole community to see. It was, it is true, a symbolic meeting. What they did is more important than what they said. One could say that there was relatively little content in the dialogue. At present, symbolic gestures of this type, reminiscent of the Assisi meeting, are very important, for they have a great symbolic power and speak better than apologetic words.

The message of the pope? Simply that God is love, quoting from I John 4:16-20, and that dialogue is an activity of love and that we must avoid all temptation to choose paths of isolation, division, and conflict. He did not name Jesus Christ, but Asia listened eagerly to the pope's word and received it with joy. This was an announcement of Good News that sets a pattern for the mission of the Church in Asia. Here, at least for a moment, the false opposition between dialogue and proclamation was bridged....

It would be wrong, we think, to take only one element of the Delhi event and see it as the only result of the Synod. The whole Synod, the rich witnessing and sharing that took place in Rome and its meaningful conclusion in Delhi, is its own message, and each element must be taken in total context. The assimilation of the Synod by the Asian Church remains the task ahead....

FINDING THE TRUE LIGHT*

John Paul II

*"Walk as children of light, for the fruit of light is found
in all that is good and right and true"* (Eph. 5:8-9).

Dear Brothers and Sisters,

Today throughout this vast country many people are celebrating the *Festival of Lights*. We rejoice with them, and in this Eucharist here in New Delhi, in India, on the continent of Asia, we too exult in the light and bear witness to the One who is "the true light that enlightens every one" (Jn. 1:8).

God, the Father of mercies, has given me the joy of coming among you to promulgate the *Post-Synodal Apostolic Exhortation Ecclesia in Asia*, the result of the labors of the Special Assembly for Asia of the Synod of Bishops held last year in Rome. What was this Synod for Asia? It was a gathering of Bishops representing the Church on this continent. What did the Bishops do? Above all, they listened in prayer to the Spirit; they reflected on the path followed so far by the Church among the peoples of Asia; they recognized the grace of the "hour" that the Church is now living on this continent; they committed the entire People of God to ever greater fidelity to the Lord and to the evangelical task which he has entrusted to all the baptized for the good of the human family.

Here today, dear brothers and sisters, you represent the Catholic community not only of India but of the whole Asian continent, and *I*

---

*Original Text: Vatican Website.

place in your hands the Post-Synodal Apostolic Exhortation as a guide for the spiritual and pastoral life of the Church on this continent as we enter a new century and a new Christian millennium.

It is fitting that this document has been signed and issued in India, the home of many of Asia's time-honored cultures, religions and spiritual traditions. These ancient Asian civilizations have shaped the lives of the peoples of this continent and have left an indelible mark on the history of the human race. Distinguished representatives of various Christian Communities and of the great religions of India are present here today. I greet them all with esteem and friendship, and I place before them my hope and dream that the next century will be a time of fruitful dialogue, leading to *a new relationship of understanding and solidarity among the followers of all religions.*

I wish to thank Archbishop Alan de Lastic, the pastor of the Archdiocese which is hosting this Eucharistic assembly, for his kind words of welcome. I greet all my brother Bishops of the Latin Church, of the Syro-Malabar Church and the Syro-Malankara Church. I embrace the Cardinals and Bishops who have come from other countries to share the joy of this occasion.

I am grateful to the large number of priests present, who share the one priesthood of Jesus Christ with the bishops and priests of Asia and the world. Dear brother priests, take as your rule of life those words of the Ordination liturgy: "Receive the Gospel of Christ whose servant you are, meditate on the Law of God, believe what you read, preach what you believe and practice what you preach."

With great affection in the Lord *I greet the men and women religious.* Whether you are engaged in contemplation or working in the active apostolate, your witness to the supremacy of the spirit places you at the very heart of the Church's life and mission in Asia. For this, I thank you and encourage you.

In a special way I entrust the fruits of the Synod to the members of the laity, for it is you above all who are called to transform society by infusing the "mind of Christ" into the mentality, customs, laws and structures of the world in which you live (cf. *EA* 22). One of the main challenges before you is to *bring the light of the Gospel to bear on the family, and on the defense of human life and dignity*. You bear witness to your faith in a world of contrasts. On the one hand there has been enormous economic and technological progress; on the other there still exist situations of extreme poverty and injustice. The Synod re-echoed the cry of the ancient prophets, the cry for justice, for the right ordering of human society, without which there can be no true worship of God (cf. Is. 1:10-17; Am. 5:21-24; *EA* 41). *The Church looks to the lay men and women of Asia to reflect the light of Christ wherever the darkness of sin, division and discrimination distorts the image of God in his children.*

"The light shines in the darkness, and the darkness has not overcome it" (Jn. 1:5). These words of Saint John in today's Gospel speak to us of Jesus Christ. His life and work are the light which illumines our journey to our transcendent destiny. The Good News of the Savior's Incarnation, and of his Death and Resurrection for our sake, illumines the Church's path as she makes her pilgrim way through history towards the fullness of Redemption.

The Synod which we are closing today rejoiced at the thought of Jesus' birth on Asian soil. The Eternal Word took flesh as an Asian! And it was on this continent, through the preaching of the Gospel in the power of the Holy Spirit, that the Church went forth to spread the Good News. With Christians throughout the world, the Church in Asia will cross the threshold of the new millennium, giving thanks for all that God has worked from those beginnings until now. Just as the first millennium saw the Cross firmly planted in the soil of Europe, and the second in that of America and Africa, so may the third Christian millennium witness *a great harvest of faith* on this vast and vital continent (cf. *EA* 1).

As we stand on the threshold of the Great Jubilee which will commemorate the two thousandth anniversary of the Birth of Jesus Christ, the community of his disciples is called to redress the great refusal mentioned in the Prologue of Saint John's Gospel: *"The world came to be through him, but the world did not know him. He came to his own, but his own did not accept him"* (Jn. 1:10-11). The Eternal Word, "the true light, which enlightens everyone, was coming into the world" (Jn. 1:9). But instead of spreading freely, that light is often hindered and obscured by darkness. In the heart of the sinner, that light is rejected. And the sins of individuals coalesce and harden into social structures of injustice, into economic and cultural imbalances which discriminate against people and force them to the margins of society. The sign that we are truly celebrating the Jubilee as the year of the Lord's favor (cf. Is. 61:2) will be *our conversion* to the light and our efforts to restore equity and to advance justice at every level of society.

"To all who received him, who believed in his name, he gave power to become children of God" (Jn. 1:12). In the Eucharist we give thanks to God the Father for his many gifts to us, and especially for the gift of his beloved Son, our Savior Jesus Christ. *Jesus Christ is the faithful and true witness* (cf. Rev. 3:14).

The Synod reminds Asian Christians that "Jesus' perfectly human life, devoted wholly to the love and service of the Father and of man, reveals that *the vocation of every human being is to receive love and give love in return"* (*EA* 13). In the Saints we marvel at the inexhaustible capacity of the human heart to love God and man, even when this involves great suffering. Does not also the legacy of so many wise teachers in India and in the other lands of Asia point in a similar direction? Such teaching is still valid today. Indeed, it is needed more than ever! The world will only be transformed if men and women of good will, and whole nations, genuinely accept that the only path worthy of the human family is the path of peace, of mutual respect, understanding and love, and solidarity with those in need.

Dear brothers and sisters, what does the Church need of her members at the dawn of a new millennium? Above all, *that you be witnesses who are convincing because you embody in your lives the message you proclaim.* As *Ecclesia in Asia* reminds us all: a fire can only be lit by something that is itself on fire. The Gospel can only be preached if bishops, clergy, those in the consecrated life, and the laity are themselves on fire with the love of Christ and burning with zeal to make him known, loved and followed (cf. *EA* 23).

This is the Synod's message: *a message of love and hope for the peoples of this continent.* May the Church in Asia heed this message so that all "may have life and have it abundantly" (Jn. 10:10). Through Jesus Christ our Lord. Amen.

LAUNCHING *ECCLESIA IN ASIA**

Luis A. G. Tagle Interview

Father Chito, you were in New Delhi for Pope John Paul's visit; what struck you most about the event?

I experienced the New Delhi visit on two levels. The first level revolved around the proclamation of the fruits of the Asian Synod. At that level, I was moved to be reunited with all the people who had attended the Synod in Rome: bishops, lay people, priests, religious. It was like a big family reunion, a gathering of long lost friends!

I believe that this is what it means to be the Church in Asia. In addition to our shared reflection and common projects, we need—even if only occasionally—this meeting of flesh and blood men and women drawn from Asia's different worlds, as well as from the different backgrounds and levels of participation in Church life. In New Delhi we experienced again what it means to be a people gathered in Christ's name, a people with a common mission. It made me feel that all the trouble and effort of going to India was worthwhile.

On the second level, I sensed that Pope John Paul's visit to New Delhi mirrored the contrasting realities of the Church in Asia. For example, we know for a fact that not all Hindus were happy about the visit; there were interviews on Indian television very definitely to this effect. This brought home to me how, in fact, the Church is not always accepted in Asia. In one interview, a prominent Hindu affirmed that Christianity destroys Indian civilization and identity. In this way the papal visit highlighted the feeling

---

*Original Text: *World Mission* 12/1 (2000): 24-28.

of many in Asia that Christianity is an alien, a foreign religion. This is what many Christians in Asia have to face everyday: an unwelcoming attitude, even an outright rejection of Jesus and Christianity as non-Asian, as hostile to things Asian.

On the other hand, I observed in many Hindus a deep respect for holiness and contemplation, and so, for holy men and women. In the midst of all the protests, there were many letters to the editors of the Indian newspapers saying things like: "Even if we Hindus disagree with the teachings of Christianity, we should still welcome the Pope, because he is a holy man, and every holy man and woman from no matter what religion deserves our respect." I saw how holiness and contemplation could be the way for Christians to dialogue with many persons in Asia and to connect with Asian cultures and peoples.

The papal visit also showed how the Church can gain respect in Asia because of its charitable work, its involvement in the lives of the poor and destitute. Over and over again I heard of the deep respect the Indian people have for Mother Teresa. Christianity as a religious system may be rejected by Hindus and Jesus perceived as a "foreign" Savior may be refused by them, but they cannot reject people who show love and genuine service to the poor, those who spend their whole lives for the love of humanity. Christians and non-Christians all agreed about the greatness of Mother Teresa. Beyond doctrinal debates there is the power of witness, of service, of selfless giving to the poor.

What has impressed you most in the Pope's Exhortation on "The Church in Asia" (Ecclesia in Asia)?

Of the many observations that suggest themselves, I would like to focus on three. First, the Pope's document is "post-synodal"; this means that it should not be read apart from what happened at the Synod of Bishops for Asia. If we isolate the document from that event, we will not understand it properly. I was lucky enough to be at the Synod and my first impression on reading the Holy Father's Exhortation is that he has tried—successfully, I believe—to be faithful to the concerns raised by the different Asian bishops on behalf of their Churches. I would go so far as to say that if we want to get a good picture of how our bishops read the signs of the times in their countries and their Churches, this document is a faithful guide.

Of course, it is not easy to do full justice to such diversity in one document. Indeed, during the Synod itself we were somewhat overwhelmed by the plurality of situations in Asia. You cannot find one concern being expressed in exactly the same way in two Asian countries. So I sympathize with the Holy Father in this difficult task of bringing things together—but I think he succeeded.

Secondly, I sense that the Pope has sought to support the views of the bishops and of the Churches of Asia, so that we can celebrate the Asian quality and roots of Jesus and Christianity. This aspect came through strongly during the Synod itself—that Jesus was born on Asian soil, that Jewish culture is an Eastern culture, that the way Jesus talked, preached and related to people were all very Asian.

Now I think we can say that in many, many different parts of *Ecclesia in Asia* there is a real celebration of all that. Against the background of the accusation that Jesus is foreign to Asia and that the Church is a European creation now exported to Asia, *Ecclesia in Asia* wants to say to the Christians and non-Christians of Asia: Jesus is one of your own!

This is a challenge for the Church. Can we now present Jesus in our preaching, in our lifestyle, in our policies, as one of us? Can we recover his way of talking and relating with people, which is very, very Asian? And, can we go back to the early Christian communities and their ideals of harmony, of sharing—ideals of eastern, Asian communities? Can we recover all that?

Yet being Asian does not mean closing yourself to the rest of the world. Part of being Asian is the capacity of being in harmony and communion with the whole of humanity—the way Jesus, born in Asia, has a universal appeal. I think it is a wonderful challenge for the Church in Asia to recover its unique identity as Asian but also to grasp its universal vocation and its potential for universal impact.

Thirdly, I am delighted to see that the missionary concerns of *Ecclesia in Asia* are really concerns for the whole of humanity. There are few things in *Ecclesia in Asia* which are inward-looking. Overall, it is a document that moves the Church away from contemplating her own face in the mirror and just analyzing her own existence. Major sections of the document are devoted to a vision of the Church at the service of the world. This is the horizon of mission you find in the document, and I was thinking to myself that, if the local Churches in Asia could only be true to this agenda, they would become a Church that is extrovert and outgoing, not a Church preoccupied with her own rights, concerns, and prerogatives. She would truly be a servant Church, a Church for others and for the world, a Church on a journey.

Ecclesia in Asia paints a picture of a truly pilgrim Church, that lives fully in the history of peoples and walks hand in hand with them, making their concerns her own. I think there is a lot of Vatican II's *Gaudium et Spes* in *Ecclesia in Asia*. The joys, the sorrows and anxieties of the men and women of our age, most especially those who are poor and afflicted in any way, these are also the concerns of the followers of Christ.

Ecclesia in Asia contains two chapters on Jesus and one on the Spirit; what is the significance of this?

I want to say that this so-called "doctrinal" section is unique to *Ecclesia in Asia* among the continental, post-synodal, apostolic exhortations. I think it is important that these chapters on Jesus and the Spirit were included, because during the Synod many bishops raised doctrinal questions, and with special reference to two points.

First, they were asking how to present Jesus more meaningfully to the peoples of Asia, and how to present him as the Savior, when we have ancient religions in Asia with their own soteriologies (ways of understanding salvation) and with their own divine figures who are considered as saviors. This is a missionary concern, but it involves the need for considerable theological clarity.

Of course, during the Synod the bishops did not have the time to develop a systematic doctrinal statement about Jesus Christ, so that task was left to the Holy Father. In the document, he has gathered together all the bishops' concerns related to Christ, and then, also looking to Christian tradition, he has sought to present a catechesis on Jesus Christ as Savior.

Even though *Ecclesia in Asia* is not, of course, a straight theological treatise, there are many solid Christological things that we can take from it. For example, I think there is a good attempt to blend Christology from below with Christology from above. There is great respect for the different ways in which Asian peoples could accept Jesus more readily—as the Enlightened One, the Guru, the Liberator of the Poor, the Contemplative—all images which will resonate with Asian sensibilities.

Naturally, we cannot expect the Holy Father to compromise in the Christological area. In fidelity to tradition and also to the views of the bishops, he has reaffirmed the Christian understanding of the faith: that Jesus is the Son of God, sent by the Father as the Savior of all. Yet, there is also much understanding of the difficulties being faced by the Asian Churches in preaching Jesus more meaningfully to the people of our times.

The section on the Holy Spirit is also important. During the Synod many bishops raised serious questions about how, in some theological circles, the Holy Spirit is being "used" to minimize the importance of Jesus. The argument goes something like this: if the Holy Spirit is present everywhere and blows where he wills, then maybe there is no need to proclaim Jesus. After all, if the Spirit is already present, we can just let things be.

Many bishops during the Synod were worried that the Holy Spirit could be isolated in this way from the Father and Jesus Christ. Pope John Paul has responded to these concerns by offering a catechesis on the Holy Spirit. He stresses that, yes, the Holy Spirit is present universally, even in ancient cultures, civilizations and religions, enabling them to promote human dignity, to do good and to fight evil in the world.

However, the Pope, again in fidelity to Vatican II and Christian tradition, cautions on two important points. First, the Holy Spirit cannot be taken in isolation from the Trinitarian economy of salvation; the Holy Spirit's action should always be referred to the Father and to Jesus. Secondly, the work of the Holy Spirit blossoms fully in the proclamation of Jesus Christ and in faith in him.

In your opinion, how should the Church in Asia go about implementing the missionary agenda presented in Ecclesia in Asia?

If we are talking about real implementation, we need first to reaffirm our faith. As the document movingly says, "the unique contribution of Christians in Asia is our faith." Indeed, many non-Christians are surprised when we Christians hesitate to talk about Jesus. They expect us to do so, because we follow Jesus and believe in him. So I think the implementation of the missionary agenda begins with this challenge: as we face the third millennium, can we Christians reaffirm our commitment to Jesus? This will not be in a triumphalistic manner, of course; but can we be secure and at peace with our faith here in Asia? Can we even have a kind of "holy pride" in our faith in Jesus Christ?

Can we retell the story of Jesus? Many people have not heard it; I'm afraid many Catholics themselves have not fully heard it. I think the implementation of the missionary agenda would require that missioners—and all Christians in Asia are called to be missioners—should engage in this interior journey of faith, and fall in love again with Jesus, his person and his mission, so as to be fascinated anew by him.

The Synod's theme was "Jesus the Savior and His Mission of Love and Service in Asia." How can we prolong that mission of love and service, especially in the very difficult situations in Asia, where people face rejection and persecution? How can we continue that mission if we are not in love with Jesus? Only love and commitment in faith, I think, will push and pull the peoples of Asia towards a commitment to mission.

Given the immense difficulties and challenges in Asia, we need a matching, proportionate intensity of love and faith in Jesus. I think the Holy Father and the bishops in the Synod hit the nail on the head when they said, "We can contribute many things to humanity in Asia, but let us not forget that the first, foremost, and unique gift that we offer is our faith in Jesus Christ." All of us in the Church—from Cardinals to children—are called to this renewal in faith as we face the third millennium. No one is exempt!

Secondly, I think we need a lot of imagination. As we read the missionary agenda outlined by the Holy Father, we may find that the details are not new. The many assemblies of the Federation of Asian Bishops' Conferences, and the many pastoral letters of the different episcopal conferences, at one time or another in the past, have already talked about various aspects of this missionary agenda. What the Holy Father did was to draw them together and to propose them on a continental level.

So what we need in the Church now is pastoral imagination. How do we develop it? There are two important components. First, the Church and the agents of missionary life in Asia should be truly immersed in the worlds of our people, the emerging cultures. I want to emphasize that this does not mean culture in the nostalgic sense; it means rather present-day culture, the worlds of Asia now. To be immersed is more than mere physical presence; it is a presence that reads trends and developments, the real signs of our times, the minds and hearts of our people, so as to be able to discern even what is not being verbalized, to feel what is being communicated by, at times, stony faces. What I am talking about is a deep penetration of the worlds of Asia. Without that, no imagination will come.

Yet for us in mission, this reading of the signs of the times must also be accompanied by the second component—an immersion in the Gospel and the Christian tradition. The Gospel contains much Asian wisdom, many images and much methodology dear to Asian people. It contains the love of God, the saving love of God, in Asian parables, in Asian images, Asian symbols. So, for me, if the Church were to be fully immersed both in the world of peoples and in the Gospel, and then allow the heart of every Christian and the heart of every community to be the place of intersection, the meeting point of these two worlds—the world of Christ and the world of our Asian people—would become the center of an explosion! Of course, hopefully this is not a harmful explosion that destroys, but rather one that opens up new vistas and new horizons. That is what I mean by imagination.

Without imagination we may look at the missionary agenda of *Ecclesia in Asia* and conclude rather dryly and maybe even sarcastically, "So what's new?" What's new about serving the poor, about dialogue, about taking care of the environment, about promoting human dignity? As topics, there is nothing novel. However, this agenda is happening in a new Asia, an Asia bombarded by many global, consumerist, modernist, sometimes even post-modernist trends. It is an Asia that has not yet even received the Good News and now is already developing a culture that does not accept the narrative of Jesus, the story of Jesus. Indeed, we need a lot of imagination!

We cannot just go on singing the old tunes. We cannot just apply the old structures, the old rules. We cannot simply use the same ways of talking that we have been used to, the same ways of presenting Christianity to people. Church people, because of their fidelity to tradition, are sometimes not known for being imaginative. Yet, I think fidelity to tradition and using our imagination can go hand in hand. They do not have to be in conflict.

Jesus is the great example of the use of imagination. When he was accomplishing his mission it was the scribes and Pharisees who were protecting the minute details of the law and who showed a lack of imagination. Jesus, instead, opened up new vistas; he brought new wine. The old law is presented by Him in new ways and the people who taste it say, "Wow, it is new wine!" I think the missionary agenda for Asia will only be pursued by people who imitate Christ, being creative and imaginative, true to the tradition and faithful to the worlds of the people among whom they live.

There is, though, a price to be paid if we allow ourselves to be the meeting point, the place of intersection, in this way. The explosion that I was talking about happened in Jesus in a rather drastic and painful manner: the untold rejection that he had to endure, and eventually the explosion of the cross. Yet, look at the imagination of God: that cross, which is supposed to be the sign of defeat and humiliation, became the explosion of new life. What I am saying is: will the Church also be ready for martyrdom in this imaginative implementation of the missionary agenda? Is she ready for the explosion of new life on the cross? We need a missionary Church that is also ready to be a martyr Church. So if we are not creative now, not imaginative now, when will be the right time?

CONTINUING PENTECOST IN ASIA
Introducing *Ecclesia in Asia*

James H. Kroeger

"The Church in Asia sings the praises of the 'God of salvation' (Ps. 68:20)." These opening words set the tone of *Ecclesia in Asia*, the post-synodal document promulgated in November, 1999. Clearly, themes of gratitude, celebration and optimism characterize *Ecclesia in Asia* (EA). The Church sings God's praises for "choosing to initiate his saving plan on Asian soil," for sending "his only-begotten Son, Jesus Christ the Savior, who took flesh as an Asian"! This Church sees "the Marvel of God's Plan in Asia" and exults "in the goodness of the continent's peoples, cultures, and religious vitality" (1).

Pope John Paul II signed the apostolic exhortation during his Asian pastoral visit to India (November 5-8, 1999). The issuance of EA was the concluding moment of the Special Assembly for Asia of the Synod of Bishops, popularly known as the "Asian Synod." This four-year project of Church reflection and renewal began with the publication of the *Lineamenta* (1996), continued with discussion on the *Instrumentum Laboris* (1998), reached its apex with the month-long Synod sessions in Rome (April 19 - May 14, 1998), and culminated with the proclamation of the post-synodal *Ecclesia in Asia* (November 6, 1999). Yes, "Asia-Church" rejoices and unceasingly proclaims God's enduring love!

The Asian Synod was a multi-faceted event on many levels. As *Ecclesia in Asia* notes, "It was indeed a moment of special grace" (3). It was also "a celebratory remembering of the Asian roots of Christianity" (4). The Synod event became "an ardent affirmation of faith in Jesus Christ the Savior" (4); and, as the local Churches of Asia gathered in Rome, "the

Synod Fathers sought to discern the principal areas of mission for the Church in Asia as she crosses the threshold of the new millennium" (18).

The Synod's theme was much debated and carefully chosen: "Jesus Christ the Savior and his Mission of Love and Service in Asia: 'That they may have Life and have it abundantly' (Jn. 10:10)." As the Pope writes, this particular formulation of the theme was to "illustrate and explain more fully that Christ is the one Mediator between God and man and the sole Redeemer of the world, to be clearly distinguished from the founders of other great religions" (2). The theme manifests the Church's faith in Jesus and his mission; he is Savior who serves and bestows abundant life; he is to be joyfully proclaimed in Asia.

Ecclesia in Asia, a rich, lengthy document, now becomes an important signpost of evangelization for the local Churches in Asia in the new millennium. An analysis of EA reveals three major sections or underlying thematics: (1) Asian Realities relevant to the Church and her Mission of Evangelization (5-9); (2) Theological-Doctrinal Aspects of Jesus Christ and the Holy Spirit (10-23); (3) The Church's Mission of Love and Service in Asia (24-49). The main body of EA is framed by an Introduction which captures the highlights of the Synod process (1-4) and a conclusion that expresses the Pope's gratitude and encouraging words as well as a final prayer to Mary, "Mother of Asia" (50-51). The entire document is focused on "seeking to discern the Spirit's word to the Churches in Asia" (51).

Asian Context. *Ecclesia in Asia* devotes its first chapter to an exploration of the concrete situation of contemporary Asia—her religious, cultural, economic, social, political, and historical realities (5-9). This inductive approach, characteristic of current Asian theological reflection, mirrors the method and experience of the Federation of Asian Bishops' Conferences (FABC). The Asian Church accepts that "a critical awareness of the diverse and complex realities of Asia is essential if the People of God on the continent are to respond to God's will for them in the new evangelization" (5).

As EA notes, "Asia is the earth's largest continent and is home to nearly two-thirds of the world's population"; its variety of peoples are "heirs to ancient cultures, religions and traditions." One is amazed "at the sheer size of Asia's population and at the intricate mosaic of its many cultures, languages, beliefs and traditions." Asia is "the cradle of the

world's major religions" and "the birthplace of many ... spiritual traditions"
(6).

Economically, socially, and politically, "situations on the Asian
continent are very diverse, defying any simple classification" (7). EA
highlights various concrete pastoral concerns: rapid change, migration,
nuclear power, tourism, population growth, poverty, women, and a host
of additional challenges. In this complex situation, the Church's one
ambition is to continue Christ's mission of service and love (cf. 50). Her
approach is that of mutual exchange and enrichment; thus, EA confirms
"the importance of dialogue as a characteristic mode of the Church's life
in Asia" (3). Mother Teresa of Calcutta is proposed as "an icon of the
service to life which the Church is offering in Asia ... [because of] her
loving and selfless care of the poorest of the poor" (7).

This "chosen" continent of Asia, with all its immensity, diversity, and
complexity, holds special meaning for the Church. God "sent his only-
begotten Son, Jesus Christ the Savior, who took flesh as an Asian" (1);
"Behold the Savior of the World is born to us, born in Asia" (2). Yes,
Asia is unique as "the birthplace of Jesus and of the Church" (5). This
Church thanks God "for choosing Asia as the earthly dwelling place of his
incarnate Son" (50; cf. 2, 9, 20). This unique gift implies a task; the
Church commits her energies to making Jesus, his Gospel of Life, and his
Community the Church truly "at home" (inculturated) in Asia and her
peoples (9, 20).

Theological Foundations. Three chapters of EA, focusing on Jesus
and the Spirit, describe a type of "doctrinal" orientation to the Church's
Asian mission. Yet, the manner of presentation is decidedly "pastoral" in
style and focus; it blends theologies "from below" and "from above." It
reads easily; the language flow is smooth; inclusive expression is partially
employed. Some insights even enjoy poetic expression: "Contemplating
Jesus in his human nature, the peoples of Asia find their deepest questions
answered, their hopes fulfilled, their dignity uplifted and their despair
conquered" (14).

The thematic of "gift" is a creative optic frequently found in these
"theological" chapters. Jesus the Savior is a gift to Asia; this faith-gift is
to be both appropriated and proclaimed. "The Church's faith in Jesus is a
gift received and a gift to be shared; it is the greatest gift which the Church
can offer to Asia" (10). "Only if the People of God recognize the gift

that is theirs in Christ will they be able to communicate that gift to others through proclamation and dialogue" (31; cf. 20). The Church in Asia must ask itself a probing question: How do we "share with our Asian brothers and sisters what we treasure as the gift containing all gifts, namely, the Good News of Jesus Christ" (19).

Proclaiming the Christian faith-gift meets unique challenges, particularly in the "multi-ethnic, multi-religious and multi-cultural situation of Asia" (21). Asia has its indigenous religions, soteriologies, and savior figures (cf. 14, 19-20). This reality demands a humble, dialogical stance on the part of the Church; "proclamation is prompted not by sectarian impulse nor the spirit of proselytism nor any sense of superiority" (20; cf. 4, 31, 46). And yet, this genuine respect and reverence for the Church's dialogue partners "does not eliminate the need for the explicit proclamation of the Gospel in its fullness" (20; cf. 31). By her very identity the Church is "a community aflame with missionary zeal to make Jesus known, loved and followed" (19).

Affirming the relevance of Jesus for Asia (1, 9, 10, 18, 50) demands a particular approach to proclamation. The Church "needs to follow a pedagogy which will introduce people step by step to the full appreciation of the mystery." She should employ "narrative methods akin to Asian cultural forms" and follow "an evocative pedagogy, using stories, parables and symbols so characteristic of Asian methodology in teaching." In a word, the Church must "evangelize in a way that appeals to the sensibilities of Asian peoples" (20). Engaging Asian peoples, their cultures and religions (FABC's triple dialogue) demands genuine commitment to inculturation (20-23) and interreligious dialogue (29-31).

EA asserts that Christology is necessarily integrated with Pneumatology as well as Trinitarian faith. It is the "uniqueness of Christ which gives him an absolute and universal significance" (14); one cannot "separate the activity of the Holy Spirit from that of Jesus the Savior" (16). The Holy Spirit, "the prime agent of evangelization," (17) is "an absolutely vital part of the mystery of Jesus and the salvation which he brings" (15). Jesus and his Spirit are only adequately comprehended within the "Trinity's plan of salvation" (15); there are no two parallel economies of salvation. There are real, complex missiological questions and the Asian Synod / EA attempted to face them.

A Missionary Community. The longest section of EA (24-49) focuses on the Church and her mission in the vast Asian continent. Four discernable themes emerge: Church as Communion for Mission (24-28), Dialogue (29-31), Human Promotion (32-41), and Agents of Evangelization (42-49). EA presents a vision as well as concrete approaches for mission; these emerge from a particular faith-stance: "the question is not whether the Church has something essential to say to the men and women of our time, but how she can say it clearly and convincingly" (29). EA recognizes "the pressing need of the local Churches in Asia to present the mystery of Christ to their peoples according to their cultural patterns and ways of thinking" (20).

"Communion Ecclesiology" finds strong expression in EA. The Church is a "privileged place of encounter" between God and people; her first purpose is "to be the sacrament of the inner union of the human person with God." She is also "the sacrament of the unity of the human race." This means that "communion and mission are inseparably connected [and] they interpenetrate and mutually imply each other." Communion is "both the source and fruit of mission." In short, "Communion gives rise to mission and mission is accomplished in communion" (24).

The Church in Asia promotes internal communion and participation on many levels: with the Successor of Peter, among various sister local Churches, dioceses, basic ecclesial communities ("a positive feature of the Church's evangelizing activity"), renewal movements, the Catholic Eastern Churches, other Christian Churches (cf. 25-27). Internal communion emanates outward toward other groups throughout Asia: the variety of peoples, cultures and religions with whom the Church shares life (25), Churches and peoples in Mainland China, North Korea, and the ex-Soviet territories of Asia (28). Regional and continental associations of Bishops that foster communion (e.g. FABC) are recognized and praised (26), but their profound insights are never directly quoted.

An inherent demand of "communion ecclesiology" is dialogue. This "desire for dialogue ... is not simply a strategy for peaceful coexistence among peoples; it is an essential part of the Church's mission..., a veritable vocation for the Church" (29). A particularly helpful section is devoted to Interreligious Dialogue (31), seen as "a part of the Church's evangelizing mission, an expression of the mission *ad gentes*."

The advent of the new millennium offers the Church "a great opportunity for interreligious dialogue and for meetings with the leaders of the great world religions." Following the lead of *Nostra Aetate*, "the *Magna Carta* of interreligious dialogue for our times," the Church in Asia is called to a double fidelity: to affirm her "belief that the fullness of salvation comes from Christ alone" and to gladly acknowledge "whatever is true and holy in the religious traditions of Buddhism, Hinduism and Islam as a reflection of that Truth which enlightens all people." Interreligious Dialogue seeks "mutual advancement ... [and] the elimination of prejudice, intolerance and misunderstandings" (31).

Dialogue demands will only increase with passing years. Persons must be formed to have "a mature and convinced Christian faith" which qualifies them "to engage in genuine interreligious dialogue." They need to be "deeply immersed in the mystery of Christ ... [and] happy in their faith community." The call to dialogue requires the Church in Asia "to provide suitable models of interreligious dialogue." In the dialogue endeavor it is imperative "to revitalize prayer and contemplation" and to give witness to "the great Christian traditions of asceticism and mysticism" (31).

The entire Chapter VI treats human promotion and Church social teaching. Striving to build a "civilization of love," the Church views all human development not only as a "technical or economic question; it is fundamentally a human and moral question" (32). An integral, holistic approach to evangelization is employed, encompassing the areas of human dignity (33), preferential love of the poor (34), health care (36), education (37), peacemaking (38), globalization (39), foreign debt (40), the environment (41). In these diverse fields, the Church resists "the culture of death" in accord with her vision of "the Gospel of Life" (35).

Agents of Evangelization. Chapter VII, entitled "Witnesses to the Gospel," focuses on the Church's missionary identity in Asia. The Church strives to be a credible witness, because "people today put more trust in witnesses than in teachers, in experience than in teaching, and in life and action than in theories"; in the Asian context "people are more persuaded by holiness of life than by intellectual argument" (42). EA asserts that it is a "genuinely religious person [who] readily wins respect and a following in Asia" (23).

Gospel witness in Asia needs holy men and women who themselves are "on fire with the love of Christ and burning with zeal to make him known more widely, loved more deeply and followed more closely." Why? "A fire can only be lit by something that is itself on fire"; Christian witnessing demands "a true missionary spirituality of prayer and contemplation" (23). Asian peoples, especially the youth, manifest this "deep thirst for spiritual values" (6). In a word, living Christian mission in Asia incorporates, in fact, demands "contemplative action and active contemplation" (23).

EA addresses a variety of Gospel witnesses: Pastors (43), religious and missionaries (44), theologians (22), laity (45), families (46), young people (47), and those whose apostolate is social communications, "the areopagus of the modern age" (48). Striking insights are often presented: "People in Asia need to see the clergy not just as charity workers and institutional administrators but as men whose minds and hearts are set on the deep things of the Spirit" (43). "The Synod Fathers were most concerned that the Church should be a participatory Church in which no one feels excluded, and they judged the wider participation of women in the life and mission of the Church in Asia to be an especially pressing need" (45).

The Pope encourages and thanks missionaries (20, 42, 44, 50), urging "the Church in Asia to send forth missionaries, even though she herself needs laborers in the vineyard" (44). Mission is to be central to each local Church; local "missionary societies of apostolic life, characterized by their special commitment to the mission *ad gentes, ad exteros* and *ad vitam*" are strongly encouraged (44). EA calls upon "the great host of Asian martyrs, old and new..., to teach the Church in Asia what it means to bear witness" (49).

Additional Emphases. The Asian Synod surfaced crucial questions facing local Churches in Asia; EA reflects several of these pastoral-missionary concerns. The question of *Jesus' Asianess* surfaces in various discussions. "Jesus is often perceived as foreign to Asia. It is paradoxical that most Asians tend to regard Jesus—born on Asian soil—as a Western rather than an Asian figure" (20). "It is indeed a mystery why the Savior of the world, born in Asia, has until now remained largely unknown to the people of the continent" (2). To address and overcome this reality, the Church must open herself to "new and surprising ways in which the face of Jesus might be presented in Asia" (20). How can Jesus be effectively proclaimed—bearing an "Asian face"?

The subject of *religious freedom* arises, because in various places in Asia "Christians are not allowed to practice their faith freely" (8); "explicit proclamation is forbidden and religious freedom is denied or systematically restricted" (23). Christians are forced "to live their faith in the midst of restrictions or even the total denial of freedom" (28). Governments are enjoined to "guarantee religious freedom for all their citizens" (28), assure "immunity from coercion" (23) in religious matters, and recognize "the right to freedom of conscience and religion and the other basic human rights" (34).

Analysis and comparison between the content of EA and the decades of pastoral reflection by *Asian Bishops (FABC)* reveal many similarities. Since 1974 in its document "Evangelization in Modern Day Asia," the FABC has promoted the local Church's triple dialogue with Asia's peoples, cultures, and religions; this vision is repeatedly found in EA (cf. 1, 15, 18, 20, 21, 24). Again, the FABC pastoral priorities enunciated over the years, particularly the focus on the family, women and the girl-child, youth, ecology, and the displaced (cf. FABC VI: 15) are also highlighted by EA (34, 37, 41, 46, 47, etc.). FABC itself is mentioned (2, 3, 26, 31), though none of its fine work is directly quoted or even noted in the copious endnotes.

The theme of *Inculturation* received much attention during the Synod, and certain particular areas were identified as requiring concentrated focus: "theological reflection, liturgy, the formation of priests and religious, catechesis and spirituality" (21). Central to inculturating the faith is the biblical word, the message of salvation, the sacred text; sacred scripture is proposed as "the basis for all missionary proclamation, catechesis, preaching and styles of spirituality" (22). One may inquire about criteria for authentic inculturation; EA notes: "The test of true inculturation is whether people become more committed to their Christian faith because they perceive it more clearly with the eyes of their own culture" (22).

The Christian *virtue of compassion* repeatedly surfaces in EA (e.g. 11, 12, 14, 20, 45, 51). The apostolic exhortation is correct in expressing the Church's mission in terms of this appealing focus. Presenting Jesus as "the Compassionate Friend of the Poor" (20) will find a resonance and reception among Asians. In the Church's mission of love and service, women evangelizers contribute greatly "to bringing the compassionate Jesus, the healer and reconciler, to Asian people, especially the poor and marginalized" (45). In Jesus, the God-Man who saves, "Divine compassion had never been so immediately accessible" (11).

As the Church in Asia enters the new millennium, she faces some very *demanding challenges*; EA highlights some important apostolates: women (7, 34, 45), youth (6, 47), nuclear power (7, 38), peacemaking and reconciliation (38), globalization (39), foreign debt (40), and the environment (41). The authenticity of the Church's "mission of service and love" (50) will indeed be tested; will it produce "a great harvest of faith ... in this vast and vital continent" (1) of Asia?

Conclusion. *Ecclesia in Asia* concludes as it began on a clear note of optimism and gratitude. "Blessed be God for the peoples of Asia, so rich in their diversity yet one in their yearning for peace and fullness of life" (50). With committed faith, "the Church in Asia joyfully makes her pilgrim way into the Third Millennium" (50). "Mary, model of all disciples and bright Star of Evangelization..., look tenderly upon the Church of your Son planted on Asian soil.... O Mary, Mother of the New Creation and Mother of Asia, pray for us, your children, now and always" (51)!

In this mood of gratitude and optimism, the local Churches of Asia accept the Holy Father's gift: *Ecclesia in Asia*. Its contents are a mixture of the old and the new (cf. Mt 13:52), a summation of Asian reflection and insights in the Vatican II era, a presentation of the mission agenda for Asia's faith-communities, a program for evangelization in the new millennium. All-in-all, EA is a much appreciated gift. Its treasures need opening in the coming years and decades; its dream for the Church— God's holy people—beckons implementation; its theme—abundant life in Jesus the Savior—requires contemplative action. Yes, Jesus' Asian disciples affirm that the Holy Spirit who moved upon Asia in times past, "moves now among Asian Christians, strengthening the witness of their faith among the peoples, cultures and religions of the continent" (18).

Contemplating God's salvific deeds and wonders during the Easter Vigil liturgy, the Universal Church proclaims in the *Exsultet*: "Rejoice, O Mother Church"! In similar fashion, the local Churches in Asia acclaim God's marvels in their midst; they joyfully affirm the Asian Synod event as a "celebratory remembering of the Asian roots of Christianity" (4). They pray that the proclamation and subsequent internalization of *Ecclesia in Asia* will confirm the Church in her servant mission to bring Christ's love and abundant life (Jn 10:10) to Asia and her peoples. *Rejoice, O Asia-Church!*

BIBLIOGRAPHICAL NOTES

Many Asian Theological Journals published several pieces on both the Asian Synod and on *Ecclesia in Asia*; individual references are too numerous to note in an article of this nature. However, to alert readers to the vast literature available, this author will list many Asian Journals with multiple articles on these topics (usually between the years 1998-2001); journals with copious articles will be indicated with an asterisk (*). Some journals even devoted entire issues to the Asian Synod or *Ecclesia in Asia*.

Important journals are: *Asia Focus* (Thailand), *Boletin Eclesiastico de Filipinas* (Philippines), *Diwa* (Philippines), *East Asian Pastoral Review* (Philippines), *Indian Currents* (India), *Indian Missiological Review* (India), *The Japan Mission Journal* (Japan), *Jeevadhara* (India), *Landas* (Philippines), *Mission Today* (India), *The New Leader* (India), *Prodipon* (Bangladesh), *Religious Life Asia* (Philippines), *Third Millennium* (India), *Vidyajyoti* (India), *Word and Worship* (India), and *World Mission* (Philippines).

CHALLENGES FOR ASIAN CHRISTIANITY*

Peter C. Phan

With the official promulgation of the apostolic exhortation *Ecclesia in Asia* by Pope John Paul II in New Delhi, India on November 6, 1999, the Special Assembly for Asia of the Synod of Bishops, which had met in Rome from April 19 to May 14, 1998, in a certain sense came to an end. Proclaimed as "a moment of special grace" (EA 3), the Synod had drawn, both during its preparatory stage and in its aftermath, both favorable and unfavorable comments, especially with regard to its *Lineamenta* and its *modus operandi*. Similarly, the immediate reception of the exhortation has been, as to be expected, mixed: it was received in some quarters with unfeigned enthusiasm; in others, with muted applause; still in others, with unalloyed disappointment.

The Asian Synod in Context. As is often the case, how one reacts to the Bishops' Synods and the ensuing apostolic exhortations largely depends on the expectations one entertains of them. As is well known, the International Bishops' Synod was established by Pope Paul VI in September 1965, shortly before the close of the Second Vatican Council, as an instrument of episcopal collegiality. The Synod, which the pope reserves the right to convoke, intends to foster a close collaboration between the bishops and the pope. It is, however, advisory and not deliberative. Since its foundation there have been eleven international synods (both ordinary and extraordinary) and eight national or regional synods, including the five continental synods called by John Paul II in *Tertio Millennio Adveniente* to celebrate the new millennium.

---

*Original Text: *East Asian Pastoral Review* 37/3 (2000): 215-232.

Unfortunately, as Michael Fahey, S.J., a highly respected American ecclesiologist, has put it tersely, "despite high hopes for their success, results of synods have been negligible. Each new Synod attracts less and less attention; the structure of their sessions has become unwieldy; they have become rituals with little practical impact on the life of the Church. In the last 30 years the institution has not been notable as a wellspring of new ideas or strategies" [Fahey, 489]. Furthermore, since the apostolic exhortations that follow these continental synods (so far three have been issued) are not the work of the synodal participants themselves (though they are supposed to incorporate the synods' "propositions"), but are composed by the pope with the assistance of a post-synodal committee, they are often suspected of having filtered the results of the synods to an officially acceptable level. Moreover, being usually quite lengthy and turgid in style, they have aroused little interest, even among the clergy and theologians; and, of course, it is totally unrealistic to expect that they will be read by the laity, at least in their entirety.

These remarks are not intended to cast a cynical eye on the Asian Synod and *Ecclesia in Asia*. On the contrary, they serve as a warning that unless concrete steps are taken to put the Synod's fifty-nine "propositions," which have been more or less incorporated into *Ecclesia in Asia*, into practice at the level of the local churches, the Asian Synod will not be unlike one of the many fireworks displays celebrating the coming of the third millennium, spectacular festivals of sounds and colors but in the end, nothing more than blurred memories of the New Year's Eve extravaganzas. What steps can and should be taken by the Asian Churches to prevent their Synod from joining the rank of its predecessors, illustrious indeed, but reduced to being a convenient quarry for doctoral dissertations, bereft of real and lasting influence on the life of the Churches of Asia?

In the following pages, what is being offered is neither an evaluation of the Asian Synod nor a commentary on *Ecclesia in Asia*. Rather, as an expatriate Vietnamese who has for a quarter of a century been engaged in the study and teaching of theology in the United States of America, and whose academic interest has focused on the Christianity of Asia, I will advance, very selectively, some reflections and proposals as to how certain teachings of the Asian Synod, as embodied in *Ecclesia in Asia*, can be implemented in Asia.

Church not *in* but *of* Asia. By any standard, *Ecclesia in Asia* is John Paul II's typical theological product, with its rather forbidding length, its frequent insistence on complete orthodoxy, its abundant citations of the pope's own writings, and its emotional peroration with a prayer to Mary. Besides an introduction and a conclusion, the exhortation is composed of seven parts dealing with the following themes: the Asian context, Jesus as Savior, the Holy Spirit as Lord and Giver of life, proclamation of Jesus in Asia (with a focus on inculturation), communion and dialogue for mission (with a focus on ecumenical and interreligious dialogue), the service of human promotion, and Christians as witnesses to the Gospel.

For an Asian reader, the inevitable question arises: Has the exhortation said anything new and important for the Churches of Asia that either had not been said before by these Churches themselves or could not have been said except thanks to the work of the Synod itself? To both parts of the question, the answer is frankly no. Except the first section on the Asian context, most of the exhortation could have been written prior to and apart from the Synod, and what the exhortation says on the other six themes has already been said, powerfully and in great detail, by the various documents of the Federation of Asian Bishops' Conferences (FABC).

This does not mean, however, that the Synod and the exhortation have not rendered a valuable service. After listing the fifteen points of agreement out of the fifty-nine propositions the Synod submitted, Luis Tagle acknowledges that there is nothing new in them in comparison with the teachings of the FABC, but he correctly insists that there was something genuinely new in the fact that these issues and concerns have been voiced in a synodal forum and recognized by the Church of Rome, and through it, have been brought to the consciousness of the universal Church [Tagle, 370-371]. What was new is not what the Asian bishops said but *that* they said it and *how* they said it at the Synod. What they said had been said, at length and with power and depth, for almost thirty years, ever since the founding of the FABC in 1972, in its numerous plenary assemblies and in the documents of its several institutes. But at the Synod, they said it again, *to the whole Church*, and with surprising *boldness* and refreshing *candor*, with what the New Testament calls *parrhésia*.

The Synod was the first official recognition that the Churches of Asia have come of age, or as a synodal participant put it, that they are not branch offices of the Roman Curia. To the universal Church the Asian bishops proclaimed, humbly but forcefully, that the Churches of Asia not only learn from but also have something to teach the Church of Rome as well as the Church universal, precisely from their experiences as Churches not simply *in* but *of* Asia. The fact that the exhortation has incorporated several elements of the Asian Synod and made them part of the papal magisterium is an eloquent witness to the value of the experiences and wisdom of the Asian Churches.

What is new, in a word, is the public recognition of the necessity and validity of the *Asianness* of the Churches of Asia. Of course, *Asianness* is a notoriously slippery concept, and the *Lineamenta* and the exhortation attempt to circumscribe it by listing several cultural and religious values that purportedly constitute the "Asian soul" or "being Asian": "love of silence and contemplation, simplicity, harmony, detachment, non-violence, discipline, frugal living, the thirst for learning and philosophical inquiry..., respect for life, compassion for all beings, closeness to nature, filial piety toward parents, elders and ancestors, and a highly developed sense of community" (EA 6). The exhortation also attends to the economic, social, and political contexts in which Christianity exists in Asia (EA 7-8). Unfortunately, when it speaks of the fact that "despite her centuries-long presence and her many apostolic endeavors, the Church in many places was still considered as foreign to Asia and indeed was often associated in people's minds with the colonial powers" (EA 9), it uses the past tense and fails to recognize that the foreignness of Christianity in Asia and the perception of its association with colonialism are *present* realities, and this not simply "in many places" but in all parts of Asia.

If the Asian Synod is to have a lasting transformative effect on the Churches of Asia, so that they may become truly *of* Asia and their association with colonialism may be removed, the most important thing, in my judgment, is that Asian Catholics take their Asianness seriously as the context of their being Christian. In practice, this means that the first and last concern for the leaders of the Asian Churches must be not how a particular policy is conformable with canonical requirements and directives coming from Rome or elsewhere, but rather how it will respond to the challenges of the Asian social, political, economic and religious contexts and whether and how it will effectively help Christians live their faith in fidelity to the Gospel and the living Christian tradition, here and now, in Asia. Determining this Asianness and making it the perspective through which the Christian faith is consistently expressed and lived should be the top priority for Asian Christianity in the post-synodal era.

Those of us who live close to the ecclesiastical centers of the Churches of the so-called Third World sometimes experience the sad irony of these

Churches trying to be "more Roman than Rome." Perhaps such a phenomenon is understandable when these Churches lack the necessary resources to be on their own, especially in countries with governments hostile to Christianity, and are still as it were in the minority. Now that the Asian Churches have come of age, however, they should be able to move to the stage of self-government, self-support, self-propagation, and self-theologizing. As the FABC Asian Colloquium on Ministries in the Church already put it in 1977: "The basic fact is that today in our Asian context we are in the process of rediscovering that the individual Christian can best survive, grow and develop as a Christian person in the midst of a self-nourishing, self-governing, self-ministering and self-propagating Christian community" [Rosales-Arévalo, 77].

To assume responsibilities in these areas, while remaining in full communion with the Church universal, demands courage, imagination, creativity, collaboration at all levels of the Church life, and above all trust in the Holy Spirit, and is much more challenging (and uncomfortable) than simply "applying" existing Church laws and traditions to the different situations of Asia. But it is only in this way that the Churches *in* Asia become truly *of* Asia. As Christian Churches, they must of course proclaim and live the Christian faith, the same *faith* handed down the ages, but not in the theological categories and with the Church structures imported from without. Rather they should do so in the modalities conceived and born from within the Asian contexts. These Asian categories and structures need not of course be totally different from those of the Churches elsewhere; however, whether they are identical with or different from these cannot and should not be determined beforehand and *a priori* but must be shaped by real experimentations in the concrete situations of each Asian country. The Churches of Asia must claim and exercise the God-given right, based on the mystery of divine incarnation (and not a concession granted by some higher ecclesiastical authority), to find out and determine for themselves how best to proclaim and live the Christian faith in Asia. Such a task is a matter of life and death for the Church, since if the Church in Asia is not Asian, it is no Church at all.

This task of becoming *Asian* Churches is all the more urgent in light of the astounding acceptance by *Ecclesia in Asia* of a point made by the Asian Synod that "Jesus is often perceived as foreign to Asia. It is paradoxical that most Asians tend to regard Jesus—born on Asian soil— as a Western rather than an Asian figure" (EA 20). While ways must be found, as the exhortation urges Asian theologians to do, "to present the mystery of Christ to their peoples according to their cultural patterns and ways of thinking" (EA 20), the most effective way to present Jesus as an Asian figure is to make the Churches authentically Asian.

A New Way of Being Church. Another way of making the point I have argued for so far is to say that for the Asian Synod to have a lasting impact, the Asian Churches must, with courage and creativity, find new ways of being Church, and hence construct an alternative ecclesiology. This is a theme repeatedly emphasized by the FABC, especially in its third and fifth plenary assemblies in Bangkok, Thailand, 1982 and Bandung, Indonesia, 1990 respectively. This ecclesiology, in a sort of Copernican revolution, de-centers the Church in the sense that it makes the center of the Christian life not the Church but the reign of God. Christians must be not ecclesiocentric but regnocentric. Their mission is not to expand the Church and its structures (*plantatio ecclesiae*) in order to enlarge the sphere of influence for the Church, but to be a transparent sign and effective instrument of the saving presence of the reign of God, the reign of justice, peace, and love, of which the Church is a seed. As the exhortation puts it well: "Empowered by the Spirit to accomplish Christ's salvation on earth, the Church is the seed of the Kingdom of God, and she looks eagerly for its final coming. Her identity and mission are inseparable from the Kingdom of God.... The Spirit reminds the Church that she is not an end unto herself: in all that she is and all that she does, she exists to serve Christ and the salvation of the world" (EA 17). The new way of being Church in Asia and the ecclesiology undergirding it are characterized by the following four features.

I. First, the Church, both at the local and universal levels, is seen primarily as "a *communion of communities*, where laity, religious and clergy recognize and accept each other as sisters and brothers" [Rosales-Arévalo, 287]. At the heart of the mystery of the Church is the bond of communion uniting God with humanity and humans with one another, of which the Eucharist is the sign and instrument *par excellence*.

Moreover, in this ecclesiology there is an explicit and effective recognition of the fundamental equality among all the members of the local Church as disciples of Jesus and among all the local Churches in so far as they are communities of Jesus' disciples and whose communion constitutes the universal Church. The communion (*koinonia*) which constitutes the Church, both at the local and universal levels, and from which flows the fundamental equality of all Christians, is rooted at its deepest level in the life of the Trinity in whom there is a perfect communion of equals. Unless this fundamental equality of all Christians is acknowledged and lived through concrete policies and actions, the Church will not become a communion of communities in Asia. Living out this fundamental equality is particularly difficult in Asia, not only because the insistence on the hierarchical structure of the Church tends to obscure and minimize it, but also because it goes against the class consciousness of many Asian societies.

Furthermore, this vision of Church as communion of communities and its corollary of fundamental equality are the *sine qua non* condition for the fulfillment of the Church's mission. Without being a communion, the Church cannot fulfill its mission, since the Church is, as intimated above, nothing more than the bond of communion between God and humanity and among humans themselves. As the exhortation puts it tersely, "communion and mission go hand in hand" (EA 24).

II.   This pastoral "discipleship of equals" leads to the second characteristic of the new way of being Church in Asia, that is, the participatory and collaborative nature of all the ministries in the Church: "It is a *participatory* Church where the gifts that the Holy Spirit gives to all the faithful—lay, religious, and cleric alike—are recognized and activated, so that the Church may be built up and its mission realized" [Rosales-Arévalo, 287]. This participatory nature of the Church must be lived out not only in the local Church but also among all the local Churches, including the Church of Rome, of course, with due recognition of the papal primacy. In this context it is encouraging to read in the exhortation the following affirmation: "It is in fact within the perspective of ecclesial communion that the universal authority of the successor of Peter shines forth more clearly, not primarily as juridical power over the local Churches, but above all as a pastoral primacy at the service of the unity of faith and life of the whole people of God" (EA 25). A "pastoral primacy" must do everything possible to foster co-responsibility and participation of all the local Churches in the triple ministry of teaching, sanctification, and service in the Church and must be held accountable to this task so that these words do not remain at the level of pious rhetoric but are productive of concrete structures and actions.

If the Asian Synod proved that the Asian Churches do have something vital to teach the Church of Rome and the Church universal, then the "magisterium" in the Church can no longer be conceived as a one-way street from Rome to the other local Churches. Instead, there must be *mutual* learning and teaching, *mutual* encouragement and correction between the Church of Rome and the other Churches, indeed among all the local Churches. Only in this way can correction be made of the widespread perception, especially in countries with the so-called national or patriotic Churches, that the Christian Church in Asia is a foreign (indeed, international) organization, comparable to a multinational corporation, that must take orders from a foreign power.

In this context it may be useful to point out that a certain language to describe the relationship between the local bishop and the Bishop of Rome, traditional though it is in some ecclesiastical circles, should be avoided to obviate misunderstanding. I refer to words such as "loyalty" and "obedience" to characterize the attitude of bishops to the pope which, to Asian ears, inevitably suggest oaths of submission of vassals to their lords in a feudal system. Besides the fact that in the Church "loyalty" is owed to no one but Christ and that the bishop is not beholden to the pope for his episcopal office nor is he the pope's vicar, it is theologically much more appropriate to describe and live the relationship between the local Church and the pope in terms of collegiality and solidarity. Only in this way can the Church's teaching office and the pope's ministry of promoting unity be effectively exercised, learning from the varied and rich experiences of being Church from all corners of the globe and welcoming respectful but frank warning and correction when errors of intellectual narrowness, moral arrogance, and spiritual blindness have been committed.

III. The third characteristic of a new way of being Church in Asia is the *dialogical* spirit: "Built in the hearts of people, it is a Church that faithfully and lovingly witnesses to the Risen Lord and reaches out to people of other faiths and persuasions in a dialogue of life towards the integral liberation of all" [Rosales-Arévalo, 287-88]. Ever since its first plenary assembly in Taipei, Taiwan, 1974, the FABC has repeatedly insisted that the primary task of the Asian Churches is the proclamation of the Gospel. But it has also maintained no less frequently that the way to fulfill this task in Asia is by way of dialogue, indeed a triple dialogue, with Asian cultures, Asian religions, and the Asians themselves, especially the poor. The exhortation reiterates the necessity of this triple dialogue.

In the dialogue with the Asian cultures (inculturation), the exhortation highlights the areas of theology, liturgy, and the Bible (EA 22). In the dialogue with other religious traditions, the document emphasizes ecumenical and interreligious dialogue. It quotes approvingly proposition 41 of the Synod: "Interreligious relations are best developed in a context of openness to other believers, a willingness to listen and the desire to respect and understand others in their differences. For all this, love of others is indispensable. This should result in collaboration, harmony and mutual enrichment" (EA 31). In the dialogue with the poor, the exhortation affirms the necessity of the preferential love of the poor (in particular, the migrants, indigenous and tribal people, women and children), defense of human life, health care, education, peacemaking, cancellation of foreign debts, and protection of the environment (EA 32-41). There is no doubt that if the Christian Church is to become truly *of* Asia, Asian Christians must be engaged, relentlessly and wholeheartedly, in this triple "dialogue of life and heart" and in this way fulfill their inalienable right and duty of proclaiming Jesus to their fellow Asians.

In this context of the proclamation of the Gospel and the triple dialogue with Asian cultures, religions and the poor, it may be appropriate to raise the vexed issue of how to proclaim Christ as the Savior and as the only Savior in Asia. The exhortation affirms that "there can be no true evangelization without the explicit proclamation of Jesus as Lord" (EA 19) and that this proclamation "is prompted not by sectarian impulse nor the spirit of proselytism nor any sense of superiority" but "in obedience to Christ's command" (EA 20). Therefore, the proclamation must be done with a twofold respect: "respect for man (*sic*) in his quest for answers to the deepest questions of his life and respect for the action of the Spirit in man" (EA 20).

As to how to proclaim that Jesus is the *only* Savior, the document frankly recognizes that this proclamation is "fraught with philosophical, cultural and theological difficulties, especially in light of the beliefs of Asia's great religions, deeply intertwined with cultural values and specific world views" (EA 20). This difficulty is compounded by the fact that, as has been mentioned above, Christ is perceived as foreign to Asia, as a Western rather than an Asian figure. Here the exhortation deserves praise for recommending (1) a *gradual* pedagogy in the proclamation that Christ is the only Savior, (2) the use of narratives to complement ontological categories in this proclamation, and (3) the legitimate variety of approaches to the proclamation of Jesus.

This is not the place to enter the theological debate regarding exclusivism, inclusivism and pluralism, but in my judgment, the issue of Jesus as the only Savior, interesting though it may be in *theology*, is a red herring in preaching and catechesis. The reason is that the immediate goal of the proclamation of the Gospel is to enable a person to accept Jesus as his or her "personal Savior," to use a favorite phrase of Pentecostal Christians, and not as the "only Savior." It is this personal and total commitment of the catechumen to Jesus that is being promoted, and not the rejection of *possible* ways in which God can reach other people, a possibility that can no longer be denied after Vatican II. The vital question before all else is not whether and how *other* people can be saved but how *I* can fully enter a personal relationship with God. Once a person has found that Jesus is the way for him or her to reach God, then out of this personal experience he or she can bear witness to this fact to others. The strength and fervor of this witness are not born out of the theological conviction that Jesus is the *only* Savior but out of the deep experience that he is the *personal* Savior for me. Were I asked in my preaching questions about other religions and savior figures, I will have to recognize, joyfully and gratefully, their various good elements and the saving presence of God's Spirit in them, but I will testify to Jesus as my way to God and invite others to try out this way for themselves. If they accept Jesus as their personal way to God, then I will have shown that Jesus is the universal and only Savior, that is, Savior for me as well as for others.

IV. The fourth and last feature of the new way of being Church in Asia is *prophecy*: The Church is "a leaven of transformation in this world and serves as a *prophetic sign* daring to point beyond this world to the ineffable Kingdom that is yet fully to come" [Rosales-Arévalo, 288]. As far as Asia is concerned, in being "a leaven of transformation in this world," Christianity must give up its ambition, so enthusiastically endorsed in many missionary quarters at the beginning of the twentieth century, to convert the majority of Asians to Christ. The report of the demise of Asian religions was premature and vastly exaggerated. In Asia, where Christians still form but a minuscule part of the population after four hundred years of mission, and where non-Christian religions have recently staged a vigorous revival, the prospect of a massive conversion of Asians to the Christian faith is utterly unlikely. Christians in Asia must come to terms with the fact that they are destined to remain for the foreseeable future a "small remnant" who must journey with adherents of other religions toward the eschatological kingdom of God.

The objective of the Church's mission of "making disciples of all nations" (Mt. 28:19) in Asia cannot therefore be adding as many members to the Church as possible, even though baptism "in the name of the Father, and of the Son, and of the Holy Spirit" (Mt. 28:19) remains the desirable outcome of the Church's mission. Rather, the primary task of the Church is to become a credible "prophetic sign" of the coming reign of God. This new focus of the Church's mission must be the light guiding the ordering of its priorities and the choice of its policies which must not aim at serving the internal interests of the Church but the proclamation of the Gospel through the triple dialogue mentioned above.

One helpful way to describe this mission of the Church is, as Thomas Thangaraj has done, to see it as part and fulfillment of the mission of humanity itself which is composed of three basic tasks: responsibility, solidarity, and mutuality. By responsibility Thangaraj means that humans are beings that go forth from themselves and back to themselves in their reflexive consciousness, interpret themselves, and with a sense of accountability take responsibility for themselves and their actions. This task they must perform in solidarity with one another and mutuality for one another. What the Christian mission adds to the mission of humanity from its faith perspective is to inform these three tasks with a new modality: *crucified* responsibility, *liberative* solidarity, and *eschatological* mutuality [Thangaraj, 49-58, 64-76].

As a consequence of this view of mission, the Churches of Asia must form not only Basic Christian Communities, which the exhortation highly recommends (EA 25), but also Basic Human Communities. Given the urgent need of Asian Christians to collaborate with their fellow Asians in the task of human promotion, the second kind of community is no less necessary than the first for the Church to become a credible prophetic sign of the reign of God. This kind of community broadens the concerns of Christians beyond the narrow walls of their Churches and puts them in constant dialogue of life and heart with followers of other religions and even non-believers.

"If the Asian Churches do not discover their own identity, they will have no future." These prophetic words of the FABC Asian Colloquium on Ministries in the Church held in Hong Kong on March 5, 1977 [Rosales-Arévalo, 70] were true then and will be even truer during the post-synodal era. Since then, the FABC has been trying to develop a pastoral approach designed to implement this Asian way of being Church called "Asian Integral Pastoral Approach towards a New Way of Being Church in Asia (ASIPA)." The goal is to develop "genuine Christian communities in Asia—Asian in their way of thinking, praying, living, communicating their own Christ-experience to others" [Rosales-Arévalo, 70].

The significance of the Asian Synod and *Ecclesia in Asia* lies, I have argued, not so much in what they say as in the recognition that the Churches of Asia have come of age and must continue to pursue the task of becoming *Asian*, relentlessly, courageously, creatively. Only in this way can the Christian Church fulfill its missionary vocation which is the task of the entire Church. It is only by living out a new way of being Church that Asian Christians will make true what the exhortation states as a fact: "Contemplating Jesus in his human nature, the peoples of Asia find their deepest questions answered, their hopes fulfilled, their dignity uplifted and their despair conquered" (EA 14).

SOURCES QUOTED

Fahey, M. "The Synod of America: Reflections of a Nonparticipant," *Theological Studies* 59/3 (1998): 486-504.

Rosales, G. & Arévalo, C. (Eds.). *For All the Peoples of Asia: Federation of Asian Bishops' Conferences Documents from 1970 to 1991.* Maryknoll, New York & Quezon City, Philippines: Orbis Books & Claretian Publications, 1992.

Tagle, L. "The Synod for Asia as Event," *East Asian Pastoral Review* 35/3-4 (1998): 366-378.

Thangaraj, T. *The Common Task: A Theology of Christian Mission.* Nashville: Abingdon Press, 1999.

A NEW THEOLOGY OF PROCLAMATION*

Josef Neuner

On November 11, 1999 Pope John Paul II proclaimed the Apostolic Exhortation *Ecclesia in Asia* (EA) in the Cathedral of Delhi, India before a large assembly of bishops from many parts of Asia. It is the concluding document of the Asian Synod celebrated in Rome April 19 until May 14, 1998. The Synod had been introduced by the *Lineamenta* (1996) which contained and unfolded the theme chosen by the Pope: "Jesus Christ the Savior and his mission of love and service in Asia."

The theme indicated the two dimensions which characterized the entire work of the Synod: the central Christian message of Jesus Christ and its actual significance for Asia. It also somehow anticipated the two trends that prevailed in the contributions of participants: (1) the need to present the full, undisguised message of faith [stressed mostly in contributions by members of the Curia] and (2) the way of presenting the message to Asian people with their cultural and religious backgrounds as well as their pressing social, political, and economic problems [these figured vastly in contributions by Asian Bishops who are confronted with the concrete situation of people in their dioceses].

The actual proceedings were based on the *Instrumentum Laboris* (1998), which already included some suggestions and criticisms that had come from various Asian bishops' conferences.

The Crucial Problem. The Synod had to face the fact what the Pope called the "mystery why the Savior of the world, born in Asia, has until now remained largely unknown to the peoples of the continent." He

---

*Original Text: *Third Millennium* 3/2 (2000): 110-116.

is relatively unknown among nations in which "religious systems such as Buddhism or Hinduism have a clearly soteriological character" (EA 2). This becomes a paradox as it is in Asia where Jesus himself was born, proclaimed his message, and gathered his first disciples. It is the only continent where Christian communities remain marginal (except in the Philippines), where there is something like collective resistance against its growth and spread, especially against conversions.

From the beginning this crucial question was clearly envisaged. Cardinal Paul Shan Kuo-hsi (Taiwan) in his inaugural address explained that Asians had no difficulty understanding Jesus as a manifestation of the divine but, given the background of their ancient national religions, they find it difficult to understand him as the only Savior. They encounter God in awareness of the harmony of the divine and human worlds that is reflected in ancient mythologies, in religious traditions, and in elaborate philosophical systems that became part of the Asian mind. Asians have to encounter Jesus in the context of their own national traditions and find him particularly in his closeness to rejected and suffering people. Such reflections recurred repeatedly during the Synod and are also taken up in the final Roman document.

The difficulty of presenting the Christian message to Asian nations is reflected also in problems connected with the publication of the post-synodal document. China refused permission for the Pope to visit Hong Kong. In our own country of India, we highly appreciated the determined efforts of the Central Government to avoid and prevent any hostile or embarrassing demonstrations against the Pope. Still, we are aware of the tense political atmosphere that surrounded the Pope's visit. All around, we realize the ever more vocal resistance against anything that seems to threaten India's cultural and religious traditions most often identified with Hinduism. EA must be read against this background.

The Synod was conscious of the need to see Christian mission in Asia within the context of Asian realities: "the Church lives and fulfils her mission in the actual circumstances of time and place. A critical awareness of the diverse and complex realities of Asia is essential if the People of God on the continent are to respond to God's will for them in the new evangelization." Thus, an assessment of the Church's mission in Asia "is conditioned by two factors: on the one hand, her self-understanding as a communion of disciples of Jesus Christ gathered round her Pastors, and on the other hand, the social, political, religious, cultural, and economic realities of Asia" (EA 5).

This process necessarily includes self-examination by the Church: "In recalling the Catholic community's humble condition, as well as the weaknesses of its members, the Synod was also *a call to conversion*, so that the Church in Asia might become ever more worthy of the graces continually being offered by God" (EA 4). This self-explanation is needed particularly at the dawn of a new era. Have there been mistakes in the past, unhealthy developments that block the Church's progress? Such questions are part of an integral renewal.

Asian Realities. EA begins with an outline of the Asian context (EA 5-9): religious-cultural realities, socio-economic situation, and political life. Mission in Asia is seen in the wide context of the Church's growth in our world: "just as in the first millennium the Cross was planted on the soil of Europe, and in the second on that of the Americas and Africa, we can pray that in the Third Christian Millennium *a great harvest of faith* will be reaped in this vast and vital continent" (EA 1). In reflection on Asian realities, special attention is paid to the differences from other continents, which is important in understanding the Church's mission, particularly at the dawn of a new millennium.

Asia is not only "the cradle of the world's major religions," but in spite of the impact of secular civilization, also keeps an atmosphere of "religious and cultural values such as love of silence and contemplation." In spite of many movements and groupings, there is still a widespread "spirit of religious tolerance and peaceful co-existence" which is frequently realized amidst "bitter tensions and violent conflicts" (EA 6).

Among socio-economic realities, the most disturbing fact remaining is the "abject poverty" in which millions of people in Asia still live in spite of widespread economic development. They are the most pressing challenges to the Church. Poverty is also connected with continued growth of population, particularly of the poor rural sections of society. The impact of global inter-relationships throughout the world has negative results: "the emergence of huge urban conglomerations, often with large depressed areas where organized crime, terrorism, prostitution, and exploitation of the weaker sections of society thrive." The rapid growth of communication techniques results in "new forms of behavior ... as a result of overexposure to mass media.... In addition, "the kinds of literature, music, and films that are proliferating on the continent," promote an atmosphere of "violence, hedonism, unbridled individualism and materialism" that strike "at the heart of Asian cultures, at the religious character of the people, families, and whole societies." Mostly affected by these movements are the weaker sections of society, especially the women; "though the awakening of women's consciousness to their dignity and rights is one of the most significant signs of the times, the poverty and exploitation of women remains a serious problem throughout Asia" (EA 7).

This survey of the Asian realities concludes with a brief presentation of the Church's development on the continent of Asia, pursued with the same energy as on other continents but with very different results. "Despite her centuries-long presence and her many apostolic endeavors, the Church in many places was still considered foreign to Asia and indeed was often associated in people's minds with the colonial powers" (EA 9).

This somewhat despondent statement, however, is followed by a positive assessment: "This was the situation on the eve of the Second Vatican Council; but thanks to the impetus provided by the Council, a new understanding of mission dawned and with it a great hope" (EA 9). Vatican II means more than a merely more practical and effective attitude towards the world of today. The new approach is based on a renewed understanding of revelation itself, as communication not only of divine truth but also of life divine. From the beginning of human history, God invites all people, from all nations and cultures to communicate with him (cf. DV 3). Most important is the renewed self-understanding of the Church and her mission for the peace and unity of the world. How has the Second Vatican Council affected the vision of the Church's mission at the dawn of a new era? How is this vision expressed in the final document of the Asian Synod?

The Synod's Answer. It was the intention of all participants in the Synod to respond to realities of Asia in the spirit of Vatican II. To communicate to the peoples of Asia the fullness of God's revelation in Jesus Christ is the Church's mission entrusted to her by Jesus Christ. This does not mean, however, to impose it as something alien; rather it is offered in answer to their intimate longings. This is the Christian message that "through the power of the Holy Spirit, we come to know that God is not distant, above and apart from man, but very near, indeed united to every person and all humanity in all of life's situations. This is the message which Christianity offers to the world, and it is a source of incomparable comfort and hope for all believers" (EA 12).

Thus, in the second, third, and fourth chapters of EA, the mission of Jesus Christ and its fulfillment through the Holy Spirit are outlined. They are presented as the answer to Asia's intimate longing for the Absolute. The Synod was unanimous in acceptance of the doctrinal basis of the Church's mission: God the Father sent his Son to be our brother and our Savior. He fulfilled the Son's mission through the outpouring of Holy Spirit.

Pastoral Focus. The main problem of the Synod was not doctrinal but pastoral: "The great question now facing the Church in Asia is *how* to share with our Asian brothers and sisters what we treasure as the gift containing all gifts, namely, the Good News of Jesus Christ" (EA 19). We are not surprised that the approach to this question differed in the perspective of the "Roman Center" and of the Asian bishops. The latter, of course, came from an actual encounter with Asian nations, which are struggling for renewal of this vast continent that has slowly and painfully emancipated itself from the colonial grip of Western dominance.

Rome is the "Center" of the Church and stands for unity, which must be protected and safeguarded against divisive and disintegrating forces. From early centuries the Church had to struggle for unity in doctrine. The laborious search for unity was sealed in doctrinal formulas of great councils in which the substance of Trinitarian and Christological mysteries was defined. The modern encounter with great world religions contains new challenges. The Second Vatican Council has recognized from the beginning the presence and action of the Holy Spirit among all nations and religions. Will encounter with world religions relativize the unique mystery of Jesus Christ and his saving mediation? Therefore, one finds renewed and emphatic assertion of the centrality of Jesus Christ: "From the first moment of time to its end, Jesus is the one universal Mediator. Even for those who do not explicitly profess faith in him as the Savior, salvation comes as a grace of Jesus Christ through the communication of the Holy Spirit" (EA 14).

This is the background to the following chapters of EA, which turn to the actual proclamation of the Christian message in Asia. They open with the firm demand: "There can be no true evangelization without the explicit proclamation of Jesus Christ as Lord." The Second Vatican Council and the following missionary documents "stressed the primacy of the proclamation of Jesus Christ in all evangelizing work" (EA 19).

The pastoral concern of the Asian bishops, however, had to find an answer to the question *how* this mystery of human salvation could be presented in the Asian context in which Jesus' message was welcomed as God's gift but the uniqueness of his mediation was not easily understood. Efforts of the Synod to find an appropriate way to present the mystery of human salvation are reflected in the papal exhortation: "The presentation of Jesus Christ as the only Savior needs to follow a *pedagogy* which will introduce people step by step to the full appropriation of the mystery" (EA 20).

New Pedagogy of Proclamation. The papal exhortation recognizes this very well: "Clearly, the initial evangelization of non-Christians and the continuing proclamation of Jesus to believers will have to be different in their approach" (EA 20).

When we speak about pedagogy we think of didactical techniques needed for effective teaching, taking into account psychological and social conditions of children. In the Bible it has a deeper meaning, which is rooted in the very nature of revelation. God communicated to us not something—doctrines or norms of life—He communicates himself: "Wishing to open up the way to heavenly salvation, God manifested himself to our first parents from the very beginning" (DV 3). This self-manifestation comes to us from outside but must be perceived within. It begins with creation: "Ever since the creation of the world, God's eternal power and divine nature, invisible though they are, have been understood and seen" (Rom. 1:20). They become part of human life. In his revelation God awakens in us the awareness of his love and the meaning of the world. He becomes responsible for our life, for society, for the earth. God's revelation unfolds in the experience of life and history, which in Israel are interpreted by prophets in their warnings and in the promises of salvation.

Revelation comes to us in Jesus Christ himself, in his person, mission, and message: "Jesus perfected revelation by fulfilling it through his whole work of making himself present and manifesting himself: through his words and deeds, his signs and wonders, but especially through his death and glorious resurrection and final sending of the Spirit of Truth. He revealed that God was with us to deliver us from the darkness of sin and death and to raise us up to eternal life" (DV 4).

This text contains both the content of revelation in Jesus Christ and the "pedagogy" of the communication. The content is expressed not in terms of exclusive uniqueness but of universality, its significance for the entire world. In Jesus, God is with us. In the first covenant God's presence and assistance are assured in the promise "I will be with you" (Ex. 3:12; Judges 6:12, 16). Jesus is Emmanuel, "God with us," in person. He belongs to our world. Through him God is present also in our secular society and in our shattered history; thus, we are delivered from the darkness of sin and death.

This presence, however, is asserted not in doctrinal terms. Jesus never called himself Son of God; he even avoids the title Messiah and does not want it to be spread among the people because it would be misunderstood and misused for political purposes. People must perceive him in his preaching, in his deeds of healing and comforting, and in his destruction of the demonic powers of evil, in biblical language "casting out demons." He is revealed in his ultimate identification with the darkness of human life in his rejection, suffering, and death. He shines forth in fullness in the glorious resurrection, the final manifestation both of his salvific mission and of our ultimate human destiny in God.

Centuries were needed to express all this in doctrinal formulae, and the process is far from complete. But how can we explain all this to people who search for answers to problems of daily life? Therefore, EA considers suggestions that had come from Asian participants in the Synod. The presentation of Jesus should be "narrative," appropriate to the Asian mind, less systematic: "In fact, the proclamation of Jesus Christ can most effectively be made by narrating his story as the Gospels do." The initial proclamation will avoid claims to authority and will present Jesus "in a way that appeals to the sensibilities of the Asian people..., intelligible to Asian minds and cultures, and at the same time faithful to Sacred Scripture and Tradition." Jesus Christ will be presented as "the Teacher of Wisdom, the Healer, the Liberator, the Spiritual Guide, the Enlightened One, the Compassionate Friend of the Poor, the Good Samaritan, the Good Shepherd, the Obedient One" (EA 20).

This is the way Jesus himself proclaimed the Good News. If we appropriate the demand of explicitly proclaiming Jesus the Lord for all true evangelization, Jesus himself would not qualify as true evangelizer. Only in slow, halting steps did he introduce the disciples into the mystery of his person in a process that is concluded through the Holy Spirit, only after his death. Yet, no one would blame Jesus that he did not explicate the doctrine of his divine sonship. It would have blocked his mission as it was beyond the mental horizon of his audience. His revelation remains "implicit"; he truly reveals himself and nothing could later be "added" to this revelation though its fullness was grasped only in a slow growth. This is biblical pedagogy.

Must this pedagogy not be applied in the Asian situation? For Asians with their vast cultural and religious history, with riches of philosophical and spiritual scriptures, with treasures of religious art and architecture, it is impossible to be confronted with the claim of exclusive uniqueness of Jesus Christ as the only Savior and Mediator. It would seem appropriate for the Church to follow Jesus' own example: in her life and work she must make God's work of salvation visible and tangible and in steps lead to the fullness of Jesus' message and person. She must become transparent to the divine mystery which is embodied in her—truly become Christ's body, his continued presence and action in our world. This procedure would also correspond with the principles laid down by the Vatican Council in its *Declaration on Religious Freedom*: "Truth is to be sought after in a manner proper to the dignity of the human person and his social nature. The inquiry is to be free, carried on with the aid of teaching or instruction, communication, and dialogue ... thus to assist one another in the quest for truth" (DH 3).

Such pedagogy begins with the situation and needs of people, not with the remedy, which we intend to offer as the doctrinal system of our faith. Dogmas are the concluding end of proclamation not its beginning. If they are put first they become for many a deterrent as they do not understand them and close themselves to the message as something alien to them. Even if they are accepted, they may be assumed without truly understanding them. We do not become Christians by repeating the Creed, the meaning of which often remains blurred; we must encounter Jesus Christ with growing faith.

The Mission of Love and Service. This pedagogy of leading people towards personal contact with Jesus was actually at the heart of Asian Bishops in their many suggestions of concrete approaches to proclamation of Jesus; they are taken up in the post-synodal exhortation.

First, there is the importance of the Church as community rather than as institution. God desires "that the whole human race may become one People of God, form one Body of Christ, and be built up into one Temple of the Holy Spirit." This links all believers in love and so makes the Church "the sacrament of *the unity of the human race*" (EA 24). This communion must be fostered within the Church herself, among various rites and particular Churches, with other Christians through ecumenical dialogue and collaboration, and by reaching out to other religions.

The Christian message must be communicated through the service of human promotion, in various activities of education, in the many forms of healing ministry, and in social service. It was the peculiar feature of the Second Vatican Council that it reached out to the actual world and was aware of "the joys and hopes, the griefs and anxieties of the people of this age, especially those who are poor and in any way afflicted" (GS 1; EA 32). The social commitment of the Christian faithful is "an integral part of their evangelizing mission" (EA 32). It must, however, extend "far beyond questions of economy and technology. It begins and ends with the integrity of the human person created in the image of God and endowed with God-given dignity and inalienable human rights" (EA 33). In her social ministry "the Church shows a preferential love for the poor and the voiceless, because the Lord has identified himself with them in a special way" (EA 34); very special concern must be given to refugees and immigrants, the aboriginal population, to children, and women (EA 34).

The educational work of the Church is seen in close connection with the Church's mission. "Catholic education must become still more closely directed towards human promotion, providing an environment where students receive not only the formal elements of schooling but, more broadly, an integral human formation based upon the teachings of Christ" (EA 37). This has nothing to do with proselytizing; it implies a formation towards a genuine understanding and realization of human life.

The decisive feature of Gospel-pedagogy is witness. All mission documents after the Council place Christian witness at the center of all evangelizing work: "there can be no true proclamation of the Gospel unless Christians also offer the witness of lives in harmony with the message they preach" (EA 42). Jesus never taught doctrine but proclaimed a new life in union with God and in serving love to the neighbor. His message was embodied in his person and life. So, too, Christian communities in Asia are meant to be the sacrament, the tangible sign and effective agent of the new creation. "Those who believe in Christ are still a small minority in this vast and most populous continent.... They find strength in the wondrous power of the Holy Spirit who ... ensures that the Church's presence is like the yeast which mixes with the flour in a quiet and hidden way till it is all leavened" (EA 50).

These reflections may help to understand the urgency of the request of the Asian bishops in the Synod, when they sought to give "encouragement to *theologians* in their delicate work of developing an inculturated theology, especially in the area of Christology" (EA 22). Much searching is needed in the common effort of the Church to present the mystery of our salvation in Jesus Christ meaningfully to Asia and the world of today.

INCULTURATION IN ASIA AND
*ECCLESIA IN ASIA**

Arij A. Roest Crollius

A very special relation exists between "inculturation" and Asia; in addition, inculturation has a special relevance to the Churches in Asia. In this continent, home of two-thirds of humanity, the richness and variety of cultures are greater than in any other continent. One can also state that there is no other continent where the topic of inculturation is studied so intensely and so widely by pastors and theologians as in Asia. It is no wonder, therefore, that the theme of inculturation had a prominent place in the preparation of the Special Assembly of the Synod of Bishops for Asia.

The preparation began with the Extraordinary Consistory held at the Vatican on June 13-14, 1994, where the idea of "continental synods" was emphasized and the plan for a continent-wide Synod on Asia took shape. It is significant that, when the Holy Father mentioned this plan in the apostolic letter *Tertio Millennio Adveniente* (38), he stressed the encounter of Christianity with the world's ancient local cultures and religions as a pressing issue. After the Synods for Europe (1991) and Africa (1994), a special Assembly of the Synod of Bishops for Asia did not come unexpectedly. With its convocation, a period of intensive preparation began; consultations concerning the theme were held, followed by the publication of the *Lineamenta* or "tentative guidelines" in 1996. The reactions of the different bishops' conferences in Asia to the *Lineamenta* have been sufficiently described in various publications.

---

*Original Text: *Mission Today* 2/4 (2000): 467-476.

This present article unfolds in three steps: **I.** a recall of some essential aspects of the process of inculturation; **II.** a presentation of some key points concerning inculturation as treated during the Synod; **III.** an overview of the theme of inculturation in the apostolic exhortation *Ecclesia in Asia*.

I. Essential Aspects of Inculturation. It is helpful to keep in mind three essential aspects of the process of inculturation. The first element is *inculturation ad intra* (namely, that aspect of the process of inculturation in which the Christian life of the local Church is more directly influenced). There are four areas which have to be considered in this regard: (i) the structure and discipline of the Church; (ii) theological research and modes of expressing the doctrine of the faith; (iii) liturgy and other forms of worship; (iv) spirituality and the presentation of models of sanctity.

The second aspect is *inculturation ad extra* (namely, that aspect of the process of inculturation in which the Christian life and message contribute to the growth and enrichment of the culture of its people). Here the importance of a culture of dialogue cannot sufficiently be stressed. Even if it be in an academic or theoretical way of considering things, a distinction can be made between "proclamation" and "dialogue" in the concreteness of the life of a Christian community. Amidst people of other religious convictions, proclamation cannot have any other form than witness of life and dialogue in the myriad of its manifestations. "*The Church proposes, she imposes nothing*," in full respect of the freedom of each person. This was underlined by John Paul II in his Encyclical *Redemptoris Missio* (39), as an echo of the profound meditation of Paul VI on the role of the Church in the Dialogue of Salvation (see *Ecclesiam Suam*). Between adult and civilized persons, there exists no other way to communicate a deep, personal conviction (as that of one's religious belief) than by way of personal contact, with profound respect for the life-convictions of the other. Any other manner would be one of imposition, exploitation of cultural or social inferiority, or simply indoctrination. It has to be noted, however, that an attitude of respectful sympathy not only excludes the above, but also requires the delicate task of spiritual discernment.

The third essential aspect asserts that *the primary agent of inculturation is the local Church*, under the guidance of the Bishop and in the communion of the Holy Spirit with the Church universal. Only the local Church, with its own perception of history and its unique experience of day-to-day life, can make the necessary apostolic, spiritual discernment for a fuller and more communicative Christian life.

II. Inculturation During the Synod. Without entering into details, one can observe that it was precisely on these points that, before and during the Synod, there existed a sort of "concordant discord."

With regard to the four areas of inculturation *ad intra*, several Bishops' Conferences, especially the Indonesian one, have proposed to examine the possibility of ecclesiastical structures more adapted to the particular situation of the Churches in Asia, as an "Eastern" patriarchate. One of the reasons given has been: to "relativize the primacy of the 'Western' Church and to enhance authentic inculturation of Christian faith."

As to the point mentioned above, the relation between dialogue and proclamation, the Asian bishops affirmed the intimate relationship between these two ways of sharing the Good News. When in the Encyclical *Redemptoris Missio* (57) the Holy Father says, "I am well aware that many missionaries and Christian communities find in the difficult and often misunderstood path of dialogue their only way of bearing witness to Christ and offering generous service to others," he does not mean that the path of dialogue is a sort of second-class way of bearing witness, for in the same paragraph, the Pope says, "Dialogue is a path towards the Kingdom and will certainly bear fruit, even if the times and seasons are known only to the Father (*cf.* Acts 1:7)."

With reference to the primary role of the local Church, the first reality is not that of structures and discipline, but that of the life-situation of a Church. One of the most eloquent descriptions of such a local Church is that found in a 1974 FABC Document (FABC I, 12):

> The local church is a church incarnate in a people,
> a church indigenous and inculturated. And this means
> concretely a church in continuous, humble and loving
> dialogue with the living traditions, the cultures, and
> the religions—in brief, with all the life-realities of the
> people in whose midst it has sunk its roots deeply and
> whose history and life it gladly makes its own. It seeks
> to share in whatever truly belongs to that people: its
> meanings and values, its aspirations, its thoughts and
> its language, as well as its artistry. Even its frailties
> and failings it assumes, so that they too may be healed.

For so did God's Son assume our fallen human condition
(save only for sin) so that he might make it truly his
own, and redeem it in his paschal mystery.

In the preparatory stage of the Synod, this point has been, perhaps, most clearly stressed by the Japanese bishops, who did not hide their dissatisfaction with the *Lineamenta*.

As to the discussions on the theme of inculturation during the Synod, it would be impossible to analyze the often theologically founded and pastorally motivated interventions of the Synod Fathers on this issue. A simple survey of the themes developed in the various interventions shows that inculturation, in its challenges and accomplishments, has been a central issue of the Synod. It would be quite superficial, to make just a list of these themes in the space allotted to this article. A bird's-eye view of the way the theme of inculturation was treated during the Synod could be that of illustrating this process with one of the interventions that could be seen as representative of what many other Synod Fathers and Bishops' Conferences have voiced. We choose the one by Bishop Bernard Toshio Oshikawa, Bishop of Naha, Japan. The intervention was made on April 21, 1998, and, as in the case of all other interventions, it was published in the *Bulletin* printed by the Holy See Press Office.

The intervention, in a pastoral tone, considers inculturation as relevant to the four areas of the life of the local Church: *Christian life, Church discipline, Liturgy* and *Theology*. The text states, in clear terms, the main problem in the matter of inculturation and proposes also some practical solutions.

As the main problem Bishop Oshikawa showed that the norm for the various areas of the life of the members in a local Church in Asia "continues to be that of the Western Church." The maintaining of this Western, and therefore foreign norm, remains a "very effective block" to the service of the Gospel. From the words of the Bishop, it becomes clear that the feeling exists, that statements encouraging inculturation, ranging from the Decrees of the Second Vatican Council to the Encyclicals *Ecclesiam Suam* and *Redemptoris Missio*, have remained by and large a dead letter.

He then reiterates the conviction of John Paul II, that "inculturation is a slow journey" (RM 52), and spells out three aspects of the "Principle of Graduality." These aspects touch upon vital elements in the process of inculturation. The first underlines the wide scope of this process: it is not only a mental introduction into Christianity, but rather a process of growth of persons and communities, under the inspiration of the Gospel and drawn by Jesus Christ, into the cultural and social realities of its own people. Then, he highlights positive aspects of cultural variety within the one Catholic Church. Finally, he mentions the conflict and tension between norms that tend to favor uniformity ... [and those that promote] the growth of local Churches, with a variety of expressions in spirituality, liturgy and theology. He adds "that the Holy See redefine its role and mediate with prudence, flexibility, trust and courage a new dialogue of all the Churches in the common pilgrimage to the fullness of Christ."

One could refer to several other interventions by Asian Bishops, but this one is sufficient because of its clarity of language. It shows that the Jubilee of the year 2000 is a time for that "examination of conscience" to which the Holy Father called the Church, in order also to reconsider *the reception given to the Council*. In the matter of inculturation, one could think here of the above mentioned four aspects of the *inculturation ad intra*.

As to the Church discipline, the Council, when dealing with the "New Churches," admonishes that "the faith must be ... introduced into upright institutions and local customs by appropriate canonical legislation" (AG 19). The Council also calls new theological research a necessity: "theological investigation must necessarily be stirred up in each major socio-cultural area, as it is called. In this way, under the light of the tradition of the universal Church, a fresh scrutiny will be brought to bear on the deeds and words which God has made known, which have been consigned to sacred Scripture, and which have been unfolded by the Church Fathers and the teaching authority of the Church" (AG 22). As regards liturgy, the same Conciliar Decree prescribes that "the faith must be ... celebrated in a liturgy which harmonizes with the genius of the people" (AG 19). Finally, as to the spiritual ways and customs of other religions, the Council invites Christians to witness to the Christian faith and life through dialogue, in order to "acknowledge, preserve and promote the spiritual and moral goods found among these [followers of other religions], as well as the values in their society and culture" (NA 3). No wonder then, that the final document of the Synod, *Ecclesia in Asia*, takes up these major themes, enriches them, and suggests several points of pastoral application within the context of the Churches in Asia.

This might also be the right moment to call to mind the unmistakably clear words of the Second Vatican Council, in its Decree on Ecumenism.

The Council addresses itself to the "Eastern sons of the Catholic Church" and solemnly "declares that this entire heritage of spirituality and liturgy, of discipline and theology, in their various traditions, belongs to the full apostolic and catholic character of the Church" (UR 17). It is evident that there is a difference in the historical situations of the Churches in West Asia and those more to the East (with due exception made to the venerable "Eastern" Churches in Iraq, China and India). However, it would not be beyond one's imagination to think of a closer juridical link of a given national Bishops' Conference in East Asia with one of the Patriarchates toward the West of the Asian Continent, rather than with the Patriarchate of the West. The differences in mentality as expressed in spirituality, church structures, theology and liturgy might require much re-education. In these matters, one has to take into account past historical developments and the present trends of globalization according to a "Western" model—with the evident reactions these provoke in a "struggle for survival" of other cultures. In this same context, one might also call to mind the attempts to invite African Bishops to enter into more firm bonds with the (African) Coptic Catholic Patriarchate of Alexandria in the early 1960s.

III. Inculturation in *Ecclesia in Asia*. Concerning this ongoing, worldwide process of cultural change and the endeavor of inculturation which tries to keep pace with these developments, the post-synodal apostolic exhortation *Ecclesia in Asia* contains a number of important statements. Some of the key issues are treated in the following paragraphs.

(a) Very important is the affirmation of the dignity of the human person, in a world that shows the conflicting tendencies of "liberal" individualism and degrading collectivism. The exhortation calls "for a radical change of both mentality and structures in favor of the human person" (EA 32).

(b) This not only strengthens the efforts of Christians and of all humans of good will to take "imaginative and creative steps to overcome both dehumanizing underdevelopment" and the "overdevelopment" which leads to a consumerist culture (EA 32), but also calls for evangelization through "personal contact" (EA 20). This might indicate a way of overcoming the false dilemma between "proclamation" and "dialogue."

(c) In the inculturation endeavor of the Churches in Asia, "communion and dialogue are two essential aspects of the Church's mission, which have their infinitely transcendent exemplar in the mystery of the Trinity, from whom all mission comes and to whom it must be directed" (EA 31). This "infinitely transcendent exemplar" is also the source of communion in word and love. As has been judiciously noted by A. Wolanin in *Following Christ in Mission*, this Divine Source and Exemplar "includes not only the *divine missions ad extra*, but also and above all, the Trinity as communion of Persons" (p. 38).

(d) The exhortation thus leads to new, essential, but also more inculturated accentuations in the mission of the Churches in Asia. *"Mission is contemplative action and active contemplation"* (EA 23), and the Pope adds, as a fruit also of his personal experience of meeting with representatives of non-Christian spiritual traditions, particularly those of Asia, that "the future of mission depends to a great extent on contemplation" (EA 23). As to the formation of evangelizers in the cultural contexts of Asia, seminary professors and staff are encouraged, "to seek a profound understanding of the elements of spirituality and prayer akin to the Asian soul, and to involve themselves more deeply in the Asian peoples' search for a fuller life" (EA 22).

(e) Based on the dignity of the human person and its call to transcendent communion, sought in faith, service and religious experience, inculturation in Asia can take on original features in the present historical and cultural setting of the Churches an Asia. The apostolic exhortation speaks of the inculturation of *liturgy*, also in multi-cultural societies. *Spirituality* receives special attention. *Ecclesia in Asia*, expressing a concern for the formation of "men and women in the consecrated life," makes it clear, "that the spirituality and lifestyle of consecrated persons needs to be sensitive to the religious and cultural heritage of the people among whom they live and whom they serve, always presupposing the necessary discernment of what conforms to the Gospel and what does not" (EA 22). The test of genuine inculturation of *theology* is to see "whether people become more committed to their Christian faith because they perceive it more clearly with the eyes of their own culture" (EA 22). Regarding the groups that are *victims of exploitation and discrimination*, the exhortation sees a special task of inculturation: "They need support and care in order to preserve their human dignity and their cultural and religious heritage" (EA 34). Thus, they can "become the evangelizers of their own culture and society" (EA 34). *Education* in its various forms, from schools to universities, has "an important role in evangelization, inculturating the faith, teaching the ways of openness and respect, and fostering interreligious understanding" (EA 37).

We conclude this short survey with a brief mention of the processes of globalization—economic, political and cultural. With regard to cultural globalization, the apostolic exhortation highlights its negative effects, and calls for more efficient endeavors towards *"the ethical and moral aspects of globalization"* (EA 39). This would involve, for all concerned Christians in Asia, a deepening of their understanding of *catholicity*, also in its cultural values and attitudes. In dialogue with the many cultures and religions of Asia, the Catholic Church can greatly contribute to a new "culture of globalization" which will yield fruits of peace and justice in this vast Continent, and enrich the cultures of the entire world.

INTERRELIGIOUS DIALOGUE IN
*ECCLESIA IN ASIA**

Sebastiano D'Ambra

When Pope John Paul II traveled to New Delhi at the beginning of November 1999 to entrust his post-Synodal exhortation *Ecclesia in Asia* (EA) to the Asian Church, the welcome given him by the Indian people was marred by protests against his visit from some Hindu groups. These incidents, though sad, challenge all to reflect on the different situations where the Christian message is not welcome in Asia. After two thousand years of Christianity, Asia still finds it difficult to welcome the Church's mission, in spite of the fact that Jesus' message is already present in Asia in a real though mysterious way.

In this context, EA offers a new opportunity to rediscover the Church's mission and to understand the spiritual aspirations of the different peoples of Asia. My special focus here is to see how this document can inspire the Church in Asia to be open to interreligious dialogue.

Focus on Asia. In its seven chapters, EA offers a good synthesis of the teaching of the Church and of her concern for Asian people today. We are reminded that "Asia is the earth's largest continent and is home to nearly two-thirds of the world's population" (6). We are called to "recognize the ancient religious traditions and civilizations, the profound philosophies and the wisdom which have made Asia what it is today" (4). In addition, we should recall "the Catholic community's humble condition, as well as the weakness of its members" (4). The Asian Synod itself issued "*a call to conversion,* so that the Church in Asia might become ever

---

*Original Text: *World Mission* 12/4 (2000): 23-26.

more worthy of the graces continually being offered by God" (4). This "humility" of the Church in Asia is a good starting point for genuine dialogue in Asia today.

God's Ways. Personally, I believe that the light of the Gospel is present in the life of the Asian peoples in a mysterious way, although not as we might expect. The statistic which tell us that Catholics in Asia are less than two percent of the total population can not be taken as a measure of the presence of God's plan of salvation in this continent. In dialogue we do not have to be worried about statistics, if we believe that God is guiding the history of humanity. Interreligious dialogue helps us to extend the concept of community (*koinonia*) to all God's creatures and to believe that the transformation (*metanoia*) of people's hearts happens according to God's own time and style.

After two thousand years of Christianity we have to accept that God is moving in Asia in a way that is not according to the understanding we ourselves had in the past concerning the proper approach to other cultures and religions. I say this without in any way diminishing the value of the missionary zeal of the past, which has also mysteriously entered the life of the peoples of Asia and become light of their light.

Nevertheless, it can be considered providential that the Asian cultures and religions are still alive today. It means that in a spirit of dialogue we can be allowed gradually to discover the hidden mystery of this reality, and thus to share in the richness of God's own dialogue, as this develops in the encounter between the Oriental religious experience and the experience nurtured in the West. As EA remarks: "The presentation of Jesus Christ as the only Savior needs to follow a *pedagogy* which will introduce people step by step to the full appreciation of the mystery" (20).

Only gradually, only "step by step," can we understand and appreciate the mystery of God's dialogue as it emerges in humanity's religious experience. This "step-by-step" approach must be a basic Christian attitude of dialogue with people of different cultures and religions. Interreligious dialogue in Asia is challenged to read the signs of the times that reveal the unique pedagogy of God.

Striking Statements. In this basic perspective, I am struck by three major statements about dialogue in EA's fifth chapter, entitled

"Communion and Dialogue for Mission": **(1)** "All this demands of the Catholic community a sincere examination of conscience, the courage to seek reconciliation and a renewed commitment to dialogue" (24); **(2)** "The desire for dialogue, however, is not simply a strategy for peaceful coexistence among peoples; it is an essential part of the Church's mission because it has its origin in the Father's loving dialogue of salvation with humanity through the Son in the power of the Holy Spirit" (29); **(3)** "The dialogue which the Church proposes is grounded in the logic of the Incarnation" (29).

We are invited to begin from a "sincere examination of conscience." This also means rethinking our missionary approach in Asia. A lot has been written in this area, but the results are still limited, because we need to start from the life and aspirations of Asia's people. We have to be grateful to EA because it has emphasized Asian spirituality, encouraging Christians to see in it an important element of dialogue.

Some of EA's statements on this point are especially striking: "people [of Asia] are more persuaded by holiness of life than by intellectual argument" (42). "A genuinely religious person readily wins respect and a following in Asia. Prayer, fasting and various forms of asceticism are held in high regard. Renunciation, detachment, humility, simplicity and silence are considered great values by the followers of all religions" (23). "People in Asia need to see the clergy not just as charity workers and institutional administrators but as men whose minds and hearts are set on the deep things of the Spirit (cf. Rom. 8:5)" (43).

Many other quotations could be listed here, but these are enough to make an examination of conscience. We have to accept the mystery of God's plan and to be more humble in our theological reflection, giving more space to spirituality. Christians are invited to see in this a way to dialogue: "Their silent example of poverty and abnegation, of purity and sincerity, of self-sacrifice in obedience, can become an eloquent witness capable of touching all people of good will and leading to fruitful dialogue with surrounding cultures and religions, and with the poor and the defenseless" (44).

EA also calls for "the courage to seek reconciliation and a renewed commitment to dialogue" (24). I have met a lot of Christians in Asia who are not ready to move in dialogue, either because they are afraid or are not ready to make the first step along the road of reconciliation. This is true especially in some areas where there is still a situation of conflict between people of different religions.

Thank God, though, there are also many examples of the "courage" EA calls for. I have many Muslim and Christian friends who were educated in an atmosphere of suspicion and hatred, but who, once they start the conversion to genuine interreligious dialogue, are able to discover the beauty of this new pilgrimage with people of other cultures and religions.

Often this involves a painful struggle, which can be interior or exterior to the person. I remember that when Father Salvatore Carzedda PIME was killed in Zamboanga City [Philippines] because of his commitment to dialogue in the Silsilah Movement, the Muslim and Christian members and friends of the movement experienced both interior and exterior struggle. They suffered because of the death of a dear friend and companion in dialogue; they were also subjected to threats. At that time, we found an interior strength that united us and helped us to renew our commitment saying: *Padayon!* [Move on! Continue].

Loving Origin. EA emphasizes that Christians are not in dialogue only to seek peace, but that dialogue is "an essential part of the Church's mission because it has its origin in the Father's loving dialogue of salvation" (29). The document does not enter into the many aspects of theological research on dialogue, but it does encourage this research, adding: "Theological work must always be guided by respect for the sensibilities of Christians, so that by a gradual growth into inculturated forms of expressing the faith people are neither confused nor scandalized" (22). This concern was, I sense, considered important in the way EA presented its message to the Church in Asia.

If we really believe that "dialogue is an essential part of the Church's mission" today (29), we have to conclude that mission has to change, especially in Asia. In fact, it would not be true to say that dialogue is already considered an essential part of mission in Asia; at most, we might be able to say that it is still at the planning stage. EA, instead, emphasizes that dialogue is "essential" and adds this challenge: "The Church ... must be open to the new and surprising ways in which the face of Jesus might be presented in Asia" (20).

Indeed, we are at the beginning of this new pilgrimage that can be considered an adventure of dialogue, because we have to be ready to face, with joy, the new "surprising ways" mentioned by EA. What is important is to be guided by faith and to move in dialogue because we believe in it, not so much because we expect immediate results. In this adventure the vision of God's own dialogue must enlighten our own path.

Emptiness and Silence. For me, the third statement I noted above is the most inspiring element that I found in EA: "The dialogue which the Church proposes is grounded in the logic of the Incarnation" (29). The Incarnation of Christ is a mysterious self-emptying (*kenosis*) of God (Phil. 2:5-11). This point can help the Church deepen her reflection on dialogue in Asia, focusing on the element of *kenosis* as important in continuing a positive theological and spiritual search with people of all religions in Asia.

This will be possible if Christians take to heart the example of John the Baptist, who went to the desert to prepare the way of the Lord, through the preaching of conversion of heart. In the desert of our own lives, in silence and prayer, we have to find what is the way of the Lord in Asia. Meanwhile, we continue our mission of sharing God's love through Jesus Christ, and the people of other religions continue in their ways, in an attitude of mutual respect, appreciation and mutual compassion.

To the Christians, the document says that they "must retain a clear Christian identity to be a Christian leaven in Asian societies" (37). To become "leaven" is a form of "incarnation." The crucial question is: Are the Catholic Church and its members, to whom EA is addressed, ready to become "leaven" in Asia? Are we ready to become powerless? Are we ready, in the process of Christian "incarnation," to lose that form of Christian identity, at present perceived negatively by non-Christians, in order to grow in Asia? These and similar questions need a silent and prayerful attitude, and maybe the best place to continue this reflection is in front of the Blessed Sacrament, the mysterious Eucharistic silence of God with us. We continue the reflection, living in this pluralistic society, ready to see the mysterious presence of God in each person who moves with a sincere heart and mind according to his/her own faith and "sustained by the grace of the Holy Spirit" (25).

9

ECCLESIA IN ASIA: AN ASIAN DOCUMENT?*

Michael Amaladoss

The document *Ecclesia in Asia* is a strong affirmation of the need for a new drive for evangelizing Asia and expresses a fervent hope that Asia will turn to Christ in the third millennium. The document is comprehensive in the sense that any questions or problems that Asians or others might raise concerning Asia can be found mentioned somewhere in the document. One can pick up encouraging quotes to support any activity in which the Church is engaged.

The part of the document of human promotion is an exhaustive list of the economic and social problems in Asia. It lists a lot of concrete challenges with which Christians in Asia will have to be busy in the coming century. There is a small paragraph on Iraq expressing great sympathy for its suffering people. The document also evokes the particularly difficult situations of the different Churches in Asia, including China, North Korea, and the Middle East. The situation of Jerusalem is also mentioned and the pope expresses his desire to go there.

The number of references to the propositions [of the Synod Fathers] in the footnotes shows that efforts have been made to take into account the many practical concerns expressed by the Asian bishops during the Synod. The call to be a witnessing and participative Church in the final section is also welcome.

After a first part that exposes a Trinitarian theology of evangelization, there are sections on proclamation, communion, and human promotion. Inculturation is taken up as part of proclamation; interreligious dialogue

---

*Original Text: *Asia Focus* 15/44 (1999): 3.

becomes an aspect of communion; the perspective of "liberation" seems carefully avoided in the section on human promotion. With regard to evangelization, the framework is that Asia is waiting for fulfillment and we have the truth and the fullness in Christ—a very simple and clear scenario and paradigm.

The special pluralisitc situation of Asia with its developed cultures and religions and any providential role that they may have in the divine plan are not taken into account. There is no sensitivity to the different way in which the "great" religions of Asia have reacted and are reacting to the Gospel as compared to the cosmic religions of Europe, America and Africa.

The many questions that Asian bishops and theologians have raised in the past twenty-five years regarding the goal, the focus, the dimensions, the motivations and methods of evangelization regarding the experience and understanding of the mystery of Jesus Christ in the context of religious pluralism are not reflected here. Their search is ignored. The effort rather seems to be to make a strong reaffirmation of traditional approaches in the face of Asian doubts and hesitations, without any attempt to dialogue with Asia.

There is a reference in passing to the sharing of Asian bishops about the special difficulties in Asia in speaking an exclusive language concerning Jesus Christ. But there is no attempt to explore the reasons for this and meet their concerns and difficulties.

Inculturation is encouraged. But, set in the context of proclamation, this is a point of view from above rather than from below. It has more to do with "adaptation" of the Gospel to the various cultures of Asia than with a free and creative response of the Asian peoples to the Gospel. The rich cultures of Asia are left with a few "seeds of the Word" that the Church will eventually pick up and "fulfill." The usual warnings are repeated.

The perspective of communion and the exploration of interreligious dialogue in that context is interesting. Dialogue is encouraged in traditional terms. But, after the strong statement on evangelization in the document's first part, which is repeated again in number 31, I wonder if anyone from the great religions of Asia would be interested in dialoguing. The Church has nothing to get, nothing to learn. It can only give. I wonder if there is any room for real dialogue anymore. The "preparation-fulfillment" paradigm is not the ideal context for dialogue.

There had been some voices at the Synod about the rightful autonomy of the Asian Churches within the communion of the universal Church. These requests have been quietly ignored. Rather, the role of the central agencies in preserving tradition and unity are stressed.

The pope's brief presentation in the Delhi archdiocese cathedral had a different tone. It spoke of *kenosis* and of the cross. It was less triumphalistic. He even mentioned "liberation" in relation to justice.

The exhortation is a document for Asia. It is not an Asian document. It is not the voice of Asia. The tone and style are very un-Asian. The method is *a priori* and from above. One can compare it with any document of the Federation of Asian Bishops' Conferences or even with the special message of the bishops at the end of the Synod.

Asians today are trying to reflect on their faith by starting from their experience of life in Asia and by exploring appropriate pastoral and missionary strategies. This approach is implicitly questioned. The document does evoke the situation of Asia in the beginning, but then it goes on to make a strong *a priori* statement on the mission to evangelize Asia. The reflection is more dogmatic than contextual.

Dialogue is seen more as a method that does not affect the content in any way. The Church was born in Asia as the document points out and it has been present in Asia longer than it has been present in northern Europe, America or sub-Saharan Africa. But, it has not yet learned to speak in an Asian voice in the Asian context to Asian experience. A strong reaffirmation of traditional teaching will not make the Asian experience of the richness and pluralism of its cultures and religions and the questions it raises go away.

10

IMPLEMENTING *ECCLESIA IN ASIA**

Local Church Responses

The following presentation integrates the voices of spokesmen from three of Asia's local Churches on how *Ecclesia in Asia* should challenge the local faith-communities and how they can proceed with the concrete implementation of the apostolic exhortation. The first response comes from Vietnamese Nguyen Van Noi, coordinator of lay volunteer Catholics who educate young couples on marital issues in parishes of Ho Chi Minh City Archdiocese. Secondly, Archbishop Matthias U Shwe of Taunggyi, Myanmar (Shan State) describes his hopes for his "little flock" (43,000 Catholics among 1.7 million people) as they respond to *Ecclesia in Asia*. Finally, Redemptorist Bishop George Yod Phimphisan of Udon Thani, Thailand, President of the Thailand Bishops' Conference, reflects on how the Asian Synod and its final document can be concretized in Thailand (J. Kroeger).

Nguyen Van Noi. A major concern of Church leaders in Vietnam is how to implement *Ecclesia in Asia* in a Vietnamese setting.... First, it is imperative that the Church in Vietnam seek ways to further integrate into the Asian Church and learn from other Asian Churches. In the last thirty years, the Federation of Asian Bishops' Conferences (FABC) has accumulated a wealth of reflection and research on how to implement the teachings of the Second Vatican Council in the Asian context. However, Church people in Vietnam are still unfamiliar with the FABC's abundant material.

The Vietnam Church's reintegration into the region would not require

---

*Original Texts: *Asia Focus* 16/29 (2000): 3; 16/42 (2000): 8; 14/29 (1998): 3.

much effort, as the Vietnam Bishops' Conference (VBC) was a founding member of the FABC in the early 1970s. VBC members and other Vietnam Church people attended the last two FABC plenary assemblies and other FABC-sponsored seminars and workshops. Moreover, the VBC made significant contributions to the 1998 Special Assembly of the Synod of Bishops for Asia, which gave birth to the landmark apostolic exhortation....

The second major task consists of exploring the spirit and spreading the content of *Ecclesia in Asia*, in which Asian Churches, including the Vietnam Church, can find key pastoral orientations to continue their faith journey alongside Asian peoples. Many bishops, clergy and laity have noted that one of the "weakest points" of the local Church stems from a serious interruption in Church thinking and collective endeavors. It is high time for the VBC to sponsor research groups in the areas of theological reflection, faith inculturation and pastoral renewal, and to explore the most appropriate ways to implement the teachings of Vatican II and the recent apostolic exhortation.

The local Church's third task is to work out concrete action plans supported by appropriate mechanisms to implement the exhortation. To benefit the local Church, any attempt at reflection or research should lead to concrete action. In other words, any attempt to deepen the mystery of the triune God as communion or the innate equality of all God's people should lead to tangible changes....

The spirit of communion and equality should be applied to Church structures—the VBC, priests' councils, and diocesan and parish pastoral councils. Catholics in Vietnam can find in FABC documents an ecclesiology that promotes the concept of a "participatory Church." Each member of such a Church has rights and obligations, and should play a part in contributing to its growth. This is the Asian way to apply Vatican II ecclesiology so as to promote the concept of Church as "People of God." It requires the building up of Basic Ecclesial Communities and a "non-dominant," democratic and community-centered leadership style that counters individualism and authoritarianism.

The fourth task is for the Church in Vietnam to readjust her relationships with religious, cultural, social and political entities in the country. Catholics in Vietnam continue to be a minority that is expected to interact with more ancient religions and cultural traditions, with the entire national community, and with past and present political systems.

The readjustment must conform with the spirit of dialogue fostered by the Gospel, Vatican II and *Ecclesia in Asia*. In more concrete terms, the Church in Vietnam must embark on a triple dialogue with the nation's cultural and religious traditions, and with the poor in contemporary Vietnamese society.

The last task consists of forming a cadre of mature and competent laity and returning to them their legitimate role in all Church activities. A well-known overseas Vietnamese theologian once wrote me, "I am strongly convinced that if Vietnamese laity are not given adequate formation in accordance with Vatican II teachings, the Church in Vietnam will not see any outcome for its future." This task needs to be concretized by well-structured formation, training programs and suitable mechanisms that foster the specific role and mission of laity within the Church and society. One such new mechanism could focus on encouraging the emergence of Basic Ecclesial Communities in a particularly Vietnamese setting.

Matthias U Shwe. In my opinion, two important aspects of evangelization mentioned in *Ecclesia in Asia* are inculturation and interreligious dialogue. In my archdiocese we have done something in an informal manner, as far as inculturation is concerned. For instance, we use the native language in local music and liturgy. We use ethnic tribal dance in religious celebrations and native language translations of the Scriptures in workshops.

With regard to interreligious dialogue we are not able to do anything on the official level, even to hold serious discussions. However, on a practical level, we live peacefully with Buddhists, fostering understanding and collaborating in development projects that help all the people. For example, our *Zetemins* [little evangelizers] are opening and teaching in schools and health-care centers in Buddhist villages. Our orphanages and dispensaries accept non-Catholics. We care for displaced people regardless of their race or religion. We always keep the welfare of non-Catholics in mind in all our pastoral, social and development planning.

I understand integral human development as the spiritual-social-economic development of a person and the person's community. For instance, we have started a scheme of low-interest loans for youth, women and Catholic activists in various parishes and communities. The Karuna Animation Team conducts courses on the social doctrine of the Church, while catechists and lay leaders run occasional AsIPA [Asian Integrated

Pastoral Approach] sessions for them. In this way we make it a point that the persons involved and the beneficiaries of the social-economic development do not lose sight of the spiritual and moral aspects of development. We also see that the development of an individual has a positive impact on the community or society as a whole....

My hopes in the next ten years are: • That the faithful are deepened in their faith, especially through love for the Word of God and the Eucharist; • That the Good News of Jesus Christ is heard by all the people of the archdiocese through our social-charitable works and the witness of the life of our Catholics; • That the archdiocese becomes self-reliant with trained personnel and becoming less dependent on outside sources for finances; • That each Catholic family will be able to live a decent life and be able to contribute spiritually and materially to the growth and progress of the Church; • That the archdiocese will be able to send out missionaries: priests, Religious, and laypeople; • That the vast archdiocese be divided in two, when the faith has reached maturity and the number of Catholics has doubled.

I hope that the "little flock" will grow in their spiritual life and remain united and committed in their faith, joyful in their life and service for their sisters and brothers, especially the poor and disadvantaged. In this way they will bear witness to the Good News of Jesus Christ like the first Christians.

George Yod Phimphisan. The results of efforts by the Church in Asia to live Asian realities over the last quarter century were evident during the Special Assembly of the Synod of Bishops for Asia.

The Federation of Asian Bishops' Conferences (FABC) has developed many pastoral orientations that became part of the language used during the Synod. Phrases such as "communion of communities," "new way of being Church in Asia," etc., were often cited in the Synod hall. FABC member conferences were well prepared to present a unified view on many issues. They shared their pastoral ministries based on lived experiences in their respective Churches.

The central vision of the Church in Asia is to establish "a truly local Church," which can be characterized as a Church incarnated in the people, a Church indigenous and inculturated. Its model of evangelization is formed by the histories, traditions and cultures of Asian peoples. In the process of evangelization, Asian bishops have engaged in a "triple dialogue"—dialogue with cultures, other religions and the poor. These pastoral orientations were mentioned in the "Message of the Synod" for the whole Church in Asia.

The Synod for Asia has concluded. For the Church in Thailand [and all Asia's local Churches], the real challenge now is to renew the Church.... How can the Church be more relevant to present Thai society? How can we eliminate the so-called "foreignness" of the Thai Church? ... How can we make the Church more relevant to our young people? How can we make use of our Catholic schools, which are very popular and well known, to be means of evangelization? How can we make priestly and religious lives more meaningful for young people who are called to become priests or Religious?

How can we have true dialogue with our Buddhist sisters and brothers? How can we animate and encourage laypeople to take a more active role in the Church, and Church leaders to encourage them to do so?

These are some of the questions and issues that we have to face. Many of these issues were discussed at the Synod by our sisters and brothers from other parts of Asia. We see the end of the Synod [and the proclamation of *Ecclesia in Asia*] as the beginning of our efforts to make the Thai Church truly an instrument "of Christ's Mission of Love and Service" in Thailand.

Part Three

Ecclesia in Asia

Text - Notes

POST-SYNODAL APOSTOLIC EXHORTATION

ECCLESIA IN ASIA

OF THE HOLY FATHER JOHN PAUL II

TO THE BISHOPS,

PRIESTS AND DEACONS,

MEN AND WOMEN IN THE CONSECRATED LIFE

AND ALL THE LAY FAITHFUL

ON JESUS CHRIST THE SAVIOR

AND HIS MISSION OF LOVE AND SERVICE IN ASIA:

"... THAT THEY MAY HAVE LIFE,

AND HAVE IT ABUNDANTLY" (Jn. 10:10)

TABLE OF CONTENTS

NOTE: This text of *Ecclesia in Asia*, originating from the Vatican Website, is in full concordance with the text issued by the Libreria Editrice Vaticana, Vatican City (ISBN 88-209-2847-7). Minor corrections have been entered, Scripture quotes and English usage have been made uniform, and the individual paragraph numbers (e.g. 6a, 6b, 6c, etc.) have been supplied to facilitate research and location of data (J. Kroeger).

INTRODUCTION

1. The Marvel of God's Plan in Asia

1a. The Church in Asia sings the praises of the "God of salvation" (Ps. 68:20) for choosing to initiate his saving plan on Asian soil, through men and women of that continent. It was in fact in Asia that God revealed and fulfilled his saving purpose from the beginning. He guided the patriarchs (cf. Gen. 12) and called Moses to lead his people to freedom (cf. Ex. 3:10). He spoke to his chosen people through many prophets, judges, kings and valiant women of faith. In "the fullness of time" (Gal. 4:4), he sent his only-begotten Son, Jesus Christ the Savior, who took flesh as an Asian! Exulting in the goodness of the continent's peoples, cultures, and religious vitality, and conscious at the same time of the unique gift of faith which she has received for the good of all, the Church in Asia cannot cease to proclaim: "Give thanks to the Lord for he is good, for his love endures for ever" (Ps. 118:1).

1b. Because Jesus was born, lived, died and rose from the dead in the Holy Land, that small portion of Western Asia became a land of promise and hope for all mankind. Jesus knew and loved this land. He made his own the history, the sufferings and the hopes of its people. He loved its people and embraced their Jewish traditions and heritage. God in fact had long before chosen this people and revealed himself to them in preparation for the Savior's coming. And from this land, through the preaching of the Gospel in the power of the Holy Spirit, the Church went forth to make "disciples of all nations" (Mt. 28:19). With the Church throughout the world, the Church in Asia will cross the threshold of the Third Christian Millennium marveling at all that God has worked from those beginnings until now, and strong in the knowledge that "just as in the first millennium the Cross was planted on the soil of Europe, and in the second on that of the Americas and Africa, we can pray that in the Third Christian Millennium *a great harvest of faith* will be reaped in this vast and vital continent."[1]

2. Background to the Special Assembly

2a. In my Apostolic Letter *Tertio Millennio Adveniente*, I set out a program for the Church to welcome the Third Millennium of Christianity, a program centered on the challenges of the new evangelization. An important feature of that plan was the holding of *continental Synods* so that Bishops could address the question of evangelization according to the particular situation and needs of each continent. This series of Synods, linked by the common theme of the new evangelization, has proved an important part of the Church's preparation for the Great Jubilee of the Year 2000.

2b. In that same letter, referring to the Special Assembly for Asia of the Synod of Bishops, I noted that in that part of the world "the issue of the encounter of Christianity with ancient local cultures and religions is a pressing one. This is a great challenge for evangelization, since religious systems such as Buddhism or Hinduism have a clearly soteriological character."[2] It is indeed a mystery why the Savior of the world, born in Asia, has until now remained largely unknown to the people of the continent. The Synod would be a providential opportunity for the Church in Asia to reflect further on this mystery and to make a renewed commitment to the mission of making Jesus Christ better known to all. Two months after the publication of *Tertio Millennio Adveniente*, speaking to the Sixth Plenary Assembly of the Federation of Asian Bishops' Conferences, in Manila, the Philippines, during the memorable Tenth World Youth Day celebrations, I reminded the Bishops: "If the Church in Asia is to fulfil its providential destiny, evangelization as the joyful, patient and progressive preaching of the saving Death and Resurrection of Jesus Christ must be your absolute priority."[3]

2c. The positive response of the Bishops and of the particular Churches to the prospect of a Special Assembly for Asia of the Synod of Bishops was evident throughout the preparatory phase. The Bishops communicated their desires and opinions at every stage with frankness and a penetrating knowledge of the continent. They did so in full awareness of the bond of communion which they share with the universal Church. In line with the original idea of *Tertio Millennio Adveniente* and following the proposals of the Pre-Synodal Council which evaluated the views of the Bishops and the particular Churches on the Asian continent, I chose as the Synod's theme: *Jesus Christ the Savior and his Mission of Love and Service in Asia: "That they may have Life and have it abundantly"* (Jn 10:10). Through this particular formulation of the theme, I hoped that the Synod might "illustrate and explain more fully the truth that Christ is the one Mediator between God and man and the sole Redeemer of the world, to be clearly distinguished from the founders of other great religions."[4] As we approach the Great Jubilee, the Church in Asia needs to be able to proclaim with renewed vigor: *Ecce natus est nobis Salvator mundi*, "Behold the Savior of the World is born to us," born in Asia!

3. The Celebration of the Special Assembly

3a. By the grace of God, the Special Assembly for Asia of the Synod of Bishops took place from 18 April to 14 May 1998 in the Vatican. It came after the Special Assemblies for Africa (1994) and America (1997), and was followed at the year's end by the Special Assembly for Oceania (1998). For almost a month, the Synod Fathers and other participants, gathered around the Successor of Peter and sharing in the gift of hierarchical communion, gave concrete voice and expression to the Church in Asia. It was indeed a moment of special grace.[5] Earlier meetings of Asian Bishops had contributed to preparing the Synod and making possible an atmosphere of intense ecclesial and fraternal communion. Of particular relevance in this respect were the past Plenary Assemblies and Seminars sponsored by the Federation of Asian Bishops' Conferences and its offices, which periodically brought together great numbers of Asian Bishops and fostered personal as well as ministerial bonds between them. I had the privilege of being able to make a visit to some of these meetings, at times presiding at the opening or closing Solemn Eucharistic Celebrations. On those occasions I was able to observe directly the *encounter in dialogue* of the particular Churches, including the Eastern Churches, in the person of their Pastors. These and other regional assemblies of Asia's Bishops served providentially as remote preparation for the Synod Assembly.

3b. The actual celebration of the Synod itself confirmed the importance of dialogue as a *characteristic mode of the Church's life in Asia*. A sincere and honest sharing of experiences, ideas and proposals proved to be the way to a genuine meeting of spirits, a communion of minds and hearts which, in love, respects and transcends differences. Particularly moving was the encounter of the new Churches with the ancient Churches which trace their origins to the Apostles. We experienced the incomparable joy of seeing the Bishops of the particular Churches in Myanmar, Vietnam, Laos, Cambodia, Mongolia, Siberia and the new republics of Central Asia sitting beside their Brothers who had long desired to encounter them and to dialogue with them. Yet there was also a sense of sadness at the fact that Bishops from Mainland China could not be present. Their absence was a constant reminder of the heroic sacrifices and suffering which the Church continues to endure in many parts of Asia.

3c. The encounter in dialogue of the Bishops and the Successor of Peter, entrusted with the task of strengthening his brothers (cf. Lk. 22:32), was truly a confirmation in faith and mission. Day after day the Synod Hall and meeting rooms were filled with accounts of deep faith, self-sacrificing love, unwavering hope, long-suffering commitment, enduring courage and merciful forgiveness, all of which eloquently disclosed the truth of Jesus' words: "I am with you always" (Mt. 28:20). The Synod was a moment of grace because it was an encounter with the Savior who continues to be present in his Church through the power of the Holy Spirit, experienced in a fraternal dialogue of life, communion and mission.

4. Sharing the Fruits of the Special Assembly

4a. Through this Post-Synodal Apostolic Exhortation, I wish to share with the Church in Asia and throughout the world the fruits of the Special Assembly. This document seeks to convey the wealth of that great spiritual event of communion and episcopal collegiality. The Synod was a *celebratory remembering* of the Asian roots of Christianity. The Synod Fathers remembered the first Christian community, the early Church, Jesus' little flock on this immense continent (cf. Lk. 12:32). They remembered what the Church has received and heard from the beginning (cf. Rev. 3:3), and, having remembered, they celebrated God's "abundant goodness" (Ps. 145:7) which never fails. The Synod was also an occasion to recognize the ancient religious traditions and civilizations, the profound philosophies and the wisdom which have made Asia what it is today. Above all, the peoples of Asia themselves were remembered as the continent's true wealth and hope for the future. Throughout the Synod those of us present were witnesses of an extraordinarily fruitful meeting between the old and new cultures and civilizations of Asia, marvelous to behold in their diversity and convergence, especially when symbols, songs, dances and colors came together in harmonious accord around the one Table of the Lord in the opening and closing Eucharistic Liturgies.

4b. This was not a celebration motivated by pride in human achievements, but one conscious of what the Almighty has done for the Church in Asia (cf. Lk. 1:49). In recalling the Catholic community's humble condition, as well as the weaknesses of its members, the Synod was also *a call to conversion*, so that the Church in Asia might become ever more worthy of the graces continually being offered by God.

4c. As well as a remembrance and a celebration, the Synod was *an ardent affirmation of faith in Jesus Christ the Savior*. Grateful for the gift of faith, the Synod Fathers found no better way to celebrate the faith than to affirm it in its integrity, and to reflect on it in relation to the context in which it has to be proclaimed and professed in Asia today. They emphasized frequently that the faith is already being proclaimed with trust and courage on the continent, even amid great difficulties. In the name of so many millions of men and women in Asia who put their trust in no one other than the Lord, the Synod Fathers confessed: "We have believed and come to know that you are the Holy One of God" (Jn. 6:69). In the face of the many painful questions posed by the suffering, violence, discrimination and poverty to which the majority of Asian peoples are subjected, they prayed: "I believe, help my unbelief" (Mk. 9:24).

4d. In 1995, I invited the Bishops of Asia gathered in Manila to "open wide to Christ the doors of Asia."[6] Taking strength from the mystery of communion with the countless and often unheralded martyrs of the faith in Asia, and confirmed in hope by the abiding presence of the Holy Spirit, the Synod Fathers courageously called all Christ's disciples in Asia to a new *commitment to mission*. During the Synod Assembly, the Bishops and participants bore witness to the character, spiritual fire and zeal which will assuredly make Asia the land of a bountiful harvest in the coming millennium.

CHAPTER ONE: THE ASIAN CONTEXT

5. Asia, the Birthplace of Jesus and of the Church

5a. The Incarnation of the Son of God, which the whole Church will solemnly commemorate in the Great Jubilee of the Year 2000, took place in a definite historical and geographical context. That context exercised an important influence on the life and mission of the Redeemer as man. "In Jesus of Nazareth, God has assumed the features typical of human nature, including a person's belonging to a particular people and a particular land.... The physical particularity of the land and its geographical determination are inseparable from the truth of the human flesh assumed by the Word."[7] Consequently, knowledge of the world in which the Savior "dwelt among us" (Jn. 1:14) is an important key to a more precise understanding of the Eternal Father's design and of the immensity of his love for every creature: "For God so loved the world that he gave his only Son, that whoever believes in him should not perish but have eternal life" (Jn. 3:16).

5b. Likewise, the Church lives and fulfils her mission in the actual circumstances of time and place. A critical awareness of the diverse and complex realities of Asia is essential if the People of God on the continent are to respond to God's will for them in the new evangelization. The Synod Fathers insisted that the Church's mission of love and service in Asia is conditioned by two factors: on the one hand, her self-understanding as a community of disciples of Jesus Christ gathered around her Pastors, and on the other hand, the social, political, religious, cultural and economic realities of Asia.[8] The situation of Asia was examined in detail during the Synod by those who have daily contact with the extremely diversified realities of such an immense continent. The following is, in synthesis, the result of the Synod Fathers' reflections.

6. Religious and Cultural Realities

6a. Asia is the earth's largest continent and is home to nearly two-thirds of the world's population, with China and India accounting for almost half the total population of the globe. The most striking feature of the continent is the variety of its peoples who are "heirs to ancient cultures, religions and traditions."[9] We cannot but be amazed at the sheer size of Asia's population and at the intricate mosaic of its many cultures, languages, beliefs and traditions, which comprise such a substantial part of the history and patrimony of the human family.

6b. Asia is also the cradle of the world's major religions—Judaism, Christianity, Islam and Hinduism. It is the birthplace of many other spiritual traditions such as Buddhism, Taoism, Confucianism, Zoroastrianism, Jainism, Sikhism and Shintoism. Millions also espouse traditional or tribal religions, with varying degrees of structured ritual and formal religious teaching. The Church has the deepest respect for these traditions and seeks to engage in sincere dialogue with their followers. The religious values they teach await their fulfillment in Jesus Christ.

6c. The people of Asia take pride in their religious and cultural values, such as love of silence and contemplation, simplicity, harmony, detachment, non-violence, the spirit of hard work, discipline, frugal living, the thirst for learning and philosophical enquiry.[10] They hold dear the values of respect for life, compassion for all beings, closeness to nature, filial piety towards parents, elders and ancestors, and a highly developed sense of community.[11] In particular, they hold the family to be a vital source of strength, a closely knit community with a powerful sense of solidarity.[12] Asian peoples are known for their spirit of religious tolerance and peaceful co-existence. Without denying the existence of bitter tensions and violent conflicts, it can still be said that Asia has often demonstrated a remarkable capacity for accommodation and a natural openness to the mutual enrichment of peoples in the midst of a plurality of religions and cultures. Moreover, despite the influence of modernization and secularization, Asian religions are showing signs of great vitality and a capacity for renewal, as seen in reform movements within the various religious groups. Many people, especially the young, experience a deep thirst for spiritual values, as the rise of new religious movements clearly demonstrates.

6d. All of this indicates an innate spiritual insight and moral wisdom in the Asian soul, and it is the core around which a growing sense of "being Asian" is built. This "being Asian" is best discovered and affirmed not in confrontation and opposition, but in the spirit of complementarity and harmony. In this framework of complementarity and harmony, the Church can communicate the Gospel in a way which is faithful both to her own Tradition and to the Asian soul.

7. Economic and Social Realities

7a. On the subject of economic development, situations on the Asian continent are very diverse, defying any simple classification. Some countries are highly developed, others are developing through effective economic policies, and others still find themselves in abject poverty, indeed among the poorest nations on earth. In the process of development, materialism and secularism are also gaining ground, especially in urban areas. These ideologies, which undermine traditional, social and religious values, threaten Asia's cultures with incalculable damage.

7b. The Synod Fathers spoke of the rapid changes taking place within Asian societies and of the positive and negative aspects of these changes. Among them are the phenomenon of urbanization and the emergence of huge urban conglomerations, often with large depressed areas where organized crime, terrorism, prostitution, and the exploitation of the weaker sectors of society thrive. Migration too is a major social phenomenon, exposing millions of people to situations which are difficult economically, culturally and morally. People migrate within Asia and from Asia to other continents for many reasons, among them poverty, war and ethnic conflicts, the denial of their human rights and fundamental freedoms. The establishment of giant industrial complexes is another cause of internal and external migration, with accompanying destructive effects on family life and values. Mention was also made of the construction of nuclear power plants with an eye to cost and efficiency but with little regard for the safety of people and the integrity of the environment.

7c. Tourism also warrants special attention. Though a legitimate industry with its own cultural and educational values, tourism has in some cases a devastating influence upon the moral and physical landscape of many Asian countries, manifested in the degradation of young women and even children through prostitution.[13] The pastoral care of migrants, as well as that of tourists, is difficult and complex, especially in Asia where basic structures for this may not exist. Pastoral planning at all levels needs to take these realities into account. In this context we should not forget the migrants from Catholic Eastern Churches who need pastoral care according to their own ecclesiastical traditions.[14]

7d. Several Asian countries face difficulties related to population growth, which is "not merely a demographic or economic problem but especially a moral one."[15] Clearly, the question of population is closely linked to that of human promotion, but false solutions that threaten the dignity and inviolability of life abound and present a special challenge to the Church in Asia. It is perhaps appropriate at this point to recall the Church's contribution to the defence and promotion of life through health care, social development and education to benefit peoples, especially the poor. It is fitting that the Special Assembly for Asia paid tribute to the late Mother Teresa of Calcutta, "who was known all over the world for her loving and selfless care of the poorest of the poor."[16] She remains an icon of the service to life which the Church is offering in Asia, in courageous contrast to the many dark forces at work in society.

7e. A number of Synod Fathers underlined the external influences being brought to bear on Asian cultures. New forms of behavior are emerging as a result of over-exposure to the mass media and the kinds of literature, music and films that are proliferating on the continent. Without denying that the means of social communication can be a great force for good,[17] we cannot disregard the negative impact which they often have. Their beneficial effects can at times be outweighed by the way in which they are controlled and used by those with questionable political, economic and ideological interests. As a result, the negative aspects of the media and entertainment industries are threatening traditional values, and in particular the sacredness of marriage and the stability of the family. The effect of images of violence, hedonism, unbridled individualism and materialism "is striking at the heart of Asian cultures, at the religious character of the people, families and whole societies."[18] This is a situation which poses a great challenge to the Church and to the proclamation of her message.

7f. The persistent reality of poverty and the exploitation of people are matters of the most urgent concern. In Asia there are millions of oppressed people who for centuries have been kept economically, culturally and politically on the margins of society.[19] Reflecting upon the situation of women in Asian societies, the Synod Fathers noted that "though the awakening of women's consciousness to their dignity and rights is one of the most significant signs of the times, the poverty and exploitation of women remains a serious problem throughout Asia."[20] Female illiteracy is much higher than that of males; and female children are more likely to be aborted or even killed after birth. There are also millions of indigenous or tribal people throughout Asia living in social, cultural and political isolation from the dominant population.[21] It was reassuring to hear the Bishops at the Synod mention that in some cases these matters are receiving greater attention at the national, regional and international levels, and that the Church is actively seeking to address this serious situation.

7g. The Synod Fathers pointed out that this necessarily brief reflection upon the economic and social realities of Asia would be incomplete if recognition were not also given to the extensive economic growth of many Asian societies in recent decades: a new generation of skilled workers, scientists and technicians is growing daily and their great number augurs well for Asia's development. Still, not all is stable and solid in this progress, as has been made evident by the most recent and far-reaching financial crisis suffered by a number of Asian countries. The future of Asia lies in cooperation, within Asia and with the nations of other continents, but building always on what Asian peoples themselves do with a view to their own development.

8. Political Realities

8a. The Church always needs to have an exact understanding of the political situation in the different countries where she seeks to fulfil her mission. In Asia today the political panorama is highly complex, displaying an array of ideologies ranging from democratic forms of government to theocratic ones. Military dictatorships and atheistic ideologies are very much present. Some countries recognize an official state religion that allows little or no religious freedom to minorities and the followers of other religions. Other States, though not explicitly theocratic, reduce minorities to second-class citizens with little safeguard for their fundamental human rights. In some places Christians are not allowed to practice their faith freely and proclaim Jesus Christ to others.[22] They are persecuted and denied their rightful place in society. The Synod Fathers remembered in a special way the people of China and expressed the fervent hope that all their Chinese

Catholic brothers and sisters would one day be able to exercise their religion in freedom and visibly profess their full communion with the See of Peter.[23]

8b. While appreciating the progress which many Asian countries are making under their different forms of government, the Synod Fathers also drew attention to the widespread corruption existing at various levels of both government and society.[24] Too often, people seem helpless to defend themselves against corrupt politicians, judiciary officials, administrators and bureaucrats. However, there is a growing awareness throughout Asia of people's capacity to change unjust structures. There are new demands for greater social justice, for more participation in government and economic life, for equal opportunities in education and for a just share in the resources of the nation. People are becoming increasingly conscious of their human dignity and rights and more determined to safeguard them. Long dormant ethnic, social and cultural minority groups are seeking ways to become agents of their own social advancement. The Spirit of God helps and sustains people's efforts to transform society so that the human yearning for a more abundant life may be satisfied as God wills (cf. Jn. 10:10).

9. The Church in Asia: Past and Present

9a. The history of the Church in Asia is as old as the Church herself, for it was in Asia that Jesus breathed the Holy Spirit upon his disciples and sent them to the ends of the earth to proclaim the Good News and gather communities of believers. "As the Father has sent me, even so I send you" (Jn. 20:21; see also Mt. 28:18-20;. Mk. 16:15-18; Lk. 24:47; Acts 1:8). Following the Lord's command, the Apostles preached the word and founded Churches. It may help to recall some elements of this fascinating and complex history.

9b. From Jerusalem, the Church spread to Antioch, to Rome and beyond. It reached Ethiopia in the South, Scythia in the North and India in the East, where tradition has it that Saint Thomas the Apostle went in the year 52 AD and founded Churches in South India. The missionary spirit of the East Syrian community in the third and fourth centuries, with its center at Edessa, was remarkable. The ascetic communities of Syria were a major force of evangelization in Asia from the third century onwards. They provided spiritual energy for the Church, especially during times of persecution. At the end of the third century, Armenia was the first nation as a whole to embrace Christianity, and is now preparing to celebrate the 1700th anniversary of its baptism. By the end of the fifth century, the Christian message had reached the Arab kingdoms, but for many reasons, including the divisions among Christians, the message failed to take root among these peoples.

9c. Persian merchants took the Good News to China in the fifth century. The first Christian Church was built there at the beginning of the seventh century. During the T'ang dynasty (618-907 AD), the Church flourished for nearly two centuries. The decline of this vibrant Church in China by the end of the First Millennium is one of the sadder chapters in the history of God's People on the continent.

9d. In the thirteenth century the Good News was announced to the Mongols and the Turks and to the Chinese once more. But Christianity almost vanished in these regions for a number of reasons, among them the rise of Islam, geographical isolation, the absence of an appropriate adaptation to local cultures, and perhaps above all a lack of preparedness to encounter the great religions of Asia. The end of the fourteenth century saw the drastic diminution of the Church in Asia, except for the isolated community in South India. The Church in Asia had to await a new era of missionary endeavor.

9e. The apostolic labors of Saint Francis Xavier, the founding of the Congregation of *Propaganda Fide* by Pope Gregory XV, and the directives for missionaries to respect and appreciate local cultures all contributed to achieving more positive results in the course of the sixteenth and seventeenth centuries. Again in the nineteenth century there was a revival of missionary activity. Various religious congregations dedicated themselves wholeheartedly to this task. *Propaganda Fide* was reorganized. Greater emphasis was placed upon building up the local Churches. Educational and charitable works went hand in hand with the preaching of the Gospel. Consequently, the Good News continued to reach more people, especially among the poor and the underprivileged, but also here and there among the social and intellectual elite. New attempts were made to inculturate the Good News, although they proved in no way sufficient. Despite her centuries-long presence and her many apostolic endeavors, the Church in many places was still considered as foreign to Asia, and indeed was often associated in people's minds with the colonial powers.

9f. This was the situation on the eve of the Second Vatican Council; but thanks to the impetus provided by the Council, a new understanding of mission dawned and with it a great hope. The universality of God's plan of salvation, the missionary nature of the Church and the responsibility of everyone in the Church for this task, so strongly reaffirmed in the Council's Decree on the Church's Missionary Activity *Ad Gentes*, became the framework of a new commitment. During the Special Assembly, the Synod Fathers testified to the recent growth of the ecclesial community among many different peoples in various parts of the continent, and they appealed for further missionary efforts in the years to come, especially as new possibilities for the proclamation of the Gospel emerge in the Siberian region and the Central Asian countries which have recently gained their independence, such as Kazakhstan, Uzbekistan, Kyrgyzstan, Tajikistan and Turkmenistan.[25]

9g. A survey of the Catholic communities in Asia shows a splendid variety by reason of their origin and historical development, and the diverse spiritual and liturgical traditions of the various Rites. Yet all are united in proclaiming the Good News of Jesus Christ, through Christian witness, works of charity and human solidarity. While some particular Churches carry out their mission in peace and freedom, others find themselves in situations of violence and conflict, or feel threatened by other groups, for religious or other reasons. In the vastly diversified cultural world of Asia, the Church faces multiple philosophical, theological and pastoral challenges. Her task is made more difficult by the fact of her being a minority, with the only exception the Philippines, where Catholics are in the majority.

9h. Whatever the circumstances, the Church in Asia finds herself among peoples who display an intense yearning for God. The Church knows that this yearning can only be fully satisfied by Jesus Christ, the Good News of God for all the nations. The Synod Fathers were very keen that this Post-Synodal Apostolic Exhortation should focus attention on this yearning and encourage the Church in Asia to proclaim with vigor in word and deed that *Jesus Christ is the Savior.*

9i. The Spirit of God, always at work in the history of the Church in Asia, continues to guide her. The many positive elements found in the local Churches, frequently highlighted in the Synod, strengthen our expectation of a "new springtime of Christian life."[26] One solid cause of hope is the increasing number of better trained, enthusiastic and Spirit-filled lay people, who are more and more aware of their specific vocation within the ecclesial community. Among them the lay catechists deserve special recognition and praise.[27] The apostolic and charismatic movements too are a gift of the Spirit, bringing new life and vigor to the formation of lay men and women, families and the young.[28] Associations and ecclesial movements devoted to the promotion of human dignity and justice make accessible and tangible the universality of the evangelical message of our adoption as children of God (cf. Rom. 8:15-16).

9j. At the same time, there are Churches in very difficult circumstances, "experiencing intense trials in the practice of their faith."[29] The Synod Fathers were moved by reports of the heroic witness, unshaken perseverance and steady growth of the Catholic Church in China, by the efforts of the Church in South Korea to offer assistance to the people of North Korea, the humble steadfastness of the Catholic community in Vietnam, the isolation of Christians in such places as Laos and Myanmar, the difficult co-existence with the majority in some predominantly Islamic states.[30] The Synod paid special attention to the situation of the Church in the Holy Land and in the Holy City of Jerusalem, "the heart of Christianity,"[31] a city dear to all the children of Abraham. The Synod Fathers expressed the belief that the peace of the region, and even the world, depends in large measure on the peace and reconciliation which have eluded Jerusalem for so long.[32]

9k. I cannot bring to an end this brief survey of the situation of the Church in Asia, though far from complete, without mentioning the Saints and Martyrs of Asia, both those who have been recognized and those known only to God, whose example is a source of "spiritual richness and a great means of evangelization."[33] They speak silently but most powerfully of the importance of holiness of life and readiness to offer one's life for the Gospel. They are the teachers and the protectors, the glory of the Church in Asia in her work of evangelization. With the whole Church I pray to the Lord to send many more committed laborers to reap the harvest of souls which I see as ready and plentiful (cf. Mt. 9:37-38). At this moment, I call to mind what I wrote in *Redemptoris Missio*: "God is opening before the Church the horizons of a humanity more fully prepared for the sowing of the Gospel."[34] This vision of a new and promising horizon I see being fulfilled in Asia, where Jesus was born and where Christianity began.

CHAPTER TWO: JESUS THE SAVIOR: A GIFT TO ASIA

10. The Gift of Faith

10a. As the Synod discussion of the complex realities of Asia unfolded, it became increasingly obvious to all that the Church's unique contribution to the peoples of the continent is the proclamation of Jesus Christ, true God and true man, the one and only Savior for all peoples.[35] What distinguishes the Church from other religious communities is her faith in Jesus Christ; and she cannot keep this precious light of faith under a bushel (cf. Mt. 5:15), for her mission is to share that light with everyone. "[The Church] wants to offer the new life she has found in Jesus Christ to all the peoples of Asia as they search for the fullness of life, so that they can have the same fellowship with the Father and his Son Jesus Christ in the power of the Spirit."[36] This faith in Jesus Christ is what inspires the Church's evangelizing work in Asia, often carried out in difficult and even dangerous circumstances. The Synod Fathers noted that proclaiming Jesus as the only Savior can present particular difficulties in their cultures, given that many Asian religions teach divine self-manifestations as mediating salvation. Far from discouraging the Synod Fathers, the challenges facing their evangelizing efforts were an even greater incentive in striving to transmit "the faith that the Church in Asia has inherited from the Apostles and holds with the Church of all generations and places."[37] Indeed they expressed the conviction that "the heart of the Church in Asia will be restless until the whole of Asia finds its rest in the peace of Christ, the Risen Lord."[38]

10b. The Church's faith in Jesus is a gift received and a gift to be shared; it is the greatest gift which the Church can offer to Asia. Sharing the truth of Jesus Christ with others is the solemn duty of all who have received the gift of faith. In my Encyclical Letter *Redemptoris Missio*, I wrote that "the Church, and every individual Christian within her, may not keep hidden or monopolize this newness and richness which has been received from God's bounty in order to be communicated to all mankind."[39] In the same Letter I wrote: "Those who are incorporated in the Catholic Church ought to sense their privilege and for that very reason their greater obligation of *bearing witness to the faith and to the Christian life* as a service to their brothers and sisters and as a fitting response to God."[40]

10c. Deeply convinced of this, the Synod Fathers were equally conscious of their personal responsibility to grasp through study, prayer and reflection the timeless truth of Jesus in order to bring its power and vitality to bear on the present and future challenges of evangelization in Asia.

11. Jesus Christ, the God-Man Who Saves

11a. The Scriptures attest that Jesus lived an authentically human life. The Jesus whom we proclaim as the only Savior walked the earth as the God-Man in full possession of a human nature. He was like us in all things except sin. Born of a Virgin Mother in humble surroundings at Bethlehem, he was as helpless as any other infant, and even suffered the fate of a refugee fleeing the wrath of a ruthless leader (cf. Mt. 2:13-15). He was subject to human parents who did not always understand his ways, but in whom he trusted and whom he lovingly obeyed (cf. Lk. 2:41-52). Constantly at prayer, he was in intimate relationship with God whom he addressed as *Abba*, "Father," to the dismay of his listeners (cf. Jn. 8:34-59).

11b. He was close to the poor, the forgotten and the lowly, declaring that they were truly blessed, for God was with them. He ate with sinners, assuring them that at the Father's table there was a place for them when they turned from their sinful ways and came back to him. Touching the unclean and allowing them to touch him, he let them know the nearness of God. He wept for a dead friend, he restored a dead son to his widowed mother, he welcomed children, and he washed the feet of his disciples. Divine compassion had never been so immediately accessible.

11c. The sick, the lame, the blind, the deaf and the dumb all experienced healing and forgiveness at his touch. As his closest companions and co-workers he chose an unusual group in which fishermen mixed with tax collectors, Zealots with people untrained in the Law, and women also. A new family was being created under the Father's all-embracing and surprising love. Jesus preached simply, using examples from everyday life to speak of God's love and his Kingdom; and the people recognized that he spoke with authority.

11d. Yet he was accused of being a blasphemer, a violator of the sacred Law, a public nuisance to be eliminated. After a trial based on false testimony (cf. Mk. 14:56), he was sentenced to die as a criminal on the Cross and, forsaken and humiliated, he seemed a failure. He was hastily buried in a borrowed tomb. But on the third day after this death, and despite the vigilance of the guards, the tomb was found empty! Jesus, risen from the dead, then appeared to his disciples before returning to the Father from whom he had come.

11e. With all Christians, we believe that this particular life, in one sense so ordinary and simple, in another sense so utterly wondrous and shrouded in mystery, ushered into human history the Kingdom of God and "brought its power to bear upon every facet of human life and society beset by sin and death."[41] Through his words and actions, especially in his suffering, death and resurrection, Jesus fulfilled the will of his Father to reconcile all humanity to himself, after original sin had created a rupture in the relationship between the Creator and his creation. On the Cross, he took upon himself the sins of the world—past, present and future. Saint Paul reminds us that we were dead as a result of our sins and his death has brought us to life again: "God made [us] alive together with him, having forgiven us all our trespasses, having cancelled the bond which stood against us with its legal demands; this he set aside, nailing it to the cross" (Col. 2:13-14). In this way, salvation was sealed once and for all. Jesus is our Savior in the fullest sense of the word because his words and works, especially his resurrection from the dead, have revealed him to be the Son of God, the pre-existent Word, who reigns for ever as Lord and Messiah.

12. The Person and Mission of the Son of God

12a. The "scandal" of Christianity is the belief that the all-holy, all-powerful and all-knowing God took upon himself our human nature and endured suffering and death to win salvation for all people (cf. 1 Cor. 1:23). The faith we have received declares that Jesus Christ revealed and accomplished the Father's plan of saving the world and the whole of humanity because of "*who he is*" and "*what he does because of who he is.*" "*Who he is*" and "*what he does*" acquire their full meaning only when set within the mystery of the Triune God. It has been a constant concern of my Pontificate to remind the faithful of the communion of life of the Blessed Trinity and the unity of the three Persons in the plan of creation and redemption. My Encyclical Letters *Redemptor Hominis, Dives in Misericordia* and *Dominum et Vivificantem* are reflections on the Son, the Father and the Holy Spirit respectively and on their roles in the divine plan of salvation. We cannot however isolate or separate one Person from the others, since each is revealed only within the communion of life and action of the Trinity. The saving action of Jesus has its origin in the communion of the Godhead, and opens the way for all who believe in him to enter into intimate communion with the Trinity and with one another in the Trinity.

12b. "He who has seen me has seen the Father," Jesus claims (Jn. 14:9). In Jesus Christ alone dwells the fullness of God in bodily form (cf. Col. 2:9), establishing him as the unique and absolute saving Word of God (cf. Heb. 1:1-4). As the Father's definitive Word, Jesus makes God and his saving will known in the fullest way possible. "No one comes to the Father but by me," Jesus says (Jn. 14:6). He is "the Way, and the Truth, and the Life" (Jn. 14:6), because, as he himself says, "the Father who dwells in me does his works" (Jn. 14:10). Only in the person of Jesus does God's word of salvation appear in all its fullness, ushering in the final age (cf. Heb. 1:1-2). Thus, in the first days of the Church, Peter could proclaim: "There is salvation in no one else, for there is no other name under heaven given among men by which we must be saved" (Acts 4:12).

12c. The mission of the Savior reached its culmination in the Paschal Mystery. On the Cross, when "he stretched out his arms between heaven and earth in the everlasting sign of [the Father's] covenant,"[42] Jesus uttered his final appeal to the Father to forgive the sins of humanity: "Father, forgive them; for they know not what they do" (Lk. 23:34). Jesus destroyed sin by the power of his love for his Father and for all mankind. He took upon himself the wounds inflicted on humanity by sin, and he offered release through conversion. The first fruits of this are evident in the repentant thief hanging beside him on another cross (cf. Lk. 23:43). His last utterance was the cry of the faithful Son: "Father, into your hands I commit my spirit" (Lk. 23:46). In this supreme expression of love he entrusted his whole life and mission into the hands of the Father who had sent him. Thus he handed over to the Father the whole of creation and all humanity, to be accepted finally by him in compassionate love.

12d. Everything that the Son is and has accomplished is accepted by the Father, who then offers this gift to the world in the act of raising Jesus from the dead and setting him at his right hand, where sin and death have power no more. Through Jesus' Paschal Sacrifice *the Father irrevocably offers reconciliation and fullness of life to the world*. This extraordinary gift could only come through the beloved Son, who alone was capable of fully responding to the Father's love, rejected by sin. In Jesus Christ, through the power of the Holy Spirit, we come to know that God is not distant, above and apart from man, but is very near, indeed united to every person and all humanity in all of life's situations. This is the message which Christianity offers to the world, and it is a source of incomparable comfort and hope for all believers.

13. Jesus Christ: the Truth of Humanity

13a. How does the humanity of Jesus and the ineffable mystery of the

Incarnation of the Son of the Father shed light on the human condition? The Incarnate Son of God not only revealed completely the Father and his plan of salvation; he also "fully reveals man to himself."[43] His words and actions, and above all his Death and Resurrection, reveal the depths of what it means to be human. Through Jesus, man can finally know the truth of himself. Jesus' perfectly human life, devoted wholly to the love and service of the Father and of man, reveals that the vocation of every human being is to receive love and give love in return. In Jesus we marvel at the inexhaustible capacity of the human heart to love God and man, even when this entails great suffering. Above all, it is on the Cross that Jesus breaks the power of the self-destructive resistance to love which sin inflicts upon us. On his part, the Father responds by raising Jesus as the first-born of all those predestined to be conformed to the image of his Son (cf. Rom. 8:29). At that moment, Jesus became once and for all both the revelation and the accomplishment of a humanity re-created and renewed according to the plan of God. In Jesus then, we discover the greatness and dignity of each person in the heart of God who created man in his own image (cf. Gen. 1:26), and we find the origin of the new creation which we have become through his grace.

13b. The Second Vatican Council taught that "by his Incarnation, he, the Son of God, in a certain way united himself with each individual."[44] In this profound insight the Synod Fathers saw the ultimate source of hope and strength for the people of Asia in their struggles and uncertainties. When men and women respond with a living faith to God's offer of love, his presence brings love and peace, transforming the human heart from within. In *Redemptor Hominis* I wrote that "the redemption of the world—this tremendous mystery of love in which creation is renewed—is, at its deepest root, the fullness of justice in a human Heart—the Heart of the First-born Son—in order that it may become justice in the hearts of many human beings, predestined from eternity in the First-born Son to be children of God and called to grace, called to love."[45]

13c. Thus, the mission of Jesus not only restored communion between God and humanity; it also established a new communion between human beings alienated from one another because of sin. Beyond all divisions, Jesus makes it possible for people to live as brothers and sisters, recognizing a single Father who is in heaven (cf. Mt. 23:9). In him, a new harmony has emerged, in which "there is neither Jew nor Greek, ...neither slave nor free, ...neither male nor female, for you are all one in Christ Jesus" (Gal. 3:28). Jesus is our peace, "who has made us both one, and has broken down the dividing wall of hostility" (Eph. 2:14). In all that he said and did, Jesus was the Father's voice, hands and arms, gathering all God's children into one family of love. He prayed that his disciples might live in communion just as he is in communion with the Father (cf. Jn. 17:11). Among his last words we hear him say: "As the Father has loved me, so have I loved you; abide in my love.... This is my commandment, that you love one another as I have loved you" (Jn. 15:9, 12). Sent by the God of communion and being truly God and truly man, Jesus established communion between heaven and earth in his very person. It is our faith that "in him all the fullness of God was pleased to dwell, and through him to reconcile to himself all things, whether on earth or in heaven, making peace by the blood of his Cross" (Col. 1:19-20). Salvation can be found in the person of the Son of God made man and the mission entrusted to him alone as the Son, a mission of service and love for the life of all. Together with the Church throughout the world, the Church in Asia proclaims the truth of faith: "There is one God, and there is one mediator between God and men, the man Christ Jesus who gave himself as a ransom for all" (1 Tim. 2:5-6).

14. The Uniqueness and Universality of Salvation in Jesus

14a. The Synod Fathers recalled that the pre-existent Word, the eternally begotten Son of God, "was already present in creation, in history and in every human yearning for good."[46] Through the Word, present to the cosmos even before the Incarnation, the world came to be (cf. Jn. 1:1-4, 10; Col. 1:15-20). But as the incarnate Word who lived, died and rose from the dead, Jesus Christ is now proclaimed as the fulfillment of all creation, of all history, and of all human yearning for fullness of life.[47] Risen from the dead, Jesus Christ "is present to all and to the whole of creation in a new and mysterious way."[48] In him, "authentic values of all religious and cultural traditions, such as mercy and submission to the will of God, compassion and rectitude, non-violence and righteousness, filial piety and harmony with creation find their fullness and realization."[49] From the first moment of time to its end, Jesus is the one universal Mediator. Even for those who do not explicitly profess faith in him as the Savior, salvation comes as a grace from Jesus Christ through the communication of the Holy Spirit.

14b. We believe that Jesus Christ, true God and true man, is the one Savior because he alone—the Son—accomplished the Father's universal plan of salvation. As the definitive manifestation of the mystery of the Father's love for all, Jesus is indeed unique, and "it is precisely this uniqueness of Christ which gives him an absolute and universal significance, whereby, while belonging to history, he remains history's center and goal."[50]

14c. No individual, no nation, no culture is impervious to the appeal of Jesus who speaks from the very heart of the human condition. "It is his life that speaks, his humanity, his fidelity to the truth, his all-embracing love. Furthermore, his death on the Cross speaks—that is to say the inscrutable depth of his suffering and abandonment."[51] Contemplating Jesus in his human nature, the peoples of Asia find their deepest questions answered, their hopes fulfilled, their dignity uplifted and their despair conquered. Jesus is the Good News for the men and women of every time and place in their search for the meaning of existence and for the truth of their own humanity.

CHAPTER THREE: THE HOLY SPIRIT:
LORD AND GIVER OF LIFE

15. The Spirit of God in Creation and History

15a. If it is true that the saving significance of Jesus can be understood only in the context of his revelation of the Trinity's plan of salvation, then it follows that the Holy Spirit is an absolutely vital part of the mystery of Jesus and of the salvation which he brings. The Synod Fathers made frequent references to the role of the Holy Spirit in the history of salvation, noting that a false separation between the Redeemer and the Holy Spirit would jeopardize the truth of Jesus as the one Savior of all.

15b. In Christian Tradition, the Holy Spirit has always been associated with life and the giving of life. The Nicene-Constantinopolitan Creed calls the Holy Spirit "the Lord, the Giver of Life." It is not surprising, therefore, that many interpretations of the creation account in Genesis have seen the Holy Spirit in the mighty wind that swept over the waters (cf. Gen. 1:2). The Holy Spirit is present from the first moment of creation, the first manifestation of the love of the Triune God, and is always present in the world as its life-giving force.[52] Since creation is the beginning of history, the Spirit is in a certain sense a hidden power at work in history, guiding it in the ways of truth and goodness.

15c. The revelation of the person of the Holy Spirit, the mutual love of the Father and the Son, is proper to the New Testament. In Christian thought he is seen as the wellspring of life for all creatures. Creation is God's free communication of love, a communication which, out of nothing, brings everything into being. There is nothing created that is not filled with the ceaseless exchange of love that marks the innermost life of the Trinity, filled that is with the Holy Spirit: "the Spirit of the Lord has filled the world" (Wis. 1:7). The presence of the Spirit in creation generates order, harmony and interdependence in all that exists.

15d. Created in the image of God, human beings become the dwelling-place of the Spirit in a new way when they are raised to the dignity of divine adoption (cf. Gal. 4:5). Reborn in Baptism, they experience the presence and power of the Spirit, not just as the Author of Life but as the One who purifies and saves, producing fruits of "love, joy, peace, patience, kindness, goodness, faithfulness, gentleness, self-control" (Gal. 5:22-23). These fruits of the Spirit are the sign that "God's love has been poured into our hearts through the Holy Spirit who has been given to us" (Rom. 5:5). When accepted in freedom, this love makes men and women visible instruments of the unseen Spirit's ceaseless activity. It is above all this new capacity to give and receive love which testifies to the interior presence and power of the Holy Spirit. As a consequence of the transformation and re-creation which he produces in people's hearts and minds, the Spirit influences human societies and cultures.[53] "Indeed, the Spirit is at the origin of the noble ideals and undertakings which benefit humanity on its journey through history. 'The Spirit of God with marvelous foresight directs the course of the ages and renews the face of the earth'."[54]

15e. Following the lead of the Second Vatican Council, the Synod Fathers drew attention to the multiple and diversified action of the Holy Spirit who continually sows the seeds of truth among all peoples, their religions, cultures and philosophies.[55] This means that these religions, cultures and philosophies are capable of helping people, individually and collectively, to work against evil and to serve life and everything that is good. The forces of death isolate people, societies and religious communities from one another, and generate the suspicion and rivalry that lead to conflict. The Holy Spirit, by contrast, sustains people in their search for mutual understanding and acceptance. The Synod was therefore right to see the Spirit of God as the prime agent of the Church's dialogue with all peoples, cultures and religions.

16. The Holy Spirit and the Incarnation of the Word

16a. Under the Spirit's guidance, the history of salvation unfolds on the stage of the world, indeed of the cosmos, according to the Father's eternal plan. That plan, initiated by the Spirit at the very beginning of creation, is revealed in the Old Testament, is brought to fulfillment through the grace of Jesus Christ, and is carried on in the new creation by the same Spirit until the Lord comes again in glory at the end of time.[56] The Incarnation of the Son of God is the supreme work of the Holy Spirit: "The conception and birth of Jesus Christ are in fact the greatest work accomplished by the Holy Spirit in the history of creation and salvation: the supreme grace—'the grace of union,' source of every other grace."[57] The Incarnation is the event in which God gathers into a new and definitive union with himself not only man but the whole of creation and all of history.[58]

16b. Having been conceived in the womb of the Virgin Mary by the Spirit's power (cf. Lk. 1:35; Mt. 1:20), Jesus of Nazareth, the Messiah and only Savior, was filled with the Holy Spirit. The Spirit descended upon him at his baptism (cf. Mk. 1:10) and led him into the wilderness to be strengthened before his public ministry (cf. Mk. 1:12; Lk. 4:1; Mt. 4:1). In the synagogue at Nazareth he began his prophetic ministry by applying to himself Isaiah's vision of the Spirit's anointing which leads to the preaching of good news to the poor, freedom to captives and a time acceptable to the Lord (cf. Lk. 4:18-19). By the power of the Spirit, Jesus healed the sick and cast out demons as a sign that the Kingdom of God had come (cf. Mt. 12:28). After rising from the dead, he imparted to the disciples the Holy Spirit whom he had promised to pour out on the Church when he returned to the Father (cf. Jn. 20:22-23).

16c. All of this shows how Jesus' saving mission bears the unmistakable mark of the Spirit's presence: life, *new life*. Between the *sending of the Son* from the Father and the *sending of the Spirit* from the Father and the Son, there is a close and vital link.[59] The action of the Spirit in creation and human history acquires an altogether new significance in his action in the life and mission of Jesus. The "seeds of the Word" sown by the Spirit prepare the whole of creation, history and man for full maturity in Christ.[60]

16d. The Synod Fathers expressed concern about the tendency to separate the activity of the Holy Spirit from that of Jesus the Savior. Responding to their concern, I repeat here what I wrote in *Redemptoris Missio*: "[The Spirit] is ... not an alternative to Christ, nor does he fill a sort of void which is sometimes suggested as existing between Christ and the Logos. Whatever the Spirit brings about in human hearts and in the history of peoples, in cultures and religions serves as a preparation for the Gospel and can only be understood in reference to Christ, the Word who took flesh by the power of the Spirit 'so that as perfectly human he would save all human beings and sum up all things'."[61]

16e. The universal presence of the Holy Spirit therefore cannot serve as an excuse for a failure to proclaim Jesus Christ explicitly as the one and only Savior. On the contrary, the universal presence of the Holy Spirit is inseparable from universal salvation in Jesus. The presence of the Spirit in creation and history points to Jesus Christ in whom creation and history are redeemed and fulfilled. The presence and action of the Spirit both before the Incarnation and in the climactic moment of Pentecost point always to Jesus and to the salvation he brings. So too the Holy Spirit's universal presence can never be separated from his activity within the Body of Christ, the Church.[62]

17. The Holy Spirit and the Body of Christ

17a. The Holy Spirit preserves unfailingly the bond of communion between Jesus and his Church. Dwelling in her as in a temple (cf. 1 Cor. 3:16), the Spirit guides the Church, first of all, to the fullness of truth about Jesus. Then, it is the Spirit who empowers the Church to continue Jesus' mission, in the first place by witnessing to Jesus himself, thus fulfilling what he had promised before his death and resurrection, that he would send the Spirit to his disciples *so that they might bear witness to him* (cf. Jn. 15:26-27). The work of the Spirit in the Church is also to testify that believers are the adopted children of God destined to inherit salvation, the promised fullness of communion with the Father (cf. Rom. 8:15-17). Endowing the Church with different charisms and gifts, the Spirit makes the Church grow in communion as one body made up of many different parts (cf. 1 Cor. 12:4; .Eph. 4:11-16). The Spirit gathers into unity all kinds of people, with their different customs, resources and talents, making the Church a sign of the communion of all humanity under the headship of Christ.[63] The Spirit shapes the Church as a community of witnesses who, through his power, bear testimony to Jesus the Savior (cf. Acts 1:8). In this sense, the Holy Spirit is the prime agent of evangelization. From this the Synod Fathers could conclude that, just as the earthly ministry of Jesus was accomplished in the power of the Holy Spirit, "the same Spirit has been given to the Church by the Father and the Son at Pentecost to bring to completion Jesus' mission of love and service in Asia."[64]

17b. The Father's plan for the salvation of man does not end with the death and resurrection of Jesus. By the gift of Christ's Spirit, the fruits of his saving mission are offered through the Church to all peoples of all times through the proclamation of the Gospel and loving service of the human family. As the Second Vatican Council observed, "the Church is driven by the Holy Spirit to do her part for the full realization of the plan of God, who has constituted Christ as the source of salvation for the whole world."[65] Empowered by the Spirit to accomplish Christ's salvation on earth, the Church is the seed of the Kingdom of God and she looks eagerly for its final coming. Her identity and mission are inseparable from the Kingdom of God which Jesus announced and inaugurated in all that he said and did, above all in his death and resurrection. The Spirit reminds the Church that she is not an end unto herself: in all that she is and all that she does, she exists to serve Christ and the salvation of the world. In the present economy of salvation the workings of the Holy Spirit in creation, in history and in the Church are all part of the one eternal design of the Trinity over all that is.

18. The Holy Spirit and the Church's Mission in Asia

18a. The Spirit who moved upon Asia in the time of the patriarchs and prophets, and still more powerfully in the time of Jesus Christ and the early Church, moves now among Asian Christians, strengthening the witness of their faith among the peoples, cultures and religions of the continent. Just as the great dialogue of love between God and man was prepared for by the Spirit and accomplished on Asian soil in the mystery of Christ, so the dialogue between the Savior and the peoples of the continent continues today by the power of the same Holy Spirit at work in the Church. In this process, Bishops, priests, religious and lay men and women all have an essential role to play, remembering the words of Jesus, which are both a promise and a mandate: "You shall receive power when the Holy Spirit has come upon you; and you shall be my witnesses in Jerusalem and in all Judea and Samaria and to the end of the earth" (Acts 1:8).

18b. The Church is convinced that deep within the people, cultures and religions of Asia there is a thirst for "living water" (cf. Jn. 4:10-15), a thirst which the Spirit himself has created and which Jesus the Savior alone can fully satisfy. The Church looks to the Holy Spirit to continue to prepare the peoples of Asia for the saving dialogue with the Savior of all. Led by the Spirit in her mission of service and love, the Church can offer an encounter between Jesus Christ and the peoples of Asia as they search for the fullness of life. In that encounter alone is to be found the living water which springs up to eternal life, namely, the knowledge of the one true God and Jesus Christ whom he has sent (cf. Jn 17:3).

18c. The Church well knows that she can accomplish her mission only in obedience to the promptings of the Holy Spirit. Committed to being a genuine sign and instrument of the Spirit's action in the complex realities of Asia, she must discern, in all the diverse circumstances of the continent, the Spirit's call to witness to Jesus the Savior in new and effective ways. The full truth of Jesus and the salvation he has won is always a gift, never the result of human effort. "It is the Spirit himself bearing witness with our spirit that we are children of God, and if children, then heirs, heirs of God and fellow heirs with Christ" (Rom. 8:16-17). Therefore the Church ceaselessly cries out, "Come, Holy Spirit! Fill the hearts of your faithful and enkindle in them the fire of your love!" This is the fire which Jesus casts upon the earth. The Church in Asia shares his zeal that this fire be re-kindled now (cf. Lk. 12:49). With this ardent desire, the Synod Fathers sought to discern the principal areas of mission for the Church in Asia as she crosses the threshold of the new millennium.

CHAPTER FOUR: JESUS THE SAVIOR: PROCLAIMING THE GIFT

19. The Primacy of Proclamation

19a. On the eve of the Third Millennium, the voice of the Risen Christ echoes anew in the heart of every Christian: "All authority in heaven and on earth has been given to me. Go, therefore, and make disciples of all nations, baptizing them in the name of the Father and of the Son and of the Holy Spirit, teaching them to observe all that I have commanded you; and lo, I am with you always, to the close of the age" (Mt. 28:18-20). Certain of the unfailing help of Jesus himself and the presence and power of his Spirit, the Apostles set out immediately after Pentecost to fulfil this command: "they went forth and preached everywhere, while the Lord worked with them" (Mk. 16:20). What they announced can be summed up in the words of Saint Paul: "For what we preach is not ourselves, but Jesus Christ as Lord, with ourselves as your servants for Jesus' sake" (2 Cor. 4:5). Blessed with the gift of faith, the Church, after two thousand years, continues to go out to meet the peoples of the world in order to share with them the Good News of Jesus Christ. She is a community aflame with missionary zeal to make Jesus known, loved and followed.

19b. There can be no true evangelization without the explicit proclamation of Jesus as Lord. The Second Vatican Council and the Magisterium since then, responding to a certain confusion about the true nature of the Church's mission, have repeatedly stressed the primacy of the proclamation of Jesus Christ in all evangelizing work. Thus Pope Paul VI explicitly wrote that "there is no true evangelization if the name, the teaching, the life, the promises, the Kingdom and the mystery of Jesus of Nazareth, the Son of God, are not proclaimed."[66] This is what generations of Christians have done down the centuries. With understandable pride the Synod Fathers recalled that "many Christian communities in Asia have preserved their faith down the centuries against great odds and have clung to this spiritual heritage with heroic perseverance. For them to share this immense treasure is a matter of great joy and urgency."[67]

19c. At the same time the participants in the Special Assembly testified over and over again to the need for a renewed commitment to the proclamation of Jesus Christ precisely on the continent which saw the beginning of that proclamation two thousand years ago. The words of the Apostle Paul become still more pointed, given the many people on that continent who have never encountered the person of Jesus in any clear and conscious way: "Everyone who calls upon the name of the Lord will be saved. But how are they to call upon him in whom they have not believed? And how are they to believe in him of whom they have never heard? And how are they to hear without a preacher?" (Rom. 10:13-14). The great question now facing the Church in Asia is *how* to share with our Asian brothers and sisters what we treasure as the gift containing all gifts, namely, the Good News of Jesus Christ.

20. Proclaiming Jesus Christ in Asia

20a. The Church in Asia is all the more eager for the task of proclamation knowing that "through the working of the Spirit, there already exists in individuals and peoples an expectation, even if an unconscious one, of knowing the truth about God, about man, and about how we are to be set free from sin and death."[68] This insistence on proclamation is prompted not by sectarian impulse nor the spirit of proselytism nor any sense of superiority. The Church evangelizes in obedience to Christ's command, in the knowledge that every person has the right to hear the Good News of the God who reveals and gives himself in Christ.[69] To bear witness to Jesus Christ is the supreme service which the Church can offer to the peoples of Asia, for it responds to their profound longing for the Absolute, and it unveils the truths and values which will ensure their integral human development.

20b. Deeply aware of the complexity of so many different situations in Asia, and "speaking the truth in love" (Eph. 4:15), the Church proclaims the Good

News with loving respect and esteem for her listeners. Proclamation which respects the rights of consciences does not violate freedom, since faith always demands a free response on the part of the individual.[70] Respect, however, does not eliminate the need for the explicit proclamation of the Gospel in its fullness. Especially in the context of the rich array of cultures and religions in Asia it must be pointed out that "neither respect and esteem for these religions nor the complexity of the questions raised are an invitation to the Church to withhold from these non-Christians the proclamation of Jesus Christ."[71] While visiting India in 1986, I stated clearly that "the Church's approach to other religions is one of genuine respect.... This respect is twofold: respect for man in his quest for answers to the deepest questions of his life, and respect for the action of the Spirit in man."[72] Indeed, the Synod Fathers readily recognized the Spirit's action in Asian societies, cultures and religions, through which the Father prepares the hearts of Asian peoples for the fullness of life in Christ.[73]

20c. Yet even during the consultations before the Synod many Asian Bishops referred to *difficulties in proclaiming Jesus as the only Savior*. During the Assembly, the situation was described in this way: "Some of the followers of the great religions of Asia have no problem in accepting Jesus as a manifestation of the Divine or the Absolute, or as an 'enlightened one.' But it is difficult for them to see Him as the only manifestation of the Divine."[74] In fact, the effort to share the gift of faith in Jesus as the only Savior is fraught with philosophical, cultural and theological difficulties, especially in light of the beliefs of Asia's great religions, deeply intertwined with cultural values and specific world views.

20d. In the opinion of the Synod Fathers, the difficulty is compounded by the fact that Jesus is often perceived as foreign to Asia. It is paradoxical that most Asians tend to regard Jesus—born on Asian soil—as a Western rather than an Asian figure. It was inevitable that the proclamation of the Gospel by Western missionaries would be influenced by the cultures from which they came. The Synod Fathers recognized this as an unavoidable fact in the history of evangelization. At the same time they took advantage of the occasion "to express in a very special way their gratitude to all the missionaries, men and women, religious and lay, foreign and local, who brought the message of Jesus Christ and the gift of faith. A special word of gratitude again must be expressed to all the particular Churches which have sent and still send missionaries to Asia."[75]

20e. Evangelizers can take heart from the experience of Saint Paul who engaged in dialogue with the philosophical, cultural and religious values of his listeners (cf. Acts 14:13-17; 17:22-31). Even the Ecumenical Councils of the Church which formulated doctrines binding on the Church had to use the linguistic, philosophical and cultural resources available to them. Thus these resources become a shared possession of the whole Church, capable of expressing her Christological doctrine in an appropriate and universal way. They are part of the heritage of faith which must be appropriated and shared again and again in the encounter with the various cultures.[76] Thus the task of proclaiming Jesus in a way which enables the peoples of Asia to identify with him, while remaining faithful both to the Church's theological doctrine and to their own Asian origins is a paramount challenge.

20f. The presentation of Jesus Christ as the only Savior needs to follow a *pedagogy* which will introduce people step by step to the full appropriation of the mystery. Clearly, the initial evangelization of non-Christians and the continuing proclamation of Jesus to believers will have to be different in their approach. In initial proclamation, for example, "the presentation of Jesus Christ could come as the fulfillment of the yearnings expressed in the mythologies and folklore of the Asian peoples."[77] In general, narrative methods akin to Asian cultural forms are to be preferred. In fact, the proclamation of Jesus Christ can most effectively be made by narrating his story, as the Gospels do. The ontological notions involved, which must always be presupposed and expressed in presenting Jesus, can be complemented by more relational, historical and even cosmic perspectives. The Church, the Synod Fathers noted, must be open to the new and surprising ways in which the face of Jesus might be presented in Asia.[78]

20g. The Synod recommended that subsequent catechesis should follow "an evocative pedagogy, using stories, parables and symbols so characteristic of Asian methodology in teaching."[79] The ministry of Jesus himself shows clearly the value of *personal contact*, which requires the evangelizer to take the situation of the listener to heart, so as to offer a proclamation adapted to the listener's level of maturity, and in an appropriate form and language. In this perspective, the Synod Fathers stressed many times the need to evangelize in a way that appeals to the sensibilities of Asian peoples, and they suggested images of Jesus which would be intelligible to Asian minds and cultures and, at the same time, faithful to Sacred Scripture and Tradition. Among them were "Jesus Christ as the Teacher of Wisdom, the Healer, the Liberator, the Spiritual Guide, the Enlightened One, the Compassionate Friend of the Poor, the Good Samaritan, the Good Shepherd, the Obedient One."[80] Jesus could be presented as the Incarnate Wisdom of God whose grace brings to fruition the "seeds" of divine Wisdom already present in the lives, religions and peoples of Asia.[81] In the midst of so much suffering among Asian peoples, he might best be proclaimed as the Savior "who can provide meaning to those undergoing unexplainable pain and suffering."[82]

20h. The faith which the Church offers as a gift to her Asian sons and daughters cannot be confined within the limits of understanding and expression of any single human culture, for it transcends these limits and indeed challenges all cultures to rise to new heights of understanding and expression. Yet at the same time the Synod Fathers were well aware of the pressing need of the local Churches in Asia to present the mystery of Christ to their peoples according to their cultural patterns and ways of thinking. They pointed out that such an inculturation of the faith on their continent involves rediscovering the Asian countenance of Jesus and identifying ways in which the cultures of Asia can grasp the universal saving significance of the mystery of Jesus and his Church.[83] The penetrating insight into peoples and their cultures, exemplified in such men as Giovanni da Montecorvino, Matteo Ricci and Roberto de Nobili, to mention only a few, needs to be emulated at the present time.

21. The Challenge of Inculturation

21a. Culture is the vital space within which the human person comes face to face with the Gospel. Just as a culture is the result of the life and activity of a human group, so the persons belonging to that group are shaped to a large extent by the culture in which they live. As persons and societies change, so too does the culture change with them. As a culture is transformed, so too are persons and societies transformed by it. From this perspective, it becomes clearer why evangelization and inculturation are naturally and intimately related to each other. The Gospel and evangelization are certainly not identical with culture; they are independent of it. Yet the Kingdom of God comes to people who are profoundly linked to a culture, and the building of the Kingdom cannot avoid borrowing elements from human cultures. Thus Paul VI called the split between the Gospel and culture the drama of our time, with a profound impact upon both evangelization and culture.[84]

21b. In the process of encountering the world's different cultures, the Church not only transmits her truths and values and renews cultures from within, but she also takes from the various cultures the positive elements already found in them. This is the obligatory path for evangelizers in presenting the Christian faith and making it part of a people's cultural heritage. Conversely, the various cultures, when refined and renewed in the light of the Gospel, can become true expressions of the one Christian faith. "Through inculturation the Church, for her part, becomes a more intelligible sign of what she is, and a more effective instrument of mission."[85] This engagement with cultures has always been part of the Church's pilgrimage through history. But it has a special urgency today in the multi-ethnic, multi-religious and multi-cultural situation of Asia, where Christianity is still too often seen as foreign.

21c. It is good to remember at this point what was said repeatedly during the Synod: that the Holy Spirit is the prime agent of the inculturation of the Christian faith in Asia.[86] The same Holy Spirit who leads us into the whole truth makes possible a fruitful dialogue with the cultural and religious values of different peoples, among whom he is present in some measure, giving men and women with a sincere heart the strength to overcome evil and the deceit of the Evil One, and indeed offering everyone the possibility of sharing in the Paschal Mystery in a manner known to God.[87] The Spirit's presence ensures that the dialogue unfolds in truth, honesty, humility and respect.[88] "In offering to others the Good News of the Redemption, the Church strives to understand their culture. She seeks to know the minds and hearts of her hearers, their values and customs, their problems and difficulties, their hopes and dreams. Once she knows and understands these various aspects of culture, then she can begin the dialogue of salvation; she can offer, respectfully but with clarity and conviction, the Good News of the Redemption to all who freely wish to listen and to respond."[89] Therefore the people of Asia who, as Asians, wish to make the Christian faith their own, can rest assured that their hopes, expectations, anxieties and sufferings are not only embraced by Jesus, but become the very point at which the gift of faith and the power of the Spirit enter the innermost core of their lives.

21d. It is the task of the Pastors, in virtue of their charism, to guide this dialogue with discernment. Likewise, experts in sacred and secular disciplines have important roles to play in the process of inculturation. *But the process must involve the entire People of God*, since the life of the Church as a whole must show forth the faith which is being proclaimed and appropriated. To ensure that this is done soundly, the Synod Fathers identified certain areas for particular attention—theological reflection, liturgy, the formation of priests and religious, catechesis and spirituality.[90]

22. Key Areas of Inculturation

22a. The Synod expressed encouragement to *theologians* in their delicate work of developing an inculturated theology, especially in the area of Christology.[91] They noted that "this theologizing is to be carried out with courage, in faithfulness to the Scriptures and to the Church's Tradition, in sincere adherence to the Magisterium and with an awareness of pastoral realities."[92] I too urge theologians to work in a spirit of union with the Pastors and the people, who—in union with one another and never separated from one another—"reflect the authentic *sensus fidei* which must never be lost sight of."[93] Theological work must always be guided by respect for the sensibilities of Christians, so that by a gradual growth into inculturated forms of expressing the faith people are neither confused nor scandalized. In every case inculturation must be guided by compatibility with the Gospel and communion with the faith of the universal Church, in full compliance with the Church's Tradition and with a view to strengthening people's faith.[94] The test of true inculturation is whether people become more committed to their Christian faith because they perceive it more clearly with the eyes of their own culture.

22b. The *Liturgy* is the source and summit of all Christian life and mission.[95]

It is a decisive means of evangelization, especially in Asia, where the followers of different religions are so drawn to worship, religious festivals and popular devotions.[96] The liturgy of the Oriental Churches has for the most part been successfully inculturated through centuries of interaction with the surrounding culture, but the more recently established Churches need to ensure that the liturgy becomes an ever greater source of nourishment for their peoples through a wise and effective use of elements drawn from the local cultures. Yet liturgical inculturation requires more than a focus upon traditional cultural values, symbols and rituals. There is also a need to take account of the shifts in consciousness and attitudes caused by the emerging secularist and consumer cultures which are affecting the Asian sense of worship and prayer. Nor can the specific needs of the poor, migrants, refugees, youth and women be overlooked in any genuine liturgical inculturation in Asia.

22c. The national and regional Bishops' Conferences need to work more closely with the Congregation for Divine Worship and the Discipline of the Sacraments in the search for effective ways of fostering appropriate forms of worship in the Asian context.[97] Such cooperation is essential because the Sacred Liturgy expresses and celebrates the one faith professed by all and, being the heritage of the whole Church, cannot be determined by local Churches in isolation from the universal Church.

22d. The Synod Fathers stressed particularly the importance of the biblical word in passing on the message of salvation to the peoples of Asia, where the transmitted word is so important in preserving and communicating religious experience.[98] It follows that an effective biblical apostolate needs to be developed in order to ensure that the sacred text may be more widely diffused and more intensively and prayerfully used among the members of the Church in Asia. The Synod Fathers urged that it be made the basis for all missionary proclamation, catechesis, preaching and styles of spirituality.[99] Efforts to translate the Bible into local languages need to be encouraged and supported. Biblical formation should be considered an important means of educating people in the faith and equipping them for the task of proclamation. Pastorally oriented courses on the Bible, with due emphasis on applying its teachings to the complex realities of Asian life, ought to be incorporated into formation programmes for the clergy, for consecrated persons and for the laity.[100] The Sacred Scriptures should also be made known among the followers of other religions; the word of God has an inherent power to touch the hearts of people, for through the Scriptures the Holy Spirit reveals God's plan of salvation for the world. Moreover, the narrative styles found in many books of the Bible has an affinity with the religious texts typical of Asia.[101]

22e. Another key aspect of inculturation upon which the future of the process in large part depends is *the formation of evangelizers*. In the past, formation often followed the style, methods and programs imported from the West, and while appreciating the service rendered by that mode of formation, the Synod Fathers recognized as a positive development the efforts made in recent times to adapt the formation of evangelizers to the cultural contexts of Asia. As well as a solid grounding in biblical and patristic studies, seminarians should acquire a detailed and firm grasp of the Church's theological and philosophical patrimony, as I urged in my Encyclical Letter *Fides et Ratio*.[102] On the basis of this preparation, they will then benefit from contact with Asian philosophical and religious traditions.[103] The Synod Fathers also encouraged seminary professors and staff to seek a profound understanding of the elements of spirituality and prayer akin to the Asian soul, and to involve themselves more deeply in the Asian peoples' search for a fuller life.[104] To this end, emphasis was placed on the need to ensure the proper formation of seminary staff.[105] The Synod also expressed concern for the formation of men and women in the consecrated life, making it clear that the spirituality and lifestyle of consecrated persons needs to be sensitive to the religious and cultural heritage of the people among whom they live and whom they serve, always presupposing the necessary discernment of what conforms to the Gospel and what does not.[106] Moreover, since the inculturation of the Gospel involves the entire People of God, the role of the laity is of paramount importance. It is they above all who are called to transform society, in collaboration with the Bishops, clergy and religious, by infusing the "mind of Christ" into the mentality, customs, laws and structures of the secular world in which they live.[107] A wider inculturation of the Gospel at every level of society in Asia will depend greatly on the appropriate formation which the local Churches succeed in giving to the laity.

23. Christian Life as Proclamation

23a. The more the Christian community is rooted in the experience of God which flows from a living faith, the more credibly it will be able to proclaim to others the fulfilment of God's Kingdom in Jesus Christ. This will result from faithfully listening to the word of God, from prayer and contemplation, from celebrating the mystery of Jesus in the sacraments, above all in the Eucharist, and from giving example of true communion of life and integrity of love. The heart of the particular Church must be set on the contemplation of Jesus Christ, God-made-Man, and strive constantly for a more intimate union with him whose mission she continues. *Mission is contemplative action and active contemplation.* Therefore, a missionary who has no deep experience of God in prayer and contemplation will have little spiritual influence or missionary success. This is an insight drawn from my own priestly ministry and, as I have written elsewhere, my contact with representatives of the non-Christian spiritual traditions, particularly those of Asia, has confirmed me in the view that the future of mission depends to a great extent on contemplation.[108] In Asia, home to great religions where individuals and entire peoples are thirsting for the divine, the Church is called to be a praying Church, deeply spiritual even as she engages in immediate human and social concerns. All Christians need a true missionary spirituality of prayer and contemplation.

23b. A genuinely religious person readily wins respect and a following in Asia. Prayer, fasting and various forms of asceticism are held in high regard. Renunciation, detachment, humility, simplicity and silence are considered great values by the followers of all religions. Lest prayer be divorced from human promotion, the Synod Fathers insisted that "the work of justice, charity and compassion is interrelated with a genuine life of prayer and contemplation, and indeed it is this same spirituality that will be the wellspring of all our evangelizing work."[109] Fully convinced of the importance of authentic witnesses in the evangelization of Asia, the Synod Fathers stated: "The Good News of Jesus Christ can only be proclaimed by those who are taken up and inspired by the love of the Father for his children, manifested in the person of Jesus Christ. This proclamation is a mission needing holy men and women who will make the Savior known and loved through their lives. A fire can only be lit by something that is itself on fire. So, too, successful proclamation in Asia of the Good News of salvation can only take place if Bishops, clergy, those in the consecrated life and the laity are themselves on fire with the love of Christ and burning with zeal to make him known more widely, loved more deeply and followed more closely."[110] Christians who speak of Christ must embody in their lives the message that they proclaim.

23c. In this regard, however, a particular circumstance in the Asian context demands attention. The Church realizes that *the silent witness of life* still remains the only way of proclaiming God's Kingdom in many places in Asia where explicit proclamation is forbidden and religious freedom is denied or systematically restricted. The Church consciously lives this type of witness, seeing it as the "taking up of her cross" (cf. Lk. 9:23), all the while calling upon and urging governments to recognize religious freedom as a fundamental human right. The words of the Second Vatican Council are worth repeating here: "the human person has a right to religious freedom. Such freedom consists in this, that all should have such immunity from coercion by individuals, or by social groups, or by any human power, that no one should be forced to act against his conscience in religious matters, nor prevented from acting according to his conscience, whether in private or in public, whether alone or in association with others, within due limits."[111] In some Asian countries, this statement still has to be acknowledged and put into effect.

23d. Clearly, then, the proclamation of Jesus Christ in Asia presents many complex aspects, both in content and in method. The Synod Fathers were keenly aware of the legitimate variety of approaches to the proclamation of Jesus, provided that the faith itself is respected in all its integrity in the process of appropriating and sharing it. The Synod noted that "evangelization today is a reality that is both rich and dynamic. It has various aspects and elements: witness, dialogue, proclamation, catechesis, conversion, baptism, insertion into the ecclesial community, the implantation of the Church, inculturation and integral human promotion. Some of these elements proceed together, while some others are successive steps or phases of the entire process of evangelization."[112] In all evangelizing work, however, it is *the complete truth of Jesus Christ* which must be proclaimed. Emphasizing certain aspects of the inexhaustible mystery of Jesus is both legitimate and necessary in gradually introducing Christ to a person, but this cannot be allowed to compromise the integrity of the faith. In the end, a person's acceptance of the faith must be grounded on a sure understanding of the person of Jesus Christ, as presented by the Church in every time and place, the Lord of all who is "the same yesterday, today and for ever" (Heb. 13:8).

CHAPTER FIVE: COMMUNION AND DIALOGUE FOR MISSION

24. Communion and Mission Go Hand in Hand

24a. In accordance with the Father's eternal design, the Church, foreshadowed from the world's beginning, prepared for in the old Covenant, instituted by Christ Jesus and made present to the world by the Holy Spirit on the day of Pentecost, "progresses on her pilgrimage amid this world's persecutions and God's consolations,"[113] as she strives towards her perfection in the glory of heaven. Since God desires "that the whole human race may become one People of God, form one Body of Christ, and be built up into one temple of the Holy Spirit,"[114] the Church is in the world "the visible plan of God's love for humanity, the sacrament of salvation."[115] The Church cannot therefore be understood merely as a social organization or agency of human welfare. Despite having sinful men and women in her midst, the Church must be seen as the privileged place of encounter between God and man, in which God chooses to reveal the mystery of his inner life and carry out his plan of salvation for the world.

24b. The mystery of God's loving design is made present and active in the community of the men and women who have been buried with Christ by baptism into death, so that as Christ was raised from the dead by the glory of the Father, they might walk in newness of life (cf. Rom. 6:4). At the heart of the mystery of the Church is the bond of communion which unites Christ the Bridegroom to all the baptized. Through this living and life-giving communion, "Christians no longer belong to themselves but are the Lord's very own."[116] United to the Son in the Spirit's bond of love, Christians are united to the Father, and from this communion flows the communion which Christians share with one another through Christ in the Holy Spirit.[117] The Church's first purpose then is to be the sacrament of *the inner union of the human person with God*, and, because people's communion with one another is rooted in that union with God, the Church is also the sacrament of *the unity of the human race*.[118] In her this unity is already begun; and at the same time she is the "sign and instrument" of the full realization of the unity yet to come.[119]

24c. It is an essential demand of life in Christ that whoever enters into communion with the Lord is expected to bear fruit: "He who abides in me, and I in him, he it is that bears much fruit" (Jn. 15:5). So true is this that the person who does not bear fruit does not remain in communion: "Each branch of mine that bears no fruit [my Father] takes away" (Jn. 15:2). Communion with Jesus, which gives rise to the communion of Christians among themselves, is the indispensable condition for bearing fruit; and communion with others, which is the gift of Christ and his Spirit, is the most magnificent fruit that the branches can give. In this sense, communion and mission are inseparably connected. They interpenetrate and mutually imply each other, so that "communion represents both the source and fruit of mission: communion gives rise to mission and mission is accomplished in communion."[120]

24d. Using the theology of communion, the Second Vatican Council could describe the Church as the pilgrim People of God to whom all peoples are in some way related.[121] On this basis the Synod Fathers stressed the mysterious link between the Church and the followers of other Asian religions, noting that they are "related to [the Church] in varying degrees and ways."[122] In the midst of so many different peoples, cultures and religions "the life of the Church as communion assumes greater importance."[123] In effect, the Church's service of unity has a specific relevance in Asia where there are so many tensions, divisions and conflicts, caused by ethnic, social, cultural, linguistic, economic and religious differences. It is in this context that the local Churches in Asia, in communion with the Successor of Peter, need to foster greater communion of mind and heart through close cooperation among themselves. Vital also to their evangelizing mission are their relations with other Christian Churches and ecclesial communities, and with the followers of other religions.[124] The Synod therefore renewed the commitment of the Church in Asia to the task of improving both ecumenical relations and interreligious dialogue, recognizing that building unity, working for reconciliation, forging bonds of solidarity, promoting dialogue among religions and cultures, eradicating prejudices and engendering trust among peoples are all essential to the Church's evangelizing mission on the continent. All this demands of the Catholic community a sincere examination of conscience, the courage to seek reconciliation and a renewed commitment to dialogue. At the threshold of the Third Millennium it is clear that the Church's ability to evangelize requires that she strive earnestly to serve the cause of unity in all its dimensions. Communion and mission go hand in hand.

25. Communion within the Church

25a. Gathered around the Successor of Peter, praying and working together, the Bishops of the Special Assembly for Asia personified as it were the communion of the Church in all the rich diversity of the particular Churches over which they preside in charity. My own presence at the Synod's General Sessions was both a welcome opportunity to share the joys and hopes, the difficulties and anxieties of the Bishops, and an intense and deeply-felt exercise of my own ministry. It is in fact within the perspective of ecclesial communion that the universal authority of the Successor of Peter shines forth more clearly, not primarily as juridical power over the local Churches, but above all as a pastoral primacy at the service of the unity of faith and life of the whole People of God. Fully aware that "the Petrine office has a unique ministry in guaranteeing and promoting the unity of the Church,"[125] the Synod Fathers acknowledged the service which the Dicasteries of the Roman Curia and the Holy See's Diplomatic Service render to the local Churches, in the spirit of communion and collegiality.[126] An essential feature of this service is the respect and sensitivity which these close co-workers of the Successor of Peter show towards the legitimate diversity of the local Churches and the variety of cultures and peoples with which they are in contact.

25b. Each particular Church must be grounded in the witness of ecclesial communion which constitutes its very nature as Church. The Synod Fathers chose to describe the Diocese as *a communion of communities* gathered around the Shepherd, where clergy, consecrated persons and the laity are engaged in a "dialogue of life and heart" sustained by the grace of the Holy Spirit.[127] It is primarily in the Diocese that the vision of a communion of communities can be actualized in the midst of the complex social, political, religious, cultural and economic realities of Asia. Ecclesial communion implies that each local Church should become what the Synod Fathers called a "participatory Church," a Church, that is, in which all live their proper vocation and perform their proper role. In order to build up the "communion for mission" and the "mission of communion," every member's unique charism needs to be acknowledged, developed and effectively utilized.[128] In particular there is a need to foster greater involvement of the laity and consecrated men and women in pastoral planning and decision-making, through such participatory structures as Pastoral Councils and Parish Assemblies.[129]

25c. In every Diocese, *the parish* remains the ordinary place where the faithful gather to grow in faith, to live the mystery of ecclesial communion and to take part in the Church's mission. Therefore, the Synod Fathers urged Pastors to devise new and effective ways of shepherding the faithful, so that everyone, especially the poor, will feel truly a part of the parish and of God's People as a whole. Pastoral planning with the lay faithful should be a normal feature of all parishes.[130] The Synod singled out young people in particular as those for whom "the parish should provide greater opportunity for fellowship and communion ...

by means of organized youth apostolates and youth clubs."[131] No one should be excluded *a priori* from sharing fully in the life and mission of the parish because of their social, economic, political, cultural or educational background. Just as each follower of Christ has a gift to offer the community, so the community should show a willingness to receive and benefit from the gift of each one.

25d. In this context, and drawing on their pastoral experience, the Synod Fathers underlined the value of *basic ecclesial communities* as an effective way of promoting communion and participation in parishes and Dioceses, and as a genuine force for evangelization.[132] These small groups help the faithful to live as believing, praying and loving communities like the early Christians (cf. Acts 2:44-47; 4:32-35). They aim to help their members to live the Gospel in a spirit of fraternal love and service, and are therefore a solid starting point for building a new society, the expression of *a civilization of love*. With the Synod, I encourage the Church in Asia, where possible, to consider these basic communities as a positive feature of the Church's evangelizing activity. At the same time they will only be truly effective if—as Pope Paul VI wrote—they live in union with the particular and the Universal Church, in heartfelt communion with the Church's Pastors and the Magisterium, with a commitment to missionary outreach and without yielding to isolationism or ideological exploitation.[133] The presence of these small communities does not do away with the established institutions and structures, which remain necessary for the Church to fulfil her mission.

25e. The Synod also recognized the role of *renewal movements* in building communion, in providing opportunities for a more intimate experience of God through faith and the sacraments, and in fostering conversion of life.[134] It is the responsibility of Pastors to guide, accompany and encourage these groups so that they may be well integrated into the life and mission of the parish and Diocese. Those involved in associations and movements should offer their support to the local Church and not present themselves as alternatives to Diocesan structures and parish life. Communion grows stronger when the local leaders of these movements work together with the Pastors in a spirit of charity for the good of all (cf. 1 Cor. 1:13).

26. Solidarity among the Churches

26a. This communion *ad intra* contributes to *solidarity among the particular Churches themselves*. Attention to local needs is legitimate and indispensable, but communion requires that the particular Churches remain open to one another and collaborate with one another, so that in their diversity they may preserve and clearly manifest the bond of communion with the universal Church. Communion calls for mutual understanding and a coordinated approach to mission, without prejudice to the autonomy and rights of the Churches according to their respective theological, liturgical and spiritual traditions. History however shows how divisions have often wounded the communion of the Churches in Asia. Down the centuries, relations between particular Churches of different ecclesiastical jurisdictions, liturgical traditions and missionary styles have sometimes been tense and difficult. The Bishops present at the Synod acknowledged that even today within and among the particular Churches in Asia there are sometimes unfortunate divisions, often connected with ritual, linguistic, ethnic, caste and ideological differences. Some wounds have been partially healed, but there is not yet full healing. Recognizing that wherever communion is weakened the Church's witness and missionary work suffer, the Fathers proposed concrete steps to strengthen relations between the particular Churches in Asia. As well as the necessary spiritual expressions of support and encouragement, they suggested a more equitable distribution of priests, more effective financial solidarity, cultural and theological exchanges, and increased opportunities for partnership between Dioceses.[135]

26b. Regional and continental associations of Bishops, notably the Council of Catholic Patriarchs of the Middle East and the Federation of Asian Bishops' Conferences have helped to foster union among the local Churches and have provided venues for cooperation in resolving pastoral problems. Similarly, there are many centers of theology, spirituality and pastoral activity across Asia which foster communion and practical cooperation.[136] It must be the concern of all to see these promising initiatives develop further for the good of both the Church and society in Asia.

27. The Catholic Eastern Churches

27a. The situation of *the Catholic Eastern Churches*, principally of the Middle East and India, merits special attention. From Apostolic times they have been the custodians of a precious spiritual, liturgical and theological heritage. Their traditions and rites, born of a deep inculturation of the faith in the soil of many Asian countries, deserve the greatest respect. With the Synod Fathers, I call upon everyone to recognize the legitimate customs and the legitimate freedom of these Churches in disciplinary and liturgical matters, as stipulated by the Code of Canons of the Eastern Churches.[137] Following the teaching of the Second Vatican Council, there is an urgent need to overcome the fears and misunderstandings which appear at times between the Catholic Eastern Churches and the Latin Church, and among those Churches themselves, especially with regard to the pastoral care of their people, also outside their own territories.[138] As children of the one Church, reborn into the newness of life in Christ, believers are called to undertake all things in a spirit of common purpose, trust and unfailing charity. Conflicts must not be allowed to create division, but must instead be handled in a spirit of truth and respect, since no good can come except from love.[139]

27b. These venerable Churches are directly involved in ecumenical dialogue with their sister Orthodox Churches, and the Synod Fathers urged them to pursue this path.[140] They have also had valuable experiences in interreligious dialogue, especially with Islam. This can be helpful to other Churches in Asia and elsewhere. It is clear that the Catholic Eastern Churches possess a great wealth of tradition and experience which can greatly benefit the whole Church.

28. Sharing Hopes and Sufferings

28a. The Synod Fathers were also aware of the need for effective communion and cooperation with the local Churches present in the ex-Soviet territories of Asia, which are rebuilding in the trying circumstances inherited from a difficult period of history. The Church accompanies them in prayer, sharing their sufferings and their new-found hopes. I encourage the whole Church to lend moral, spiritual and material support, and much needed ordained and non-ordained personnel to help these communities in the task of sharing with the peoples of these lands the love of God revealed in Jesus Christ.[141]

28b. In many parts of Asia, our brothers and sisters continue to live their faith in the midst of restrictions or even the total denial of freedom. For these *suffering members of the Church*, the Synod Fathers expressed special concern and solicitude. With the Bishops of Asia, I urge our brothers and sisters of these Churches in difficult circumstances to join their sufferings to those of the crucified Lord, for we and they know that the Cross alone, when borne in faith and love, is the path to resurrection and new life for humanity. I encourage the various national Episcopal Conferences in Asia to establish an office to help these Churches; and I pledge the Holy See's continued closeness to and concern for all those who are suffering persecution for their faith in Christ.[142] I appeal to governments and the leaders of nations to adopt and implement policies that guarantee religious freedom for all their citizens.

28c. On many occasions the Synod Fathers turned their thoughts to the Catholic Church in Mainland China and prayed that the day may soon come when our beloved Chinese brothers and sisters will be completely free to practise their faith in full communion with the See of Peter and the universal Church. To you, dear Chinese brothers and sisters, I make this fervent exhortation: never allow hardship and sorrow to diminish your devotion to Christ and your commitment to your great nation.[143] The Synod also expressed a cordial sense of solidarity with the Catholic Church in Korea, and supported "the efforts of Catholics to give assistance to the people of North Korea who are deprived of the minimal means of survival, and to bring reconciliation among two countries of one people, one language and one cultural heritage."[144]

28d. Likewise, the Synod's thoughts frequently returned to the Church in Jerusalem, which has a special place in the hearts of all Christians. Indeed, the words of the Prophet Isaiah find an echo in the hearts of millions of believers throughout the world, for whom Jerusalem occupies a unique and cherished position: "Rejoice with Jerusalem, and be glad for her, all you who love her ... that you may drink deeply with delight from the abundance of her glory" (66:10-11). Jerusalem, the city of reconciliation of men with God and among themselves, has so often been a place of conflict and division. The Synod Fathers called upon the particular Churches to stand in solidarity with the Church in Jerusalem by sharing her sorrows, by praying for her and cooperating with her in serving peace, justice and reconciliation between the two peoples and the three religions present in the Holy City.[145] I renew the appeal which I have often made to political and religious leaders and to all people of good will to search for ways to ensure the peace and integrity of Jerusalem. As I have already written, it is my own fervent wish to go there on a religious pilgrimage, like my predecessor Pope Paul VI, to pray in the Holy City where Jesus Christ lived, died and rose again and to visit the place from which, in the power of the Holy Spirit, the Apostles went forth to proclaim the Gospel of Jesus Christ to the world.[146]

29. A Mission of Dialogue

29a. The common theme of the various "continental" Synods which have helped to prepare the Church for the Great Jubilee of the Year 2000 is that of the *new evangelization*. A new era of proclamation of the Gospel is essential not only because, after two millennia, a major part of the human family still does not acknowledge Christ, but also because the situation in which the Church and the world find themselves at the threshold of the new millennium is particularly challenging for religious belief and the moral truths which spring from it. There is a tendency almost everywhere to build progress and prosperity without reference to God, and to reduce the religious dimension of the human person to the private sphere. Society, separated from the most basic truth about man, namely his relationship to the Creator and to the redemption brought about by Christ in the Holy Spirit, can only stray further and further from the true sources of life, love and happiness. This violent century which is fast coming to a close bears terrifying witness to what can happen when truth and goodness are abandoned in favour of the lust for power and self-aggrandizement. The new evangelization, as a call to conversion, grace and wisdom, is the only genuine hope for a better world and a brighter future. The question is not whether the Church has something essential to say to the men and women of our time, but how she can say it clearly and convincingly!

29b. At the time of the Second Vatican Council, my predecessor Pope Paul VI declared, in his Encyclical Letter *Ecclesiam Suam*, that the question of the relationship between the Church and the modern world was one of the most important concerns of our time. He wrote that "its existence and its urgency are such as to create a burden on our soul, a stimulus, a vocation."[147] Since the Council the Church has consistently shown that she wants to pursue that relationship in a spirit of dialogue. The desire for dialogue, however, is not simply a strategy for peaceful coexistence among peoples; it is an essential part of the Church's mission because it has its origin in the Father's loving dialogue of salvation with humanity through the Son in the power of the Holy Spirit. The Church can accomplish her mission only in a way that corresponds to the way in which God acted in Jesus Christ: he became man, shared our human life and spoke in a human language to communicate his saving message. The dialogue which the Church proposes is grounded in the logic of the Incarnation. Therefore, nothing but fervent and unselfish solidarity prompts the Church's dialogue with the men and women of Asia who seek the truth in love.

29c. As the sacrament of the unity of all mankind, the Church cannot but enter into dialogue with all peoples, in every time and place. Responding to the mission she has received, she ventures forth to meet the peoples of the world, conscious of being a "little flock" within the vast throng of humanity (cf. Lk. 12:32), but also of being leaven in the dough of the world (cf. Mt. 13:33). Her efforts to engage in dialogue are directed in the first place to those who share her belief in Jesus Christ the Lord and Savior. It extends beyond the Christian world to the followers of every other religious tradition, on the basis of the religious yearnings found in every human heart. Ecumenical dialogue and interreligious dialogue constitute a veritable vocation for the Church.

30. Ecumenical Dialogue

30a. Ecumenical dialogue is a challenge and a call to conversion for the whole Church, especially for the Church in Asia where people expect from Christians a clearer sign of unity. For all peoples to come together in the grace of God, communion needs to be restored among those who in faith have accepted Jesus Christ as Lord. Jesus himself prayed and does not cease to call for the visible unity of his disciples, so that the world may believe that the Father has sent him (cf. Jn. 17:21).[148] But the Lord's will that his Church be one awaits a complete and courageous response from his disciples.

30b. In Asia, precisely where the number of Christians is proportionately small, division makes missionary work still more difficult. The Synod Fathers acknowledged that "the scandal of a divided Christianity is a great obstacle for evangelization in Asia."[149] In fact, the division among Christians is seen as a counter-witness to Jesus Christ by many in Asia who are searching for harmony and unity through their own religions and cultures. Therefore the Catholic Church in Asia feels especially impelled to work for unity with other Christians, realizing that the search for full communion demands from everyone charity, discernment, courage and hope. "In order to be authentic and bear fruit, ecumenism requires certain fundamental dispositions on the part of the Catholic faithful: in the first place, charity that shows itself in goodness and a lively desire to cooperate wherever possible with the faithful of other Churches and Ecclesial Communities; secondly, fidelity towards the Catholic Church, without however ignoring or denying the shortcomings manifested by some of her members; thirdly, a spirit of discernment in order to appreciate all that is good and worthy of praise. Finally, a sincere desire for purification and renewal is also needed."[150]

30c. While recognizing the difficulties still existing in the relationships between Christians, which involve not only prejudices inherited from the past but also judgments rooted in profound convictions which involve conscience,[151] the Synod Fathers also pointed to signs of improved relations among some Christian Churches and Ecclesial Communities in Asia. Catholic and Orthodox Christians, for example, often recognize a cultural unity with one another, a sense of sharing important elements of a common ecclesial tradition. This forms a solid basis for a continuing fruitful ecumenical dialogue into the next millennium, which, we must hope and pray, will ultimately bring an end to the divisions of the millennium that is now coming to a close.

30d. On the practical level, the Synod proposed that the national Episcopal Conferences in Asia invite other Christian Churches to join in a process of prayer and consultation in order to explore the possibilities of new ecumenical structures and associations to promote Christian unity. The Synod's suggestion that the Week of Prayer for Christian Unity be celebrated more fruitfully is also helpful. Bishops are encouraged to set up and oversee ecumenical centres of prayer and dialogue; and adequate formation for ecumenical dialogue needs to be included in the curriculum of seminaries, houses of formation and educational institutions.

31. Interreligious Dialogue

31a. In my Apostolic Letter *Tertio Millennio Adveniente* I indicated that the advent of a new millennium offers a great opportunity for interreligious dialogue and for meetings with the leaders of the great world religions.[152] Contact, dialogue and cooperation with the followers of other religions is a task which the Second Vatican Council bequeathed to the whole Church as a duty and a challenge. The principles of this search for a positive relationship with other religious traditions are set out in the Council's Declaration *Nostra Aetate*, promulgated on 28 October 1965, the Magna Carta of interreligious dialogue for our times. From the Christian point of view, interreligious dialogue is more than a way of fostering mutual knowledge and enrichment; it is a part of the Church's evangelizing mission, an expression of the mission *ad gentes*.[153] Christians bring to interreligious dialogue the firm belief that the fullness of salvation comes from Christ alone and that the Church community to which they belong is the *ordinary means* of salvation.[154] Here I repeat what I wrote to the Fifth Plenary Assembly of the Federation of Asian Bishops' Conferences: "Although the Church gladly acknowledges whatever is true and holy in the religious traditions of Buddhism, Hinduism and Islam as a reflection of that truth which enlightens all people, this does not lessen her duty and resolve to proclaim without failing Jesus Christ who is 'the way and the truth and the life'.... The fact that the followers of other religions can receive God's grace and be saved by Christ apart from the ordinary means which he has established does not thereby cancel the call to faith and baptism which God wills for all people."[155]

31b. In the process of dialogue, as I have already written in my Encyclical Letter *Redemptoris Missio*, "there must be no abandonment of principles nor false irenicism, but instead a witness given and received for mutual advancement on the road of religious inquiry and experience, and at the same time for the elimination of prejudice, intolerance and misunderstandings."[156] Only those with a mature and convinced Christian faith are qualified to engage in genuine interreligious dialogue. "Only Christians who are deeply immersed in the mystery of Christ and who are happy in their faith community can without undue risk and with hope of positive fruit engage in interreligious dialogue."[157] It is therefore important for the Church in Asia to provide suitable models of interreligious dialogue—evangelization in dialogue and dialogue for evangelization—and suitable training for those involved.

31c. Having stressed the need in interreligious dialogue for firm faith in Christ, the Synod Fathers went on to speak of the need for a *dialogue of life and heart*. The followers of Christ must have the gentle and humble heart of their Master, never proud, never condescending, as they meet their partners in dialogue (cf. Mt. 11:29). "Interreligious relations are best developed in a context of openness to other believers, a willingness to listen and the desire to respect and understand others in their differences. For all this, love of others is indispensable. This should result in collaboration, harmony and mutual enrichment."[158]

31d. To guide those engaged in the process, the Synod suggested that a directory on interreligious dialogue be drawn up.[159] As the Church explores new ways of encountering other religions, I mention some forms of dialogue already taking place with good results, including scholarly exchanges between experts in the various religious traditions or representatives of those traditions, common action for integral human development and the defence of human and religious values.[160] I repeat how important it is to revitalize prayer and contemplation in the process of dialogue. Men and women in the consecrated life can contribute very significantly to interreligious dialogue by witnessing to the vitality of the great Christian traditions of asceticism and mysticism.[161]

31e. The memorable meeting held in Assisi, the city of Saint Francis, on 27 October 1986, between the Catholic Church and representatives of the other world religions shows that religious men and women, without abandoning their own traditions, can still commit themselves to praying and working for peace and the good of humanity.[162] The Church must continue to strive to preserve and foster at all levels this spirit of encounter and cooperation between religions.

31f. Communion and dialogue are two essential aspects of the Church's mission, which have their infinitely transcendent exemplar in the mystery of the Trinity, from whom all mission comes and to whom it must be directed. One of the great "birthday" gifts which the members of the Church, and especially her Pastors, can offer the Lord of History on the two thousandth anniversary of his Incarnation is a strengthening of the spirit of *unity and communion* at every level of ecclesial life, a renewed "holy pride" in the Church's continuing fidelity to what has been handed down, and a new confidence in the unchanging grace and mission which sends her out among the peoples of the world to witness to God's saving love and mercy. Only if the People of God recognize the gift that is theirs in Christ will they be able to communicate that gift to others through *proclamation* and *dialogue*.

CHAPTER SIX: THE SERVICE OF HUMAN PROMOTION

32. The Social Doctrine of the Church

32a. In the service of the human family, the Church reaches out to all men and women without distinction, striving to build with them a civilization of love, founded upon the universal values of peace, justice, solidarity and freedom, which find their fulfilment in Christ. As the Second Vatican Council said so memorably: "The joys and the hopes, the griefs and the anxieties of the people of this age, especially those who are poor or in any way afflicted, these too are the joys and hopes, the griefs and anxieties of the followers of Christ. Indeed, nothing genuinely human fails to raise an echo in their hearts."[163] The Church in Asia then, with its multitude of poor and oppressed people, is called to live a communion of life which shows itself particularly in loving service to the poor and defenceless.

32b. If in recent times the Church's Magisterium has insisted more and more upon the need to promote the authentic and integral development of the human person,[164] this is in response to the real situation of the world's peoples, as well as to an increased consciousness that not just the actions of individuals but also structures of social, political and economic life are often inimical to human well-being. The imbalances entrenched in the increasing gap between those who benefit from the world's growing capacity to produce wealth and those who are left at the margin of progress call for a radical change of both mentality and structures *in favor of the human person*. The great *moral challenge* facing nations and the international community in relation to development is to have *the courage of a new solidarity*, capable of taking imaginative and effective steps to overcome both dehumanizing underdevelopment and the "overdevelopment" which tends to reduce the person to an economic unit in an ever more oppressive consumer network. In seeking to bring about this change, "the Church does not have technical solutions to offer," but "offers her first contribution to the solution of the urgent problem of development when she proclaims the truth about Christ, about herself and about man, applying this truth to a concrete situation."[165] After all, human development is never a merely technical or economic question; it is fundamentally *a human and moral question*.

32c. The social doctrine of the Church, which proposes a set of principles for reflection, criteria for judgement and directives for action,[166] is addressed in the first place to the members of the Church. It is essential that the faithful engaged in human promotion should have a firm grasp of this precious body of teaching and make it an integral part of their evangelizing mission. The Synod Fathers therefore stressed the importance of offering the faithful—in all educational activities, and especially in seminaries and houses of formation—a solid training in the social doctrine of the Church.[167] Christian leaders in the Church and society, and especially lay men and women with responsibilities in public life, need to be well formed in this teaching so that they can inspire and vivify civil society and its structures with the leaven of the Gospel.[168] The social doctrine of the Church will not only alert these Christian leaders to their duty, but will also give them guidelines for action in favor of human development, and will free them from false notions of the human person and human activity.

33. The Dignity of the Human Person

33a. Human beings, not wealth or technology, are the prime agents and destination of development. Therefore, the kind of development that the Church promotes reaches far beyond questions of economy and technology. It begins and ends with the integrity of the human person created in the image of God and endowed with a God-given dignity and inalienable human rights. The various international declarations on human rights and the many initiatives which these have inspired are a sign of growing attention on a worldwide level to the dignity of the human person. Unfortunately, these declarations are often violated in practice. Fifty years after the solemn proclamation of the Universal Declaration of Human Rights, many people are still subjected to the most degrading forms of exploitation and manipulation, which make them veritable slaves to those who are more powerful, to an ideology, economic power, oppressive political systems, scientific technocracy or the intrusiveness of the mass media.[169]

33b. The Synod Fathers were well aware of the persistent violations of human rights in many parts of the world, and particularly in Asia, where "teeming millions are suffering from discrimination, exploitation, poverty and marginalization."[170] They expressed the need for all God's people in Asia to come to a clear awareness of the inescapable and unrenounceable challenge involved in the defence of human rights and the promotion of justice and peace.

34. Preferential Love of the Poor

34a. In seeking to promote human dignity, the Church shows a preferential love of the poor and the voiceless, because the Lord has identified himself with them in a special way (cf. Mt. 25:40). This love excludes no one, but simply embodies a priority of service to which the whole Christian tradition bears witness. "This love of preference for the poor, and the decisions which it inspires in us, cannot but embrace the immense multitudes of the hungry, the needy, the homeless, those without medical care and, above all, those without hope of a better future. It is impossible not to take account of the existence of these realities. To ignore them would mean becoming like the 'rich man' who pretended not to know the beggar Lazarus lying at his gate (cf. Lk. 16:19-31)."[171] This is especially so with regard to Asia, a continent of plentiful resources and great civilizations, but where some of the poorest nations on earth are to be found, and where more than half the population suffers deprivation, poverty and exploitation.[172] The poor of Asia and of the world will always find their best reason for hope in the Gospel command to love one another as Christ has loved us (cf. Jn. 13:34); and the Church in Asia cannot but strive earnestly to fulfil that command towards the poor, in word and in deed.

34b. Solidarity with the poor becomes more credible if Christians themselves live simply, following the example of Jesus. Simplicity of life, deep faith and unfeigned love for all, especially the poor and the outcast, are luminous signs of the Gospel in action. The Synod Fathers called on Asian Catholics to adopt a lifestyle consonant with the teachings of the Gospel, so that they may better serve the Church's mission and so that the Church herself may become a Church of the poor and for the poor.[173]

34c. In her love for the poor of Asia, the Church concerns herself especially with migrants, with indigenous and tribal peoples, with women and with children, since they are often the victims of the worst forms of exploitation. In addition, untold numbers of people suffer discrimination because of their culture, color, race, caste, economic status, or because of their way of thinking. They include those who are victimized on the basis of their conversion to Christianity.[174] I join the Synod Fathers in appealing to all nations to recognize the right to freedom of conscience and religion and the other basic human rights.[175]

34d. At the present time Asia is experiencing an unprecedented flow of refugees, asylum seekers, immigrants and overseas workers. In the countries to which they come, these people often find themselves friendless, culturally estranged, linguistically disadvantaged and economically vulnerable. They need support and care in order to preserve their human dignity and their cultural and religious heritage.[176] Despite limited resources, the Church in Asia generously seeks to be a welcoming home to the weary and heavy-burdened, knowing that in the Heart of Jesus, where no one is a stranger, they will find rest (cf. Mt. 11:28-29).

34e. In almost every Asian country, there are large aboriginal populations, some of them on the lowest economic rung. The Synod repeatedly noted that indigenous or tribal people often feel drawn to the person of Jesus Christ and to the Church as a community of love and service.[177] Herein lies an immense field of action in education and health care, as well as in promoting social participation. The Catholic community needs to intensify pastoral work among these people, attending to their concerns and to the questions of justice which affect their lives. This implies an attitude of deep respect for their traditional religion and its values; it implies as well the need to help them to help themselves, so that they can work to improve their situation and become the evangelizers of their own culture and society.[178]

34f. No one can remain indifferent to the suffering of the countless children in Asia who fall victim to intolerable exploitation and violence, not just as the result of the evil perpetrated by individuals but often as a direct consequence of corrupt social structures. The Synod Fathers identified child labor, pedophilia and the drug culture as the social evils which affect children most directly, and they saw clearly that these ills are compounded by others like poverty and ill-conceived programs of national development.[179] The Church must do all she can to overcome such evils, to act on behalf of those most exploited, and to seek to guide the little ones to the love of Jesus, for to such belongs the Kingdom of God (cf. Lk. 18:16).[180]

34g. The Synod voiced special concern for women, whose situation remains a serious problem in Asia, where discrimination and violence against women is often found in the home, in the workplace and even within the legal system. Illiteracy is most widespread among women, and many are treated simply as commodities in prostitution, tourism and the entertainment industry.[181] In their fight against all forms of injustice and discrimination, women should find an ally in the Christian community, and for this reason the Synod proposed that where possible the local Churches in Asia should promote human rights activities on behalf of women. The aim must be to bring about a change of attitude through a proper understanding of the role of men and women in the family, in society and in the Church, through greater awareness of the original complementarity between men and women, and through clearer appreciation of the importance of the feminine dimension in all things human. The contributions of women have all too often been undervalued or ignored, and this has resulted in a spiritual impoverishment of humanity. The Church in Asia would more visibly and effectively uphold women's dignity and freedom by encouraging their role in the Church's life, including her intellectual life, and by opening to them ever greater opportunities to be present and active in the Church's mission of love and service.[182]

35. The Gospel of Life

35a. The service of human development begins with the service of life itself. Life is a great gift entrusted to us by God: he entrusts it to us as a project and a responsibility. We are therefore guardians of life, not its proprietors. We receive the gift freely and, in gratitude, we must never cease to respect and defend it, from its beginning to its natural conclusion. From the moment of conception, human life involves God's creative action and remains forever in a special bond with the Creator, who is life's source and its sole end. There is no true progress, no true civil society, no true human promotion without respect for human life, especially the life of those who have no voice of their own with which to defend themselves. The life of every person, whether of the child in the womb, or of someone who is sick, handicapped or elderly, is a gift for all.

35b. The Synod Fathers wholeheartedly reaffirmed the teaching of the Second Vatican Council and the subsequent Magisterium, including my Encyclical Letter *Evangelium Vitae*, on the sanctity of human life. I join them here in calling upon the faithful in their countries, where the demographic question is often used as an argument for the need to introduce abortion and artificial population control programmes, to resist "the culture of death."[183] They can show their fidelity to God and their commitment to true human promotion by supporting and participating in programs which defend the life of those who are powerless to defend themselves.

36. Health Care

36a. Following in the steps of Jesus Christ who had compassion for all and cured "all kinds of disease and illness" (Mt. 9:35), the Church in Asia is committed to becoming still more involved in the care of the sick, since this is a vital part of her mission of offering the saving grace of Christ to the whole person. Like the Good Samaritan of the parable (cf. Lk. 10:29-37), the Church wants to care for the sick and disabled in concrete ways,[184] especially where people are deprived of elementary medical care as a result of poverty and marginalization.

36b. On numerous occasions during my visits to the Church in different parts of the world I have been deeply moved by the extraordinary Christian witness borne by religious and consecrated persons, doctors, nurses and other health care workers, especially those working with the handicapped, or in the field of terminal care, or contending with the spread of new diseases such as AIDS. Increasingly, Christian health care workers are called to be generous and self-giving in tending the victims of drug addiction and AIDS, who are often despised and abandoned by society.[185] Many Catholic medical institutions in Asia are facing pressures from public health care policies not based on Christian principles, and many of them are burdened by ever increasing financial difficulties. In spite of these problems, it is the exemplary self-giving love and dedicated professionalism of those involved that make these facilities an admirable and appreciated service to the community, and a particularly visible and effective sign of God's unfailing love. These health care workers must be encouraged and supported in the good that they do. Their continuing commitment and effectiveness is the best way to ensure that Christian values and ethics enter deeply into the health care systems of the continent and transform them from within.[186]

37. Education

37a. Throughout Asia, the Church's involvement in education is extensive and highly visible, and is therefore a key element of her presence among the peoples of the continent. In many countries, Catholic schools play an important role in evangelization, inculturating the faith, teaching the ways of openness and respect, and fostering interreligious understanding. The Church's schools often provide the only educational opportunities for girls, tribal minorities, the rural poor and less privileged children. The Synod Fathers were convinced of the need to extend and develop the apostolate of education in Asia, with an eye in particular to the disadvantaged, so that all may be helped to take their rightful place as full citizens in society.[187] As the Synod Fathers noted, this will mean that the system of Catholic education must become still more clearly directed towards human promotion, providing an environment where students receive not only the formal elements of schooling but, more broadly, an integral human formation based upon the teachings of Christ.[188] Catholic schools should continue to be places where the faith can be freely proposed and received. In the same way, Catholic universities, in addition to pursuing the academic excellence for which they are already well known, must retain a clear Christian identity in order to be a Christian leaven in Asian societies.[189]

38. Peacemaking

38a. At the end of the twentieth century the world is still threatened by forces which generate conflicts and wars, and Asia is certainly not exempt from these. Among these forces are intolerance and marginalization of all kinds—social, cultural, political, and even religious. Day by day fresh violence is inflicted upon individuals and entire peoples, and the culture of death takes hold in the unjustifiable recourse to violence to resolve tensions. Given the appalling situation of conflict in so many parts of the world, the Church is called to be deeply involved in international and interreligious efforts to bring about peace, justice and reconciliation. She continues to insist on the negotiated and non-military resolution of conflicts, and she looks to the day when nations will abandon war as a way of vindicating claims or a means of resolving differences. She is convinced that war creates more problems than it ever solves, that dialogue is the only just and noble path to agreement and reconciliation, and that the patient and wise art of peacemaking is especially blessed by God.

38b. Especially troubling in Asia is the continual race to acquire weapons of mass destruction, an immoral and wasteful expenditure in national budgets, which in some cases cannot even satisfy people's basic needs. The Synod Fathers also spoke of the vast number of landmines in Asia, which have maimed or killed hundreds of thousands of innocent people, while despoiling fertile land which could otherwise be used for food production.[190] It is the responsibility of all, especially of those who govern nations, to work more energetically for disarmament. The Synod called for a stop to the manufacture, sale and use of nuclear, chemical and biological arms and urged those who have set landmines to assist in the work of rehabilitation and restoration.[191] Above all the Synod Fathers prayed to God, who knows the depths of every human conscience, to put sentiments of peace in the hearts of those tempted to follow the ways of violence so that the biblical vision will become a reality: "they shall beat their swords into ploughshares, and their spears into pruning hooks; nation shall not lift up sword against nation, neither shall they learn war any more" (Is. 2:4).

38c. The Synod heard many testimonies concerning the sufferings of the people of Iraq, and about the fact that many Iraqis, especially children, have died because of the lack of medicines and other basic commodities deriving from the continuing embargo. With the Synod Fathers, I wish to express once again my solidarity with the Iraqi people, and I am particularly close in prayer and hope to the sons and daughters of the Church in that country. The Synod prayed that God will enlighten the minds and hearts of all those who bear responsibility for bringing about a just solution to the crisis, in order that an already sorely tried people may be spared further suffering and sorrow.[192]

39. Globalization

39a. Considering the question of human promotion in Asia, the Synod Fathers recognized the importance of the process of economic globalization. While acknowledging its many positive effects, they pointed out that globalization has also worked to the detriment of the poor,[193] tending to push poorer countries to the margin of international economic and political relations. Many Asian nations are unable to hold their own in a global market economy. And perhaps more significantly, there is also the aspect of a *cultural* globalization, made possible by the modern communications media, which is quickly drawing Asian societies into a global consumer culture that is both secularist and materialistic. The result is an eroding of traditional family and social values which until now had sustained peoples and societies. All of this makes it clear that *the ethical and moral aspects of globalization* need to be more directly addressed by the leaders of nations and by organizations concerned with human promotion.

39b. The Church insists upon the need for "globalization without marginalization."[194] With the Synod Fathers, I call upon the particular Churches everywhere, and especially those in the Western countries, to work to ensure that the Church's social doctrine has its due impact upon the formulation of ethical and juridical norms for regulating the world's free markets and for the means of social communication. Catholic leaders and professionals should urge governments and financial and trade institutions to recognize and respect such norms.[195]

40. Foreign Debt

40a. Furthermore, in her search for justice in a world marred by social and economic inequalities, the Church cannot ignore the heavy burden of debt incurred by many developing nations in Asia, with its consequent impact upon their present and future. In many cases, these countries are forced to cut down spending on the necessities of life such as food, health, housing and education, in order to service their debts to international monetary agencies and banks. This means that many people are trapped in living conditions which are an affront to human dignity. While aware of the technical complexities of this matter, the Synod recognized that this issue tests the capacity of peoples, societies and governments to value the human person and the lives of millions of human beings more highly than financial and material gain.[196]

40b. The approach of the Great Jubilee of the Year 2000 is an opportune time for the Episcopal Conferences of the world, especially of the wealthier nations, to encourage international monetary agencies and banks to explore ways of easing the international debt situation. Among the more obvious are a renegotiation of debts, with either substantial reduction or outright cancellation, as also business ventures and investments to assist the economies of the poorer countries.[197] At the same time the Synod Fathers also addressed the debtor countries. They emphasized the need to develop a sense of national responsibility, reminding them of the importance of sound economic planning, transparency and good management, and invited them to wage a resolute campaign against corruption.[198] They called upon the Christians of Asia to condemn all forms of corruption and the misappropriation of public funds by those holding political power.[199] The citizens of debtor countries have too often been victims of waste and inefficiency at home, before falling victim to the international debt crisis.

41. The Environment

41a. When concern for economic and technological progress is not accompanied by concern for the balance of the ecosystem, our earth is inevitably exposed to serious environmental damage, with consequent harm to human beings. Blatant disrespect for the environment will continue as long as the earth and its potential are seen merely as objects of immediate use and consumption, to be manipulated by an unbridled desire for profit.[200] It is the duty of Christians and of all who look to God as the Creator to protect the environment by restoring a sense of reverence for the whole of God's creation. It is the Creator's will that man should treat nature not as a ruthless exploiter but as an intelligent and responsible administrator.[201] The Synod Fathers pleaded in a special way for greater responsibility on the part of the leaders of nations, legislators, business people and all who are directly involved in the management of the earth's resources.[202] They underlined the need to educate people, especially the young, in environmental responsibility, training them in the stewardship over creation which God has entrusted to humanity. The protection of the environment is not only a *technical* question; it is also and above all an *ethical* issue. All have a moral duty to care for the environment, not only for their own good but also for the good of future generations.

41b. In conclusion, it is worth remembering that in calling on Christians to work and sacrifice themselves in the service of human development the Synod Fathers were drawing upon some of the core insights of biblical and ecclesial tradition. Ancient Israel insisted passionately upon the unbreakable bond between worship of God and care for the weak, represented typically in Scripture as "the widow, the stranger and orphan" (cf. Ex. 22:21-22; Dt. 10:18; 27:19), who in the societies of the time were most vulnerable to the threat of injustice. Time and again in the Prophets we hear the cry for justice, for the right ordering of human society, without which there can be no true worship of God (cf. Is. 1:10-17; Am. 5:21-24). In the appeal of the Synod Fathers we thus hear an echo of the Prophets filled with the Spirit of God, who wants "mercy not sacrifice" (Hos. 6:6). Jesus made these words his own (cf. Mt. 9:13), and the same is true of the Saints in every time and place. Consider the words of Saint John Chrysostom: "Do you wish to honor the body of Christ? Then do not ignore him when he is naked. Do not pay him silken honors in the temple only then to neglect him when he goes cold and naked outside. He who said: 'This is my body' is the One who also said, 'You saw me hungry and you gave me no food'.... What good is it if the Eucharistic Table groans under the weight of golden chalices, when Christ is dying of hunger? Start by satisfying his hunger, and then with what remains you may adorn the altar as well."[203] In the Synod's appeal for human development and for justice in human affairs, we hear a voice which is both old and new. It is old because it rises from the depths of our Christian tradition, which looks to that profound harmony which the Creator intends; it is new because it speaks to the immediate situation of countless people in Asia today.

CHAPTER SEVEN: WITNESSES TO THE GOSPEL

42. A Witnessing Church

42a. The Second Vatican Council taught clearly that the entire Church is missionary, and that the work of evangelization is the duty of the whole People of God.[204] Since the whole People of God is sent forth to preach the Gospel, evangelization is never an individual and isolated act; it is always an ecclesial task which has to be carried out in communion with the whole community of faith. The mission is one and indivisible, having one origin and one final purpose; but within it there are different responsibilities and different kinds of activity.[205] In every case it is clear that there can be no true proclamation of the Gospel unless Christians also offer the witness of lives in harmony with the message they preach: "The first form of witness is the very life of the missionary, of the Christian family, and of the ecclesial community, which reveal a new way of living.... Everyone in the Church, striving to imitate the Divine Master, can and must bear this kind of witness; in many cases it is the only possible way of being a missionary."[206] Genuine Christian witness is needed especially now, because "people today put more trust in witnesses than in teachers, in experience than in teaching, and in life and action than in theories."[207] This is certainly true in the Asian context, where people are more persuaded by holiness of life than by intellectual argument. The experience of faith and of the gifts of the Holy Spirit thus becomes the basis of all missionary work, in towns or villages, in schools or hospitals, among the handicapped, migrants or tribal peoples, or in the pursuit of justice and human rights. Every situation is an opportunity for Christians to show forth the power which the truth of Christ has become in their lives. Therefore, inspired by the many missionaries who bore heroic witness to God's love among the peoples of the continent in the past, the Church in Asia strives now to witness with no less zeal to Jesus Christ and his Gospel. Christian mission demands no less.

42b. Conscious of the Church's essentially missionary character and looking to a new outpouring of the dynamism of the Holy Spirit as the Church enters the new millennium, the Synod Fathers asked that this Post-Synodal Apostolic Exhortation should offer some directives and guidelines to those working in the vast field of evangelization in Asia.

43. Pastors

43a. It is the Holy Spirit who enables the Church to accomplish the mission entrusted to her by Christ. Before sending out his disciples as his witnesses, Jesus gave them the Holy Spirit (cf. Jn. 20:22), who worked through them and stirred the hearts of those who heard them (cf. Acts 2:37). The same is true of those whom he sends out now. At one level, all the baptized, by the very grace of the Sacrament, are deputed to take part in continuing the saving mission of Christ, and they are capable of this task precisely because God's love has been poured into their hearts through the Holy Spirit which has been given to them (Rom. 5:5). But on another level this common mission is accomplished through a variety of specific functions and charisms in the Church. The principal responsibility for the Church's mission has been entrusted by Christ to the Apostles and their successors. By virtue of episcopal ordination and hierarchical communion with the Head of the Episcopal College, Bishops receive the mandate and authority to teach, govern and sanctify the People of God. By the will of Christ himself, within the College of Bishops, the Successor of Peter—the rock upon which the Church is built (cf. Mt. 16:18)—exercises a special ministry of unity. Bishops therefore are to fulfil their ministry in union with the Successor of Peter, the guarantor of the truth of their teaching and of their full communion in the Church.

43b. Associated with the Bishops in the work of proclaiming the Gospel, priests are called upon at ordination to be shepherds of the flock, preachers of the good news of salvation and ministers of the sacraments. To serve the Church as Christ intends, Bishops and priests need a solid and continuing formation, which should provide opportunities for human, spiritual and pastoral renewal, as well as courses on theology, spirituality and the human sciences.[208] People in Asia need to see the clergy not just as charity workers and institutional administrators but as men whose minds and hearts are set on the deep things of the Spirit (cf. Rom. 8:5). The reverence which Asian peoples have for those in authority needs to be matched by a clear moral uprightness on the part of those with ministerial responsibilities in the Church. By their life of prayer, zealous service and exemplary conduct, the clergy witness powerfully to the Gospel in the communities which they shepherd in the name of Christ. It is my fervent prayer that the ordained ministers of the Churches in Asia will live and work in a spirit of communion and cooperation with the Bishops and all the faithful, bearing witness to the love which Jesus declared to be the true mark of his disciples (cf. Jn. 13:35).

43c. I particularly wish to underline the Synod's concern for the preparation of those who will staff and teach in seminaries and theological faculties.[209] After a thorough training in the sacred sciences and related subjects, they should receive a specific formation focused on priestly spirituality, the art of spiritual direction, and other aspects of the difficult and delicate task that awaits them in the education of future priests. This is an apostolate second to none for the Church's well-being and vitality.

44. The Consecrated Life and Missionary Societies

44a. In the Post-Synodal Apostolic Exhortation *Vita Consecrata*, I emphasized the intimate connection between the consecrated life and mission. Under its three aspects of *confessio Trinitatis*, *signum fraternitatis* and *servitium caritatis*, the consecrated life shows forth God's love in the world by its specific witness to the saving mission which Jesus accomplished by his total consecration to the Father. Recognizing that all action in the Church has its support in prayer and communion with God, the Church in Asia looks with profound respect and appreciation to the contemplative religious communities as a special source of strength and inspiration. Following the recommendations of the Synod Fathers, I strongly encourage the establishment of monastic and contemplative communities wherever possible. In this way, as the Second Vatican Council reminds us, the work of building up the earthly city can have its foundation in the Lord and can tend towards him, lest those who build labor in vain.[210]

44b. The search for God, a life of fraternal communion, and service to others are the three chief characteristics of the consecrated life which can offer an appealing Christian testimony to the peoples of Asia today. The Special Assembly for Asia urged those in the consecrated life to be witnesses to the universal call to holiness and inspiring examples to Christians and non-Christians alike of self-giving love for everyone, especially the least of their brothers and sisters. In a world in which the sense of God's presence is often diminished, consecrated persons need to bear convincing prophetic witness to the primacy of God and to eternal life. Living in community, they attest to the values of Christian fraternity and to the transforming power of the Good News.[211] All who have embraced the consecrated life are called to become leaders in the search for God, a search which has always stirred the human heart and which is particularly visible in Asia's many forms of spirituality and asceticism.[212] In the numerous religious traditions of Asia, men and women dedicated to the contemplative and ascetical life enjoy great respect, and their witness has an especially persuasive power. Their lives lived in community, in peaceful and silent testimony, can inspire people to work for greater harmony in society. No less is expected of consecrated men and women in the Christian tradition. Their silent example of poverty and abnegation, of purity and sincerity, of self-sacrifice in obedience, can become an eloquent witness capable of touching all people of good will and leading to a fruitful dialogue with surrounding cultures and religions, and with the poor and the defenceless. This makes the consecrated life a privileged means of effective evangelization.[213]

44c. The Synod Fathers recognized the vital role played by religious orders and congregations, missionary institutes and societies of apostolic life in the evangelization of Asia in past centuries. For this magnificent contribution, the Synod expressed to them the Church's gratitude and urged them not to waver in their missionary commitment.[214] I join the Synod Fathers in calling on those in the consecrated life to renew their zeal to proclaim the saving truth of Christ. All are to have appropriate formation and training, which should be Christ-centered and faithful to their founding charism, with emphasis on personal sanctity and witness; their spirituality and lifestyle should be sensitive to the religious heritage of the people among whom they live and whom they serve.[215] While maintaining respect for their specific charism, they should integrate themselves into the pastoral plan of the Diocese in which they work. The local Churches, for their part, need to foster awareness of the ideal of the religious and consecrated life, and promote such vocations. This requires that each Diocese should devise a pastoral program for vocations, including the assignment of priests and religious to full-time work among the young to help them hear and discern the call of God.[216]

44d. In the context of the communion of the universal Church, I cannot fail to urge the Church in Asia to send forth missionaries, even though she herself needs laborers in the vineyard. I am glad to see that in several Asian countries missionary institutes of apostolic life have recently been founded in recognition of the Church's missionary character and of the responsibility of the particular Churches in Asia to preach the Gospel to the whole world.[217] The Synod Fathers recommended "the establishment within each local Church of Asia, where such do not exist, of missionary societies of apostolic life, characterized by their special commitment to the mission *ad gentes, ad exteros* and *ad vitam.*"[218] Such an initiative is sure to bear abundant fruit not only in the Churches which receive the missionaries but also in the Churches which send them.

45. The Laity

45a. As the Second Vatican Council clearly indicated, the vocation of lay people sets them firmly in the world to perform the most varied tasks, and it is here that they are called to spread the Gospel of Jesus Christ.[219] By the grace and call of Baptism and Confirmation, all lay people are missionaries; and the arena of their missionary work is the vast and complex worlds of politics, economics, industry, education, the media, science, technology, the arts and sport. In many Asian countries, lay people are already serving as true missionaries, reaching out to fellow Asians who might never have contact with clergy and religious.[220] To them I express the thanks of the whole Church, and I encourage all lay people to assume their proper role in the life and mission of the People of God, as witnesses to Christ wherever they may find themselves.

45b. It is the task of the Pastors to ensure that the laity are formed as evangelizers able to face the challenges of the contemporary world, not just with worldly wisdom and efficiency, but with hearts renewed and strengthened by the truth of Christ.[221] Witnessing to the Gospel in every area of life in society, the lay faithful can play a unique role in rooting out injustice and oppression, and for this too they must be adequately formed. To this end, I join the Synod Fathers in proposing the establishment at the diocesan or national level of lay formation centers to prepare the laity for their missionary work as witnesses to Christ in Asia today.[222]

45c. The Synod Fathers were most concerned that the Church should be a participatory Church in which no one feels excluded, and they judged the wider participation of women in the life and mission of the Church in Asia to be an especially pressing need. "Woman has a quite special aptitude in passing on the faith, so much so that Jesus himself appealed to it in the work of evangelization. That is what happened to the Samaritan woman whom Jesus met at Jacob's well: he chose her for the first expansion of the new faith in non-Jewish territory."[223] To enhance their service in the Church, there should be greater opportunities for women to take courses in theology and other fields of study; and men in seminaries and houses of formation need to be trained to regard women as co-workers in the apostolate.[224] Women should be more effectively involved in pastoral programs, in diocesan and parish pastoral councils, and in diocesan synods. Their abilities and services should be fully appreciated in health care, in education, in preparing the faithful for the sacraments, in building community and in peacemaking. As the Synod Fathers noted, the presence of women in the Church's mission of love and service contributes greatly to bringing the compassionate Jesus, the healer and reconciler, to Asian people, especially the poor and marginalized.[225]

46. The Family

46a. The family is the normal place where the young grow to personal and social maturity. It is also the bearer of the heritage of humanity itself, because through the family life is passed on from generation to generation. The family occupies a very important place in Asian cultures; and, as the Synod Fathers noted, family values like filial respect, love and care for the aged and the sick, love of children and harmony are held in high esteem in all Asian cultures and religious traditions.

46b. Seen through Christian eyes, the family is "the domestic Church" (*ecclesia domestica*).[226] The Christian family, like the Church as a whole, should be a place where the truth of the Gospel is the rule of life and the gift which the family members bring to the wider community. The family is not simply the object of the Church's pastoral care; it is also one of the Church's most effective agents of evangelization. Christian families are today called to witness to the Gospel in difficult times and circumstances, when the family itself is threatened by an array of forces.[227] To be an agent of evangelization in such a time, the Christian family needs to be genuinely "the domestic Church," humbly and lovingly living out the Christian vocation.

46c. As the Synod Fathers pointed out, this means that the family should be active in parish life, partaking of the sacraments, especially the Holy Eucharist and the Sacrament of Penance, and being involved in service to others. It also means that parents should strive to make the moments when the family naturally comes together an opportunity for prayer, for Bible reading and reflection, for appropriate rituals presided over by the parents and for healthy recreation. This will help the Christian family to become a hearth of evangelization, where each member experiences God's love and communicates it to others.[228] The Synod Fathers also acknowledged that children have a role in evangelization, both in their family and in the wider community.[229] Convinced that "the future of the world and of the Church passes through the family,"[230] I once again propose for study and implementation what I wrote on the theme of the family in the Apostolic Exhortation *Familiaris Consortio*, following the Fifth Ordinary General Assembly of the Synod of Bishops in 1980.

47. Young People

47a. The Synod Fathers were particularly sensitive to the theme of youth in the Church. The many complex problems which young people now face in the changing world of Asia impel the Church to remind the young of their responsibility for the future of society and the Church, and to encourage and support them at every step to ensure that they are ready to accept that responsibility. To them the Church offers the truth of the Gospel as a joyful and liberating mystery to be known, lived and shared, with conviction and courage.

47b. If young people are to be effective agents of mission, the Church needs to offer them suitable pastoral care.[231] In agreement with the Synod Fathers, I recommend that, where possible, every diocese in Asia should appoint youth chaplains or directors to promote the spiritual formation and apostolate of young people. Catholic schools and parishes have a vital role in providing all-round formation for the young, by seeking to lead them in the way of true discipleship and developing in them the human qualities that mission requires. Organized youth apostolates and youth clubs can provide the experience of Christian friendship which is so important for the young. The parish, and associations and movements, can help young people to cope better with social pressures by offering them not only a more mature growth in the Christian life but also help in the form of career guidance, vocational training and youth counseling.

47c. The Christian formation of young people in Asia should recognize that they are not only the object of the Church's pastoral care but also "agents and co-workers in the Church's mission in her various apostolic works of love and service."[232] In parishes and dioceses, young men and women should therefore be invited to take part in the organization of activities which concern them. Their freshness and enthusiasm, their spirit of solidarity and hope can make them peacemakers in a divided world; and, on this score, it is encouraging to see young people involved in exchange programs between the particular Churches and countries in Asia and elsewhere fostering interreligious and intercultural dialogue.

48. Social Communication

48a. In an era of globalization, "the means of social communication have become so important as to be for many the chief means of information and education, of guidance and inspiration in their behavior as individuals, families and within society at large. In particular, the younger generation is growing up in a world conditioned by the mass media."[233] The world is seeing the emergence of a new culture that "originates not just from whatever content is eventually expressed, but from the very fact that there exist new ways of communicating, with new languages, new techniques and a new psychology."[234] The exceptional role played by the means of social communication in shaping the world, its cultures and ways of thinking has led to rapid and far-reaching changes in Asian societies.

48b. Inevitably, the Church's evangelizing mission too is deeply affected by the impact of the mass media. Since the mass media have an ever increasing influence even in remote areas of Asia, they can assist greatly in the proclamation of the Gospel to every corner of the continent. However, "it is not enough to use the media simply to spread the Christian message and the Church's authentic teaching. It is necessary to integrate that message into the 'new culture' created by modern communications."[235] To this end, the Church needs to explore ways of thoroughly integrating the mass media into her pastoral planning and activity, so that by their effective use the Gospel's power can reach out still further to individuals and entire peoples, and infuse Asian cultures with the values of the Kingdom.

48c. I echo the Synod Fathers' commendation of *Radio Veritas Asia*, the only continent-wide radio station for the Church in Asia, for its almost thirty years of evangelization through broadcasting. Efforts must be made to strengthen this excellent instrument of mission, through appropriate language programming, personnel and financial help from Episcopal Conferences and Dioceses in Asia.[236] In addition to radio, Catholic publications and news agencies can help to disseminate information and offer continuing religious education and formation throughout the continent. In places where Christians are a minority, these can be an important means of sustaining and nurturing a sense of Catholic identity and of spreading knowledge of Catholic moral principles.[237]

48d. I take up the recommendations of the Synod Fathers on the point of evangelization through social communications, the "areopagus of the modern age," in the hope that it may serve human promotion and the spreading of the truth of Christ and the teaching of the Church.[238] It would help if each Diocese would establish, where possible, a communications and media office. Media education, including the critical evaluation of media output, needs to be an increasing part of the formation of priests, seminarians, religious, catechists, lay professionals, students in Catholic schools and parish communities. Given the wide influence and extraordinary impact of the mass media, Catholics need to work with the members of other Churches and Ecclesial Communities, and with the followers of other religions to ensure a place for spiritual and moral values in the media. With the Synod Fathers, I encourage the development of pastoral plans for communications at the national and diocesan levels, following the indications of the Pastoral Instruction *Aetatis Novae*, with appropriate attention to the circumstances prevailing in Asia.

49. The Martyrs

49a. However important programs of formation and strategies for evangelization may be, in the end *it is martyrdom which reveals to the world the very essence of the Christian message*. The word itself, "martyr," means witness, and those who have shed their blood for Christ have borne the ultimate witness to the true value of the Gospel. In the Bull of Indiction of the Great Jubilee of the Year 2000, *Incarnationis Mysterium*, I stressed the vital importance of remembering the martyrs: "From the psychological point of view, martyrdom is the most eloquent proof of the truth of the faith, for faith can give a human face even to the most violent of deaths and show its beauty even in the midst of the most atrocious persecutions."[239] Through the ages, Asia has given the Church and the world a great host of these heroes of the faith, and from the heart of Asia there rises the great song of praise: *Te martyrum candidatus laudat exercitus*. This is the song of those who died for Christ on Asian soil in the first centuries of the Church, and it is also the joyful cry of men and women of more recent times like

Saint Paul Miki and his companions, Saint Lorenzo Ruiz and his companions, Saint Andrew Dung Lac and his companions, Saint Andrew Kim Taegon and his companions. May the great host of Asian martyrs, old and new, never cease to teach the Church in Asia what it means to bear witness to the Lamb in whose blood they have washed their shining robes (cf. Rev. 7:14)! May they stand as indomitable witnesses to the truth that Christians are called always and everywhere to proclaim nothing other than *the power of the Lord's Cross!* And may the blood of Asia's martyrs be now as always the seed of new life for the Church in every corner of the continent!

CONCLUSION

50. Gratitude and Encouragement

50a. At the end of this Post-Synodal Apostolic Exhortation which, seeking to discern the Spirit's word to the Churches in Asia (cf. Rev. 1:11), has endeavored to set forth the fruits of the Special Assembly for Asia of the Synod of Bishops, I wish to express the Church's gratitude to all of you, dear Asian brothers and sisters, who have contributed in any way to the success of this important ecclesial event. First and foremost, we again praise God for the wealth of cultures, languages, traditions and religious sensibilities of this great continent. Blessed be God for the peoples of Asia, so rich in their diversity yet one in their yearning for peace and fullness of life. Especially now, in the immediate vicinity of the 2000th anniversary of the Birth of Jesus Christ, we thank God for choosing Asia as the earthly dwelling place of his incarnate Son, the Savior of the world.

50b. I cannot fail to express my appreciation to the Bishops of Asia for their deep love of Jesus Christ, the Church and the peoples of Asia, and for their testimony of communion and generous dedication to the task of evangelization. I am grateful to all those who form the great family of the Church in Asia: the clergy, the men and women religious and other consecrated persons, the missionaries, the laity, families, the young, indigenous peoples, workers, the poor and afflicted. Deep in my heart there is a special place for those in Asia who are persecuted for their faith in Christ. They are the hidden pillars of the Church, to whom Jesus himself speaks words of comfort: "You are blessed in the Kingdom of heaven" (cf. Mt. 5:10).

50c. The words of Jesus reassure the Church in Asia: "Fear not, little flock, for it is your Father's good pleasure to give you the Kingdom" (Lk. 12:32). Those who believe in Christ are still a small minority in this vast and most populous continent. Yet far from being a timid minority, they are lively in faith, full of the hope and vitality which only love can bring. In their humble and courageous way, they have influenced the cultures and societies of Asia, especially the lives of the poor and the helpless, many of whom do not share the Catholic faith. They are an example to Christians everywhere to be eager to share the treasure of the Good News "in season and out of season" (2 Tim. 4:2). They find strength in the wondrous power of the Holy Spirit who, despite the generally small numbers of the Church in Asia, ensures that the Church's presence is like the yeast which mixes with the flour in a quiet and hidden way till it is all leavened (cf. Mt. 13:33).

50d. The peoples of Asia need Jesus Christ and his Gospel. Asia is thirsting for the living water that Jesus alone can give (cf. Jn. 4:10-15). The disciples of Christ in Asia must therefore be unstinting in their efforts to fulfil the mission they have received from the Lord, who has promised to be with them to the end of the age (cf. Mt. 28:20). Trusting in the Lord who will not fail those whom he has called, the Church in Asia joyfully makes her pilgrim way into the Third Millennium. Her only joy is that which comes from sharing with the multitude of Asia's peoples the immense gift which she herself has received—the love of Jesus the Savior. Her one ambition is to continue his mission of service and love, so that all Asians "may have life and have it abundantly" (Jn. 10:10).

51. Prayer to the Mother of Christ

51a. Faced with such a challenging mission, we turn to Mary, for whom, as the Synod Fathers said, Asian Christians have a great love and affection, revering her as their own Mother and the Mother of Christ.[240] Throughout Asia there are hundreds of Marian sanctuaries and shrines where not only the Catholic faithful gather, but also believers of other religions too.

51b. To Mary, model of all disciples and bright Star of Evangelization, I entrust the Church in Asia at the threshold of the Third Millennium of the Christian era, trusting absolutely that hers is an ear that always listens, hers a heart that always welcomes, and hers a prayer that never fails:

51c. O Holy Mary, Daughter of the Most High God, Virgin Mother of the Savior and Mother of us all, look tenderly upon the Church of your Son planted on Asian soil. Be her guide and model as she continues your Son's mission of love and service in Asia.

51d. You fully and freely accepted the Father's call to be the Mother of God; teach us to empty our hearts of all that is not of God, that we too may be filled with the Holy Spirit from on high. You pondered the mysteries of God's will in the silence of your heart; help us on our journey to discern the signs of God's powerful hand. You went quickly to visit Elizabeth and help in her days of waiting; obtain for us the same spirit of zeal and service in our evangelizing task.

You sang the praises of the Lord; lead us in joyful proclamation of faith in Christ our Savior. You had compassion on the needy and spoke to your Son on their behalf; teach us never to fear to speak of the world to Jesus and of Jesus to the world.

51e. You stood at the foot of the Cross as your Son breathed his last; be with us as we seek to be one in spirit and service with all who suffer. You prayed with the disciples in the Upper Room; help us to wait upon the Spirit and to go wherever he leads us.

51f. Protect the Church from all the powers that threaten her. Help her to be a true image of the Most Holy Trinity. Pray that through the Church's love and service all the peoples of Asia may come to know your Son Jesus Christ, the only Savior of the world, and so taste the joy of life in all its fullness. O Mary, Mother of the New Creation and Mother of Asia, pray for us, your children, now and always!

51g. Given at New Delhi, in India, on the sixth day of November in the year 1999, the twenty-second of my Pontificate.

Joannes Paulus II

ENDNOTES: *ECCLESIA IN ASIA*

(1) John Paul II, Address to the Sixth Plenary Assembly of the Federation of Asian Bishops' Conferences (FABC), Manila (15 January 1995), 11: *Insegnamenti* XVIII, 1 (1995), 159.

(2) Apostolic Letter *Tertio Millennio Adveniente* (10 November 1994), 38: AAS 87 (1995), 30.

(3) No. 11: *Insegnamenti* XVIII, 1 (1995), 159.

(4) John Paul II, Apostolic Letter *Tertio Millennio Adveniente* (10 November 1994), 38: AAS 87 (1995), 30.

(5) Cf. Special Assembly for Asia of the Synod of Bishops, *Nuntius* (Final Message), 2.

(6) Address to the Sixth Plenary Assembly of the Federation of Asian Bishops' Conferences (FABC), Manila (15 January 1995), 10: *Insegnamenti* XVIII, 1 (1995), 159.

(7) John Paul II, *Letter Concerning Pilgrimage to the Places Linked to the History of Salvation* (29 June 1999), 3: *L'Osservatore Romano* (30 June - 1 July 1999), 8.

(8) Cf. *Propositio* 3.

(9) *Propositio* 1.

(10) Cf. Special Assembly for Asia of the Synod of Bishops, *Lineamenta*, 3.

(11) Cf. *Ibid.*

(12) Cf. *Propositio* 32.

(13) Cf. Special Assembly for Asia of the Synod of Bishops, *Instrumentum Laboris*, 9.

(14) Cf. *Propositiones* 36 and 50.

(15) *Propositio* 44.

(16) *Propositio* 27.

(17) Cf. *Propositio* 45.

(18) Special Assembly for Asia of the Synod of Bishops, *Instrumentum Laboris*, 9.

(19) Cf. *Propositio* 39.

(20) *Propositio* 35.

(21) Cf. *Propositio* 38.

(22) Cf. *Propositio* 22.

(23) Cf. *Propositio* 52.

(24) Cf. Special Assembly for Asia of the Synod of Bishops, *Lineamenta*, 6.

(25) Cf. *Propositio* 56.

(26) John Paul II, Apostolic Letter *Tertio Millennio Adveniente* (10 November 1994), 18: *AAS* 87 (1995), 16.

(27) Cf. *Propositio* 29.

(28) Cf. *Propositiones* 29 and 31.

(29) *Propositio* 51.

(30) Cf. *Propositiones* 51, 52 and 53.

(31) *Propositio* 57.

(32) Cf. *Ibid.*

(33) *Propositio* 54.

(34) No. 3: *AAS* 83 (1991), 252.

(35) Cf. *Propositio* 5.

(36) Special Assembly for Asia of the Synod of Bishops, *Relatio ante disceptationem*: *L'Osservatore Romano* (22 April 1998), 5.

(37) Special Assembly for Asia of the Synod of Bishops, *Relatio post disceptationem*, 3.

(38) *Propositio* 8.

(39) No. 11: *AAS* 83 (1991), 260.

(40) *Ibid.*

(41) Special Assembly for Asia of the Synod of Bishops, *Relatio post disceptationem*, 3.

(42) *Roman Missal*: Eucharistic Prayer I for Masses of Reconciliation.

(43) John Paul II, Encyclical Letter *Redemptor Hominis* (4 March 1979), 10: *AAS* 71 (1979), 274.

(44) Pastoral Constitution on the Church in the Modern World *Gaudium et Spes*, 22.

(45) No. 9: *AAS* 71 (1979), 272f.

(46) Special Assembly for Asia of the Synod of Bishops, *Relatio post disceptationem*, 3.

(47) Cf. *Ibid.*

(48) *Ibid.*

(49) *Propositio* 5.

(50) John Paul II, Encyclical Letter *Redemptoris Missio* (7 December 1990), 6: *AAS* 83 (1991), 255.

(51) John Paul II, Encyclical Letter *Redemptor Hominis* (4 March 1979), 7: *AAS* 71 (1979), 269.

(52) Cf. John Paul II, Encyclical Letter *Dominum et Vivificantem* (18 May 1986), 54: AAS 78 (1986), 875.

(53) Cf. *Ibid.*, 59: *loc. cit.*, 885.

(54) John Paul II, Encyclical Letter *Redemptoris Missio* (7 December 1990), 28: AAS 83 (1991), 274; cf. Second Vatican Ecumenical Council, Pastoral Constitution on the Church in the Modern World *Gaudium et Spes*, 26.

(55) Cf. *Propositio* 11; Second Vatican Ecumenical Council, Decree on the Missionary Activity of the Church *Ad Gentes*, 4 and 15; Dogmatic Constitution on the Church *Lumen Gentium*, 17; Pastoral Constitution on the Church in the Modern World *Gaudium et Spes*, 11, 22 and 38; Paul II, Encyclical Letter *Redemptoris Missio* (7 December 1990), 28: *AAS* 83 (1991), 273f.

(56) Cf. Special Assembly for Asia of the Synod of Bishops, *Relatio ante disceptationem*: *L'Osservatore Romano* (22 April 1998), 5.

(57) John Paul II, Encyclical Letter *Dominum et Vivificantem*, (18 May 1986), 50: AAS 78 (1986), 870; cf. Saint Thomas Aquinas, *Summa Theologiae*, III, 2, 10-12; 6, 6; 7, 13.

(58) Cf. John Paul II, Encyclical Letter *Dominum et Vivificantem* (18 May 1986), 50: AAS 78 (1986), 870.

(59) Cf. *Ibid.*, 24: *loc. cit.*, 832.

(60) Cf. John Paul II, Encyclical Letter *Redemptoris Missio* (7 December 1990), 28: *AAS* 83 (1991), 274.

(61) No. 29: *AAS* 83 (1991), 275; cf. Second Vatican Ecumenical Council, Pastoral Constitution on the Church in the Modern World *Gaudium et Spes*, 45.

(62) Cf. John Paul II, Encyclical Letter *Redemptoris Missio* (7 December 1990), 29: *AAS* 83 (1991), 275.

(63) Cf. Second Vatican Ecumenical Council, Dogmatic Constitution on the Church *Lumen Gentium*, 13.

(64) *Propositio* 12.

(65) Dogmatic Constitution on the Church *Lumen Gentium*, 17.

(66) Apostolic Exhortation *Evangelii Nuntiandi* (8 December 1975), 22: *AAS* 68 (1976), 20.

(67) *Propositio* 8.

(68) John Paul II, Encyclical Letter *Redemptoris Missio* (7 December 1990), 45: *AAS* 83 (1991), 292.

(69) Cf. *Ibid.*, 46: *loc.cit.*, 292f.

(70) Cf. Second Vatican Ecumenical Council, Declaration on Religious Freedom *Dignitatis Humanae*, 3-4; John Paul II, Encyclical Letter *Redemptoris Missio* (7 December 1990), 39: *AAS* 83 (1991), 287; *Propositio* 40.

(71) Paul VI, Apostolic Exhortation *Evangelii Nuntiandi* (8 December 1975), 53: *AAS* 68 (1976), 41f.

(72) Address to Representatives of Non-Christians Religions, Madras (5 February 1986), 2: *AAS* 78 (1986), 767.

(73) Cf. *Propositiones* 11 and 12; John Paul II, Encyclical Letter *Redemptoris Missio* (7 December 1990), 28: *AAS* 83 (1991), 273f.

(74) Special Assembly for Asia of the Synod of Bishops, *Relatio ante disceptationem*: *L'Osservatore Romano* (22 April 1998), 5.

(75) *Propositio* 58.

(76) Cf. John Paul II, Encyclical Letter *Fides et Ratio* (14 September 1998), 72: *AAS* 91 (1999), 61.

(77) Special Assembly for Asia of the Synod of Bishops, *Relatio post disceptationem*, 15.

(78) Cf. *Ibid.*

(79) *Ibid.*

(80) *Propositio* 6.

(81) Cf. Special Assembly for Asia of the Synod of Bishops, *Relatio post disceptationem*, 6.

(82) *Ibid.*

(83) Cf. Special Assembly for Asia of the Synod of Bishops, *Relatio ante disceptationem*: *L'Osservatore Romano* (22 April 1998), 5.

(84) Cf. Apostolic Exhortation *Evangelii Nuntiandi* (8 December 1975), 20: *AAS* 68 (1976), 18f.

(85) John Paul II, Encyclical Letter *Redemptoris Missio* (7 December 1990), 52: *AAS* 83 (1991), 300.

(86) Cf. Special Assembly for Asia of the Synod of Bishops, *Relatio post disceptationem,* 9.

(87) Cf. Second Vatican Ecumenical Council, Pastoral Constitution on the Church in the Modern World *Gaudium et Spes,* 22; John Paul II, Encyclical Letter *Redemptoris Missio* (7 December 1990), 28: *AAS* 83 (1991), 273f.

(88) Cf. John Paul II, Encyclical Letter *Redemptoris Missio* (7 December 1990), 56: *AAS* 83 (1991), 304.

(89) John Paul II, Homily at the Mass for the Catholics of West Bengal, Calcutta (4 February 1986), 3: *Insegnamenti* IX, 1 (1986), 314.

(90) Cf. *Propositio* 43.

(91) Cf. *Propositio* 7.

(92) *Ibid.*

(93) John Paul II, Encyclical Letter *Redemptoris Missio* (7 December 1990), 54: *AAS* 83 (1991), 302.

(94) Cf. *Ibid.: loc. cit.,* 301.

(95) Cf. Second Vatican Ecumenical Council, Constitution on the Sacred Liturgy *Sacrosanctum Concilium,* 10; Special Assembly for Asia of the Synod of Bishops, *Relatio post disceptationem,* 14.

(96) Cf. Special Assembly for Asia of the Synod of Bishops, *Relatio post disceptationem,* 14; *Propositio* 43.

(97) Cf. *Propositio* 43.

(98) Cf. Special Assembly for Asia of the Synod of Bishops, *Relatio post disceptationem,* 13.

(99) Cf. *Propositio* 17.

(100) Cf. *Propositio* 18.

(101) Cf. *Propositio* 17.

(102) Nos. 60; 62; 105: *AAS* 91 (1999), 52f.; 54; 85f.

(103) Cf. *Propositio* 24.

(104) Cf. *Propositio* 25.

(105) Cf. *Ibid.*

(106) Cf. *Propositio* 27.

(107) Cf. *Propositio* 29.

(108) Cf. Encyclical Letter *Redemptoris Missio* (7 December 1990), 91: *AAS* 83 (1991), 338.

(109) *Propositio* 19.

(110) *Propositio* 8.

(111) Declaration on Religious Freedom *Dignitatis Humanae,* 2.

(112) *Propositio* 6.

(113) Saint Augustine, *De Civitate Dei*, XVIII, 51, 2: PL 41, 614; cf. Second Vatican Ecumenical Council, Dogmatic Constitution on the Church *Lumen Gentium*, 8.

(114) Second Vatican Ecumenical Council, Decree on the Missionary Activity of the Church *Ad Gentes*, 7; cf. Dogmatic Constitution on the Church *Lumen Gentium*, 17.

(115) Paul VI, Address to the College of Cardinals (22 June 1973): *AAS* 65 (1973), 391.

(116) John Paul II, Post-Synodal Apostolic Exhortation *Christifideles Laici* (30 December 1988), 18: *AAS* 81 (1989), 421.

(117) Cf. *Ibid.*; Second Vatican Ecumenical Council, Dogmatic Constitution on the Church *Lumen Gentium*, 4.

(118) Cf. *Catechism of the Catholic Church*, 775.

(119) Cf. *Ibid.*

(120) John Paul II, Post-Synodal Apostolic Exhortation *Christifideles Laici* (30 December 1988), 32: *AAS* 81 (1989), 451f.

(121) Cf. Dogmatic Constitution on the Church *Lumen Gentium*, 16.

(122) *Propositio* 13.

(123) *Ibid.*

(124) Cf. Special Assembly for Asia of the Synod of Bishops, *Relatio ante disceptationem*: *L'Osservatore Romano* (22 April 1998), 6.

(125) *Propositio* 13; cf. Second Vatican Ecumenical Council, Dogmatic Constitution on the Church *Lumen Gentium*, 22.

(126) Cf. *Propositio* 13.

(127) Cf. *Propositio* 15; Congregation for the Doctrine of the Faith, Letter to the Bishops of the Catholic Church on Some Aspects of the Church Understood as Communion *Communionis Notio* (28 May 1992), 3-10: *AAS* 85 (1993), 839-844.

(128) Cf. *Propositio* 15.

(129) Cf. *Ibid.*

(130) Cf. *Propositio* 16.

(131) *Propositio* 34.

(132) Cf. *Propositio* 30; cf. John Paul II, Encyclical Letter *Redemptoris Missio* (7 December 1990), 51: *AAS* 83 (1991), 298.

(133) Cf. Apostolic Exhortation *Evangelii Nuntiandi* (8 December 1975), 58: *AAS* 68 (1976), 46-49; John Paul II, Encyclical Letter *Redemptoris Missio*, 51: *AAS* 83 (1991), 299.

(134) Cf. *Propositio* 31.

(135) Cf. *Propositio* 14.

(136) Cf. Special Assembly for Asia of the Synod of Bishops, *Relatio ante disceptationem: L'Osservatore Romano* (22 April 1998), 6.

(137) Cf. *Propositio* 50.

(138) Cf. *Propositiones* 36 and 50.

(139) Cf. John Paul II, Address to the Synod of Bishops of the Syro-Malabar Church (8 January 1996), 6: *AAS* 88 (1996), 41.

(140) Cf. *Propositio* 50.

(141) Cf. *Propositio* 56.

(142) Cf. *Propositio* 51.

(143) Cf. *Propositio* 52.

(144) *Propositio* 53.

(145) Cf. *Propositio* 57.

(146) Cf. *Letter Concerning Pilgrimage to the Places Linked to the History of Salvation* (29 June 1999), 7: *L'Osservatore Romano* (30 June - 1 July 1999), 9.

(147) *AAS* 56 (1964), 613.

(148) Cf. *Propositio* 42.

(149) *Ibid.*

(150) John Paul II, Address at the General Audience (26 July 1995), 4: *Insegnamenti* XVIII, 2 (1995), 138.

(151) Cf. John Paul II, Address at the General Audience (20 January 1982), 2: *Insegnamenti* V, 1 (1982), 162.

(152) Cf. No. 53: *AAS* 87 (1995), 37.

(153) Cf. John Paul II, Encyclical Letter *Redemptoris Missio* (7 December 1990), 55: *AAS* 83 (1991), 302

(154) Cf. *Ibid.: loc. cit.*, 304.

(155) No. 4: *AAS* 83 (1991), 101f.

(156) No. 56: *AAS* 83 (1991), 304.

(157) *Propositio* 41.

(158) *Ibid.*

(159) Cf. *Ibid.*

(160) Cf. John Paul II, Encyclical Letter *Redemptoris Missio* (7 December 1990), 57: *AAS* 83 (1991), 305.

(161) Cf. John Paul II, Post-Synodal Apostolic Exhortation *Vita Consecrata* (25 March, 1996), 8: *AAS* 88 (1996), 383.

(162) Cf. John Paul II, Encyclical Letter *Sollicitudo Rei Socialis* (30 December 1987), 47: *AAS* 80 (1988), 582.

(163) Pastoral Constitution on the Church in the Modern World *Gaudium et Spes*, 1.

(164) In many ways the point of departure was the Encyclical Letter *Rerum Novarum* of Pope Leo XIII (15 May 1891) which ushered in a series of solemn Church statements on various aspects of the social question. Among these was the Encyclical Letter *Populorum Progressio* (26 March 1967) which Pope Paul VI issued in response to the teachings of the Second Vatican Council and a changed world situation. To commemorate the twentieth anniversary of that Encyclical, I released the Encyclical Letter *Sollicitudo Rei Socialis* (30 December 1987) in which, following the earlier Magisterium, I invited all the faithful to see themselves as called to a mission of service which necessarily includes the promotion of integral human development.

(165) John Paul II, Encyclical Letter *Sollicitudo Rei Socialis* (30 December 1987), 41: *AAS* 80 (1988), 570f.

(166) Cf. Congregation for the Doctrine of the Faith, Instruction on Christian Freedom and Liberation *Libertatis Conscientia* (22 March 1986), 72: *AAS* 79 (1987), 586.

(167) Cf. *Propositio* 22.

(168) Cf. *Propositio* 21.

(169) Cf. John Paul II, Post Synodal Apostolic Exhortation *Christifideles Laici* (30 December 1988), 5: *AAS* 81 (1989), 400-402; Encyclical Letter *Evangelium Vitae* (25 March 1995), 18: *AAS* 87 (1995), 419f.

(170) *Propositio* 22; cf. *Propositio* 39.

(171) John Paul II, Encyclical Letter *Sollicitudo Rei Socialis* (30 December 1987), 42: *AAS* 80 (1988), 573; cf. Congregation for the Doctrine of the Faith, Instruction on Christian Freedom and Liberation *Libertatis Conscientia* (22 March 1986), 68: *AAS* 79 (1987), 583.

(172) Cf. *Propositio* 44.

(173) Cf. *Ibid.*

(174) Cf. *Propositio* 39.

(175) Cf. *Propositio* 22.

(176) Cf. *Propositio* 36.

(177) Cf. *Propositio* 38.

(178) Cf. *Ibid.*

(179) Cf. *Propositio* 33.

(180) Cf. *Ibid.*

(181) Cf. *Propositio* 35.

(182) Cf. *Ibid.*

(183) *Propositio* 32.

(184) Cf. John Paul II, Apostolic Letter *Salvifici Doloris* (11 February 1984), 28-29: *AAS* 76 (1984), 242-244.

(185) Cf. *Propositio* 20.

(186) Cf. *Ibid.*

(187) Cf. *Propositio* 21.

(188) Cf. *Ibid.*

(189) Cf. *Ibid.*

(190) Cf. *Propositio* 23.

(191) Cf. *Ibid.*

(192) Cf. *Propositio* 55.

(193) Cf. *Propositio* 49.

(194) John Paul II, Message for the World Day of Peace (1 January 1998), 3: *AAS* 90 (1998), 50.

(195) Cf. *Propositio* 49.

(196) Cf. *Propositio* 48.

(197) Cf. *Ibid.*; John Paul II, Apostolic Letter *Tertio Millennio Adveniente* (10 November 1994), 51: *AAS* 87 (1995), 36.

(198) Cf. *Propositio* 48.

(199) Cf. *Propositio* 22; John Paul II, Encyclical Letter *Sollicitudo Rei Socialis* (30 December 1987), 44: *AAS* 80 (1988), 576f.

(200) Cf. John Paul II, Encyclical Letter *Redemptor Hominis* (4 March 1979), 15: *AAS* 71 (1979), 287.

(201) Cf. *Ibid.*

(202) Cf. *Propositio* 47.

(203) Homilies on the Gospel of Matthew, 50, 3-4: *PG* 58, 508-509.

(204) Cf. Decree on the Church's Missionary Activity *Ad Gentes*, 2 and 35.

(205) Cf. John Paul II, Encyclical Letter *Redemptoris Missio* (7 December 1990), 31: *AAS* 83 (1991), 277.

(206) *Ibid.* 42: *loc. cit.*, 289.

(207) *Ibid.*

(208) Cf. *Propositio* 25.

(209) Cf. *Ibid.*

(210) Cf. Dogmatic Constitution on the Church *Lumen Gentium*, 46.

(211) Cf. *Propositio* 27.

(212) Cf. John Paul II, Post-Synodal Apostolic Exhortation *Vita Consecrata* (25 March 1996), 103: *AAS* 88 (1996), 479.

(213) Cf. Paul VI, Apostolic Exhortation *Evangelii Nuntiandi* (8 December 1975), 69: *AAS* 68 (1976), 59.

(214) Cf. *Propositio* 27.

(215) Cf. *Ibid.*

(216) Cf. *Ibid.*

(217) Cf. *Propositio* 28.

(218) *Ibid.*

(219) Cf. Dogmatic Constitution on the Church *Lumen Gentium*, 31.

(220) Cf. *Propositio* 29.

(221) Cf. *Ibid.*

(222) Cf. *Ibid.*

(223) John Paul II, Address at the General Audience (13 July 1994), 4: *Insegnamenti* XVII, 2 (1994), 40.

(224) Cf. *Propositio* 35.

(225) Cf. *Ibid.*

(226) Second Vatican Ecumenical Council, Dogmatic Constitution on the Church *Lumen Gentium*, 11.

(227) Cf. Special Assembly for Asia of the Synod of Bishops, *Relatio ante disceptationem*: *L'Osservatore Romano* (22 April 1998), 6.

(228) Cf. *Propositio* 32.

(229) Cf. *Propositio* 33.

(230) John Paul II, Address to the Confederation of Family Advisory Bureaus of Christian Inspiration (29 November 1980), 4: *Insegnamenti* III, 2 (1980), 1454.

(231) Cf. *Propositio* 34.

(232) *Ibid.*

(233) John Paul II, Encyclical Letter *Redemptoris Missio* (7 December 1990), 37: *AAS* 83 (1991), 285.

(234) *Ibid.*

(235) *Ibid.*

(236) Cf. *Propositio* 45.

(237) Cf. *Ibid.*

(238) Cf. *Ibid.*

(239) No. 13: *AAS* 91 (1999), 142.

(240) Cf. *Propositio* 59.

Part Four

Ecclesia in Asia

Analytical Index

INDEX: *Ecclesia in Asia**

James H. Kroeger

---

*This comprehensive index (over 1,100 items) is specifically designed to be used with the annotated text of *Ecclesia in Asia* printed in this volume. Numbers refer to entire sections (e.g. 9) or to individual paragraphs (e.g. 9a, 9b, etc.). *Ecclesia in Asia* has been subdivided into numbered paragraphs in fidelity to the original paragraphs of the text to give a more precise location to the individual references (this option is followed since sections in the Vatican text often extend to several pages). This index is copyrighted by: James Kroeger [Maryknoll Box 285; Greenhills Post Office; 1502 Metro Manila, Philippines].

From Claretian Publications . . .

Asian Church Documents —
A Comprehensive Trilogy

FOR ALL THE PEOPLES
OF ASIA: I, II, III

These attractive volumes of *For All the Peoples of Asia* form a comprehensive—and indispensable—resource for understanding the remarkable growth and renewal of the Church in Asia in the post-Vatican II era. In a word, they are the basic sourcebooks for all the documents of the Federation of Asian Bishops' Conferences (FABC) for over three decades (1970-2001); they record the "Asian Pentecost" in the wake of the Second Vatican Council.